Jean-Luc Nancy among the Philosophers

Series Board

James Bernauer

Drucilla Cornell

Thomas R. Flynn

Kevin Hart

Richard Kearney

Jean-Luc Marion

Adriaan Peperzak

Thomas Sheehan

Hent de Vries

Merold Westphal

Michael Zimmerman

John D. Caputo, *series editor*

PERSPECTIVES IN
CONTINENTAL
PHILOSOPHY

IRVING GOH, EDITOR

Jean-Luc Nancy among the Philosophers

FORDHAM UNIVERSITY PRESS
New York ■ 2023

Copyright © 2023 Fordham University Press

All rights reserved. No part of this publication may be reproduced, stored in a retrieval system, or transmitted in any form or by any means—electronic, mechanical, photocopy, recording, or any other—except for brief quotations in printed reviews, without the prior permission of the publisher.

Fordham University Press has no responsibility for the persistence or accuracy of URLs for external or third-party Internet websites referred to in this publication and does not guarantee that any content on such websites is, or will remain, accurate or appropriate.

Fordham University Press also publishes its books in a variety of electronic formats. Some content that appears in print may not be available in electronic books.

Visit us online at www.fordhampress.com.

Library of Congress Cataloging-in-Publication Data available online at https://catalog.loc.gov.

Printed in the United States of America

25 24 23   5 4 3 2 1

First edition

Contents

	Introduction: Jean-Luc Nancy Passes IRVING GOH	1
1	The Iterative Cogito, or the *Sum* of Each and Every Time (Reading Descartes with Jean-Luc Nancy) GEORGES VAN DEN ABBEELE	21
2	Nancy with Hegel: The Restless Pleasures of Calculus and the Infinite Opening in Finitude JOHN H. SMITH	52
3	The World, Absolutely: On Jean-Luc Nancy (and Karl Marx) RODOLPHE GASCHÉ	75
4	Worldless: Heidegger, Simone Weil, and Anti-Judaism via Nancy ELEANOR KAUFMAN	91
5	Flesh and *Écart* in Merleau-Ponty and Nancy MARIE-EVE MORIN	111
6	Sexistence: Nancy and Lacan EMILY APTER	135
7	Sublime Seizures in Lyotard and Nancy: The Political Blooming of Art and Technology TIMOTHY MURRAY	149

8	*D'avec*: Mutations and Mutisms in Jean-Luc Nancy WERNER HAMACHER	166
9	Infinitely Passing (or, Pascal Passes) JEAN-LUC NANCY	205
	List of Contributors	*211*
	Index	*215*

Jean-Luc Nancy among the Philosophers

Introduction
Jean-Luc Nancy Passes

IRVING GOH

Jean-Luc Nancy scarcely needs any introduction today. He is now recognized as one of the most important thinkers of the twentieth and twenty-first centuries. His writings on the senses (particularly touch), community, existence (including its entanglement with sex, or "sexistence" in Nancy's more recent formulation), freedom, the deconstruction of Christianity, the world (which creates itself largely indifferent to the determining forces of globalization), aesthetics, and even the current pandemic have undoubtedly pushed "deconstruction" further toward a "postdeconstructive" dimension.[1] In other words, his writings articulate a way of thinking that not only exposes all the troubling impasses that underlie the very linguistic medium of thought but also postulates how these impasses with regard to those topics can still paradoxically play out sensorially, if not materially, in both the existing world and the world that is always in the process of coming into presence. The original contribution of Nancy's thought to contemporary intellectual discourse is only reinforced by the numerous journal special issues and edited volumes over the years committed to explicating and advancing Nancy's writings for philosophy, literature, politics, the visual arts, music, and religious thought. This book joins these collective endeavors in underscoring the importance of Nancy's thought, but it does something different at the same time. Instead of focusing singularly on Nancy, it is interested in explicating the critical philosophical relation between Nancy *and* other thinkers: thinkers such as Descartes, Hegel, Marx, Heidegger, Weil, Lacan, Merleau-Ponty, and Lyotard.

As evident, this book is not concerned with Nancy's peers such as Balibar, Badiou, Irigaray, Cixous, Rancière, Stiegler, Agamben, Esposito, or Žižek. The contemporary collections wherein they and Nancy have variously appeared together have already made manifest their philosophical proximities and distances. Neither is it preoccupied with Nancy's philosophical affinities with Derrida or Blanchot, about which much has already been written. This book has its sights set on earlier thinkers. There are thus contributions that focus on thinkers such as Descartes or Hegel whose thoughts left significant impressions on Nancy's, including those whose influence on Nancy may not be so immediately obvious to contemporary readers, such as Marx. There are contributions that turn to thinkers whose impact on Nancy is already well known, such as Heidegger, but reveal new aspects of the philosophical relations between them. And there are contributions that highlight thinkers with whom Nancy had a fraught philosophical relation, such as Lacan, but whose thoughts nevertheless play a critical role in the formation of Nancy's thinking. More specifically, this book will articulate what Nancy shares with, and where he departs from, Descartes in his deconstruction of the Subject and conceptualization of an ontological "being singular plural," Hegel in his reiteration of the infinite in terms of "transimmanence," Marx in his reaffirmation of a world free from all anthropocentric ideologies or determinations, Heidegger and Weil in his reflections on antisemitism, Lacan in his rethinking of sexual relations inextricable from existence, Merleau-Ponty in his argument for separation in touch, and Lyotard in his thinking of a sublime "ecotechnics" at the intersection of what has been deemed our "natural" world and technological advancement.

Given the book's general backward glance, let it be said at the outset that it makes no claims to tracing a genealogy of Nancy's thought. It is after all impossible to do so within a single volume, not to mention that this book does not follow any clear linear chronology. To reiterate, it attends, rather, to what could be considered—and I borrow Nancy's own phrase here—"the sharing of voices" (*le partage des voix*) that subtends his thinking/writings. In other words, it elucidates the extent to which Nancy's philosophical voice is both shared (*partagé*) and divided (*partagé*) at the same time with the selected thinkers here. Such a "sharing of voices" can be further said to be Nancy's *art* of philosophy. Certainly, when Nancy speaks of art, he is largely referring to paintings, drawings, sculpture, architecture, photography, film, installations, theater, music, and literature, and this multiplicity of aesthetic objects has led Nancy to say that there are "several arts."[2] But I want to take "art" to also mean—and I admit to taking the liberty to further multiply the notion of "several arts" in this instance—the poetic quality of Nancy's thinking/writing, that is, a philosophizing that is poetic at the same time, or else a thinking/writing that registers—this time in the precise sense Nancy intended for the phrase—a "sharing of voices" between philosophy and poetry.[3] The demonstration of such poetic or even lyrical philosophical prose, delivered furthermore in a clear and lucid voice, is arguably evident especially in *Noli me tangere* (2003), *The Fall of Sleep* (2007), and *The Equivalence of Catastrophes (After Fukushima)* (2012). I believe that it is such an "art" that helps Nancy's texts avoid the densely esoteric or even impenetrable layer that burdens so many philosophical writings; it is what makes his texts seem so readily readable or accessible, drawing readers into his thinking or writings and influencing generations of scholars.

The other way I want to think about "art" here, and to a greater extent, pertains to Nancy's reading method, which no doubt has bearings on his writing or philosophical style as well. In Nancy's early works, we witness his strongly original, if not "creative," and "deconstructive" close readings of past philosophers such that the latter become quite unrecognizable in relation to more "canonical" readings. Thus, we are introduced to a radical Descartes in *Ego Sum* (1979) and a rather exciting Kant unread of in Continental philosophy scholarship in *The Categorical Imperative* (1983). Elsewhere, we are presented with a very generous reading of Hegel in *The Speculative Remark* (1973) and again in *Hegel: The Restlessness of the Negative* (1997), which marks Nancy's distance from the critical receptions of Hegel typically found in his peers or predecessors such as Derrida and Deleuze. In later works such as *The Inoperative Community* (1983), *The Experience of Freedom* (1988), *The Sense of the World* (1993), and *Being Singular Plural* (1996)—works that are not as engaged with the history of philosophy—we begin to discern a tendency *not* to pursue any focused and close reading of any particular philosopher at any one time. Here, building upon a multiplicity of references to support his theses is the more common practice. We thus find Nancy drawing from, among others, Marx, Sartre, Bataille, and Blanchot for his thinking of community; Kant, Hegel, and Heidegger for his reaffirmation of freedom; Nietzsche, Kierkegaard, Wittgenstein, and Granel for his "deconstruction of Christianity" in the eponymous two-volume opus from 2005 and 2010; and Freud, Lacan, Spinoza, Montaigne, Schelling, and Marion for his inquiry into the ontology of sex in the more recent *Sexistence* (2017). Again, rather than a thorough or close reading of any of these thinkers, Nancy invokes them often in what seems like a touch-and-go manner (in the sense of a fleeting treatment rather than the more contemporary sense of uncertainty or riskiness). He *passes through* them, *passing through* their thoughts. (I will return to the question of *passing* soon.)

To be sure, the above is *not* to say that Nancy entirely eschews close reading or that he has no in-depth engagements with the thinkers he reads or passes through in his philosophizing. On the contrary, each of Nancy's citations of a thinker reflects a close reading already completed a priori. That is, each time he invokes a thinker, he does so in such a way that he does not need to burden his writing with any extensive demonstration of that close reading. Unquestionably and sufficiently well placed and well timed, each invocation announces both Nancy's confidence in his deep understanding of those thinkers *and* his own take on them at the same time. We could say that his style reflects a deftness in putting into relation a multiplicity of thoughts while allowing them to interlace with his own ideas in a manner at once smooth and organized, without ever losing sight of the respective (and sometimes divergent) context upon which each thought is based. Or else, in resisting any master-thinker to oversee, dictate, ground, found, or even guide his thoughts—that is, unfazed generally by what Harold Bloom calls the "anxiety of influence"—Nancy puts into practice *thinking as freedom* in his thinking/writings.[4] His style affirms his disposition as a freethinker in every sense of the word: not only free to announce the "auto-deconstruction" of religion untethered from any monotheistic/symbolic order; free to discern a world that worlds itself undetermined by any demiurge or Anthropocene; free, as will be seen in a while, to assert a sense of community devoid of any fusion, union, or communitarian project; or free to affirm that existence rebegins differently at each time; but also free to allow his philosophical views and voice to come to light, away from the shadows of past philosophers and/or those of his contemporaries. It is necessary to keep in mind that the latter freedom does not entail any negation or denial of links to other philosophers. Nancy never fails to remind us that "freedom is relation," or "relation is freedom,"[5] which is to say, that there is true freedom only if one recognizes that one is ever only in a co-immersion of freedom with others.

This returns us to the "sharing of voices" in Nancy's "art" of philosophy, in his *thinking as freedom*. Or, to use another of Nancy's phrases, it makes us attuned to the "singular plural" voice in his texts, especially his later ones, where we find a voice that is singularly or undeniably Nancy's but at the same time inflected by the plurality of other thinkers'. Put yet another way, what comes across in Nancy's style or "art" can also be considered the proliferation of surface contacts with other philosophers, whereby the limits of his thinking are exposed to, are made to encounter, or are made to *pass alongside*, those of the other philosophers. It is at the limit, after all, where thought happens. As Nancy says, "there is no thought unless it is carried to the limit of thought."[6] For him too, surface contacts can be constitutive of such limits: "it is only *on the surface of* philosophy . . . that the *logic* of freedom *passes* [my emphasis], for it answers to nothing other than the existing opening of thought."[7] And yet, he would also acknowledge that thinking "does not comprehend its own limit."[8] In other words, the limit to which thought goes, the limit that also touches the limits of other thoughts, demands to be thought and explicated. This is what this book seeks to do with regard to the limit where Nancy's "singular plural" voice is in formation, where his "sharing of voices" with other thinkers takes place.

I am leaving the task of elucidating how Nancy's "singular plural" voice is shared with and split from other philosophical voices, or of explicating what happens at the frays of the passage between Nancy and other thinkers, to the contributors to this book. For my part, I want to return to the notion of *passing* mentioned earlier. Perhaps there is no more important philosophical lexicon, no more operative philosophical vocabulary, than passing or passage in Nancy.[9] I would wager that passing or passage is effectively *the* keyword of Nancy's philosophy, especially if we take his philosophy to make sense of or touch on[10] existence as the incontrovertible fact or experience of freedom shared with other existents and the world. To put it in a crudely simple manner, passing or passage, for Nancy, is what existence does simply and ultimately.[11] It is the essence of existence, even though, to be sure, existence passes without assuming any prior or given essence; existence does not seek to live out any supposed predetermined essence. Neither does it gather or accumulate any essence in passing; passing does not accrue any essence a posteriori for existence. In passing, existence experiences the freedom of existing at each moment, experiencing how existing each time is never the same, always different from any past and future moment. This is how passing or passage, according to Nancy, does not constitute progress but "succession [strictly in the sense of one moment following another, free from any baggage of seeking to leave a legacy], appearance, disappearance, event."[12] Passing as such is existence understood properly as *existing* in its very transitivity: it is existence's essenceless essence, or it is the *essence without essence* of existence.[13] Put yet another way closer to Nancy's terms, it is the *sense* of existence, as much as it is the sense of the world, as much as it is—in a word—*sense*.

Recognizing passing or passage as the sense of existence also explains Nancy's dissatisfaction with the philosophical category of the Subject, given its classical understanding as assured of its capacity not only for rational thought but also for self-representation, an assurance founded furthermore on an indifference toward, if not negation of, others. Passing or passage renders such a self-representation impossible, revealing the notion of any absolute singularness of a Subject to be but its own fiction. This is because passing or passage brings an existent outside of itself and exposes it to the world of other existents, if its very "birth to presence" into the world has not already done so.[14] For Nancy, then, such an exposure afforded by passing or passage attests to the other existential fact of community being always already *there*. Contrary to any communitarian endeavor, and no matter if this endeavor is well intentioned in its aim to be inclusive or dissimulating in pursuing an ideology that conspires to exclude others, community has no need for any work or project for it to be established; in fact, it resists all communitarian aspirations or programs. In Nancy's words (here we can also elicit the notion of passing from his peculiar understanding of transcendence):

> Community is, in a sense, resistance itself: namely resistance to immanence. Consequently, community is transcendence: but "transcendence," which no longer has any "sacred" meaning, signifying precisely a resistance to immanence (resistance to the communion of everyone or to the exclusive passion of one or several: to all the forms and all the violences of subjectivity).[15]

It is community as such that Nancy would prefer to think about as "community without subject."[16] And because community as such is always already constituted by existents in their respective passing or passage, there can be no stable or finished unity or totality to it. This is also to say that community can be dissolving at the same time as it seems to come together through the passage of existents, because this passage includes no less than the departure of certain existents.

The passing or passage of existents in the world also surely entails forms of touching. Points of contact are inevitable when existents in their multiplicity traverse the world in various ways and at various speeds. Touch, then, is the material or corporeal reminder that we are always in the midst of a world with others, always in the midst of passing one another, and, again, that community is precisely always forming and dissolving at each time. As long as we keep in mind that each existent is always on its own trajectory of passing or passage, touch can never be an agglutinating grip. With passing or passage, touch must let go of its object; passing or passage has no time for a permanent touch. There will be no more passing or passage if touch does not withdraw itself. (This is also how Nancy reads the *noli me tangere* scene between Jesus and Mary Magdalene: the imperative "do not touch me" that Jesus addresses to Mary is necessary so that he can carry on in his passage toward resurrection.[17]) Conversely, there will be no more touch, or another touch will not be possible, if there is no distance between touching bodies, and this critical distance for touch is what passing or passage precisely allows. Passing or passage thus makes us recognize that touch is, as Nancy says, all a matter of tact, a touch-and-go affair (again in the sense of a momentary touch followed by its withdrawal).

Touch, community, freedom, existence, and sense: these are just some of the major philosophical topics or motifs of Nancy's thought, if not those for which Nancy has been known and celebrated. I believe that the above has sufficiently suggested how passing or passage figures prominently not only as the critical backdrop to these topics or motifs but also as the motor for their rethinking. The philosophical force of passing or passage precedes and traverses these topics or motifs; it drives them, inheres in them, and exceeds them, taking them along to an outside beyond what we already know or assume about them. To pass, as Nancy will remind us in his essay written specifically for this book, is to be implicated in a movement of traversing, going across, going beyond, or exceeding. More precisely, passing or passage in Nancy "unworks" those philosophical themes or motifs, rendering them "inoperative": it leaves us with a "community without community," a touch that retreats from itself, and an "in-essential" existence.

But "to pass" also signifies death. In contemporary parlance, when someone dies, we simply say, "X passed," now without the need for the supplementary preposition "away" or "on." I suspect many of us would have said on August 23, 2021: *Jean-Luc Nancy passed*.[18] In French, the verb "to pass" is rarely used when announcing someone's death; there is no French equivalent to the English construction. Nevertheless, Nancy would remind us that the verb "to pass" (*passer*) in French can also mean "to die" (*mourir*).[19] In a way, death is around the corner both in the experience *and* in the thinking of passing or passage. With regard to death, passing is certainly not without pathos. Often, such passing even weighs on us more than the existents' weight of existence when they were alive.[20] Passing as dying is not without remainder, therefore; this passing does not happen without leaving a mystery behind. "Mystery" (*mystère*) is another of Nancy's terms. According to him, there is a mystery in all of us, a mystery that is with us all along our existence, and the fact that each of us has this mystery is what makes us all common. But this mystery also marks us as uncommon (*in-commun*), since the mystery that each of us bears is unique to ourselves, underscoring the singularity of each of us. This is also how "in the passage" that is existence, "each time, what is passed or passes itself [*se passe*] is a singularity."[21] And in passing as death, what remains is this mystery of the existent's singularity. Death reminds us of this mystery, or even compounds the sense of this mystery. Or it leaves us with what Nancy also terms a *vestige*, which recalls for us how those who have passed were figures "with reproducible traits of an image," but these traits are now "undone [*défaites*], unbound [*déliés*], reduced to hints, to allusive contours."[22]

Vestige returns us to the question of genealogy, which, as said earlier, this book resists. Incidentally, vestige, according to Nancy, is not constitutive of a genealogy. Certainly, a vestige is a "remains of a step," the "act of putting one's step in the trace of steps,"[23] and the vestige in question in this book is no doubt Nancy's step in his passing or passage through the trace of steps of thinkers before him.[24] Indeed, if there is a mystery that this book touches upon in the wake of Nancy's passing, it is the vestige of Nancy's "art" of philosophy, as it seeks to unravel the "singular plural" voice that constitutes this "art," the voice that is shared (*partagé*) with the community of thinkers with which Nancy is engaged in the philosophical conversation at hand, and a voice divided (*partagé*) at the same time from the same community as Nancy distinguishes his own take on the issues.[25] But again, there is no orderly or linear, chronological pattern to this particular vestige or step; the vestige does not reveal any clear evolution from a point of origin. Vestige resists all that. As Nancy says, "The vestige does not identify its cause or its model."[26] The vestige "show[s] nothing more than its passage" within or across a field in which it finds itself, which is the field of thought or philosophy for our case here with regard to Nancy, and what is registered in this passage is "a step, a walk, a dance, or a leap, . . . a succession, an élan, a repercussion, a coming-and-going, a *transire*."[27] What this vestige reveals, then, is what happens when Nancy *passes between* the selected thinkers, and this *between*, as will be seen, "has neither a consistency nor continuity."[28] At the heart of Nancy's passage through these thinkers, the *between*-ness that bursts through in the vestige illuminates "the *inter*lacing [l'entre*croisement*] of strands whose extremities remain separate even at the center of the knot."[29] In other words, and to reiterate, what reverberates through the vestige is not genealogy, not the suggestion of a "connective tissue," "cement," or "bridge,"[30] but a complex and yet no less lyrical sharing and division of voices.

Georges Van Den Abbeele opens the book with his inquiry into the Cartesian trace in Nancy's thought by returning to the early *Ego Sum*. Van Den Abbeele considers this text to be one of Nancy's more "monographic" works, alongside *The Categorical Imperative* (which has Kantian philosophy as its backdrop), in contrast to the later "problem-oriented studies," such as those on rethinking community in *The Inoperative Community*, on contemporary secularism in *The Deconstruction of Christianity*, or on the critique of neoliberal disaster management in *The Equivalence of Catastrophes*

(After Fukushima). Van Den Abbeele notes that while the "monographic" *Ego Sum* and *The Categorical Imperative* might, at first glance, appear to be Nancy's partaking in the traditional exercise of explicating the history of philosophy, which we have seen at work too in Deleuze's earlier texts on Spinoza and Nietzsche, *Ego Sum* actually contains Nancy's idiosyncratic, "affective," and even "interruptive" reading of Descartes. Thus, instead of a stable or fixed subject assured of his capacity for rational thought and self-representation, as one is wont to think central to Descartes's thought, Nancy unravels for us an "interrupted subject." It is "interrupted" because any sense of a subject can be established only in the instance of Descartes's enunciation of *ego sum*, which is to say, only when this enunciation, through the emergence of thought or the act of thinking (*cogito*), interrupts the ceaseless passage of existence that waits for no thought or thinking. As Van Den Abbeele reads it, this also marks the performative dimension of *ego sum*, which not only challenges the latter's status as a constative but also announces how—in the true sense of a performative—each subject-formation will always be interrupted by another as long as that phrase is repeated differently each time in the act of thinking. The Cartesian *cogito*, then, according to Van Den Abbeele, is actually more *chaogito*. But to return to the relation between Nancy and Descartes: according to Van Den Abbeele, it is Nancy's reading of Descartes that will become formative of Nancy's thinking, decades later, of "being singular plural," of the relation between the body and the world, and of the very presentation of philosophy.

Nancy's intervention in the history of philosophy—this time on Hegel through *The Speculative Remark* and *Hegel: The Restlessness of the Negative*—also forms the backdrop of John H. Smith's interest in the Hegelian trace of Nancy's thought. There has been an interest in the infinite in late twentieth- to early twenty-first-century French thought, which Smith discerns from Deleuze's *The Fold* (1988) to Quentin Meillassoux's *After Finitude* (2012), with the works of Nancy (especially *The Sense of the World*) and Badiou (especially *Being and Event* [1988]) in between, and Smith argues that this line of thought owes much to Hegel. Smith thus shows in his essay how Nancy's thinking of an "infinite thinking within finitude"—where "infinite thinking" would only affirm every alterity—can be more properly understood by revisiting Hegel's philosophy. According to Smith, it is also from Hegel that Nancy will arrive at a "non-privative notion of the finite," from which we will also have Nancy's "postdeconstructive" understanding of the world, sense, and atheism. We can understand Nancy's "postdeconstructive" move to be that which, to reiterate, acknowledges its debt to Derrida's "deconstructive" thinking on the one hand, and on the other, reaches far beyond the latter, not only exposing all the troubling impasses of language itself in thought but also postulating how these impasses can paradoxically play out for both the existing world and the world to come. Nancy's "postdeconstructive" understanding of the above terms, in the aftermath of their "deconstructive" treatment, thus opens them up to a new plenitude of sense, one that is entirely different from the monolithic totality of meaning that has been imputed to them prior to the intervention of "deconstruction." As Smith underscores too, Nancy's investment in the infinite within the finite is furthermore pursued via writing, hence marking its difference with Badiou, who places his faith in mathematics.

Perhaps the thought of a "postdeconstructive" understanding of the world underlies more forcefully Rodolphe Gasché's essay, which brings Nancy's thought in relation to Marx's, a move still seldom made in scholarship on Nancy. The latter is not surprising given the at-best-scattered or *passing* references to Marx in a few selected texts by Nancy. This clearly does not faze Gasché, however, and picking up on one such reference in a footnote in Nancy's essay "Finite History," Gasché's piece sets out to explicate the presence of Marx's thought in Nancy's notions of community and/or "being-in-common." But Gasché goes even further: he argues that Nancy's thinking of the world is more indebted to Marx than to Heidegger, as is commonly assumed. In Gasché's reading, the world according to Marx is one imbued with the here and now (*hic et nunc*) of sense, truth, and value; it measures humanity's self-creation, valuation, and meaning, and the self-emancipation of this humanist world is always set against the backdrop of labor and capital. This world, in a way, is admittedly a delimited world, and in Gasché's reading of Nancy reading Marx, "one cannot follow [Marx] any longer." Instead of a delimited humanist world, the challenge is to think a more open-ended world, possibly even one with an absolute value in itself outside of labor and exchange values.

If Gasché challenges the common assumption of the proximity of Nancy's thought with Heidegger's on the idea of "world," Eleanor Kaufman's reading of Nancy, especially via *The Banality of Heidegger* (2015), written in the wake of the publications of Heidegger's *Black Notebooks*, makes us rethink Heidegger's thinking of the "world" and anti-Judaism in tandem with Simone Weil. Kaufman first reminds us that the commonly assumed hierarchy in Heidegger of the human that is rich-in-world, followed by the animal that is poor-in-world, followed by the vegetal or mineral being that is worldless, is not that straightforward, if not something less than a hierarchy in fact. Inspired by Nancy's "The Heart of Things," where Nancy clearly renounces the supposed hierarchy by arguing that a rock nevertheless stands in relation with the world as it is equally touched by a sense of the world through a lizard resting on it, Kaufman shows us that there is a certain rock ontology in Heidegger too in *The Fundamental Concepts of Metaphysics*, where he would say that the worldlessness of the rock constitutes, in Kaufman's words, its "own manner of being." In Kaufman's study, the value of worldlessness for Heidegger can be corroborated through Heidegger's reading of Paul, where the notions of "the nonworldly, the nonrelational, and the non-Jewish," alongside the affirmation of weakness, are hailed as marks of originality and/or authenticity. Heidegger's problem with the Jews, even though they are considered worldless, is that the weakness associated with this wordlessness is not a true weakness; he sees in Judaism an aspiration toward the "gigantic" that is measurable and calculable. As Kaufman tells us, such an anti-Judaism can be found in Weil too, for whom a true weakness is one that yearns for nothing except a nothingness, where one empties oneself of the world, and where there is only suffering without any eye for—or better, without any possibility for—reward. The spirit of Weil's "decreation," then, is to precipitate toward that worldless vegetal level.

We get back to the French side of philosophizing with Marie-Eve Morin's essay on Nancy and Merleau-Ponty. It is not surprising to say that much of Nancy's thought lies close to Merleau-Ponty's, given the latter's exploration into touch, sense, the body and/or flesh, the world, and painting. Interestingly enough, though, few have elucidated the connection between Nancy and Merleau-Ponty. For her part, Morin picks up on the term *écart* that has been mobilized by both Nancy and Merleau-Ponty in quite different ways toward quite different ends. In Merleau-Ponty's usage, *écart* signifies, as Morin puts it, the "chiasm or torsion between inside and outside" by which the self is "radically opened or exposed," paving the way for a self-sensing existent bearing "encroachment and promiscuity." *Écart*, for Nancy, meanwhile, is critical for his thinking of touch. It signifies precisely the distance, the separation, or the "unpassable limit" according to Morin, without which touch will not be possible: indeed, touch cannot take place if there is no distance to cross in the first place between the touching or touched bodies. Despite, or even in spite of, this conceptual difference surrounding *écart*, Morin argues that reading the two thinkers together can not only "allow us to develop a better interpretation of their respective thinking" but also present us the case whereby "each can provide a corrective to a certain tendency in the work of the other and in our interpretation of it." Thus, on the one hand, with Merleau-Ponty in mind, we might critique Nancy's "insistence on the uncrossability and unpassability of limits" as "a flattening out of the encroachments, overlaps, and envelopments, of the depths and shadows that give the world (and others) their presence in the flesh"; in so doing, we will not downplay or repress "the dimension of desire" that is however already present in Nancy. On the other hand, reading Nancy alongside Merleau-Ponty, we can present a critical take of the latter's "insistence on encroachment and promiscuity" as risking the "excess of proximity in a general regime of confusion where separation is lost"; here, Nancy would serve as a reminder of "the separation—the birth to presence—that the dehiscence of the flesh also evokes."

But if there is a thinker from whom Nancy explicitly takes his distance, even to the point of establishing a *differend* between them, it is arguably none other than Lacan, and this *differend* between Nancy and Lacan is the topic of Emily Apter's essay. As Apter notes, this *differend* is undoubtedly already present in *The Title of the Letter* (1975) that Nancy coauthored with Lacoue-Labarthe, but it becomes even clearer in Nancy's "The 'There Is' of Sexual Relation" (2001), which runs counter to Lacan's declaration that "there is no sexual relation" (*il n'y a pas de rapport sexuel*). Apter's interest lies in the thought trajectory from this particular essay to Nancy's *Sexistence*. According to Apter, it is along this trajectory that Nancy develops the thought of the "there is" of "sexistence," which is to say, the conceptualization of "sex without concepts," or else, the "theorizing [of] sexual ontology" where the insistence of the "there is" contributes to "dissolving the subjective boundaries between partners and distributing difference among man, woman, hetero, homo, and trans." This is also how, as Apter notes, ontological difference in *Sexistence* "is itself de jure sexual," and Apter will further add that it is additionally "postdual, transindividual, essentially trans." If this were not a radically progressive reading of Nancy, one that even perhaps has gender *passing* in mind, Apter goes yet further in suggesting that that very trajectory from "The 'There Is' of Sexual Relation" to *Sexistence* can be instrumental in thinking a Fourth Wave feminism: one that insists on *not* bracketing the fact that we are *not* beyond "historic struggles for parity within binary differences"; one that involves the "philosophizing in sex" that mobilizes psychoanalysis, philosophy, and translation studies.

The invocation of the term *differend* above—made current by Lyotard—indeed anticipates Timothy Murray's essay on Nancy and Lyotard, and it involves no less than another *differend*, this time surrounding the term "sublime." While Nancy and Lyotard, as Murray reminds us, have different takes on the sublime, Murray also highlights how the sublime, understood in terms of the touch in/of art, underlies both thinkers' understanding of the critical function of art, especially in the context of the increasing instrumentalization and/or digitalization of technology that Heidegger had already critiqued: the sublime contests such a "world picture" predicated upon a technologically driven rationality. For Lyotard, there is a "sublime seizure" of art in its affective touch on spectators, which arrests, interrupts, or suspends all discourses that seek to explain or explicate art, with its sense of "the not-that [*ce non-cela*]." For Nancy, there is a sublime force of art that gestures toward, as Murray cites Nancy in *The Muses*, "another *sense* of existence, [and] by the same token, another sense of 'technique.'" With these considerations, as well as returning to Lyotard's writings on the sublime and *techne* in *The Inhuman*, alongside Nancy's consideration of the *informe* or that which is yet without form but already in formation in *The Pleasure in Drawing*, Murray argues that "Lyotard joins with Nancy on building a discourse on art whose foundations contrast the state/corporate investments in technology with the *informe* of technicity as ghosted by the sublime and by what Nancy terms its affiliated '(é)motions.'" Or, placing Nancy's and Lyotard's respective consideration of a sublime technics or technics of the sublime in more contemporary terms or context, Murray will also say: "In the threatening face of ecological implosion and fascist resurgence, the texts of Nancy join the writings of Lyotard in conjoining art, technology, and philosophy to reshape the unifying sovereignties of absolutism and the deadening commodities of globalization into the transformers of plural wordliness."

Following Murray's contribution is an essay by the late Werner Hamacher. It is by grace of fortune that this book was able to receive one of Hamacher's last few finished pieces. Going beyond mortal generosity and friendship, Hamacher worked on his essay on/for Nancy in the year or so before his passing, which is to say, writing it while suffering the pains of illness. Despite that, Hamacher's essay displays no weakening, no sign of exhaustion, no letting down with regard to the rigorous and meticulous thinking about thinking through theoretical and literary texts, something so reminiscent of his earlier works, something for which some of us are nostalgic only because it reminds us what good "Continental" philosophy does, something that so few thinkers or scholars up to this day can do. Hamacher thus begins his formidably inspiring essay by positing his own version of the question "What is philosophy?" à la Deleuze and Guattari, or rather "What is called thinking?" à la Heidegger, toward whom Hamacher is clearly more inclined. For Hamacher, it all involves the "stance" of philosophy, which is to say, philosophy's encounter with its object of thought and its unique disposition, style, or gesture toward its philosophical matter. Understood as such, philosophy, accordingly, is but the reaffirmation of "a relation to itself," which Hamacher finds to underlie thinking from Heraclitus to Heidegger. And this relation, to be sure, must not be mistaken for a tautology. It is, rather, a "transition . . . from one to the other," a gathering of beings, the reverberation of the silent resonance of a "communality" involving more *and* less than an "enothering and enselfing." And as long as there is this world of existents (human, animal, vegetal, mineral, viral, etc.), this transitivity, this reverberation, never ends; the relation continues to differ from itself, always opening itself up to others even more other than what it has considered other. In other words, this relation always needs to be written anew, differently. According to Hamacher, that is what Nancy does in *Being Singular Plural*, which allows Hamacher in turn to articulate philosophy understood precisely as that relation concerning Being, whereby "Being is in each case Being-with, Being-with-another, Being-with-oneself-as-another."

If it is not already evident, Hamacher, like Murray, is attentive to Nancy's mobilization of prepositions.[31] But while Murray pursues Nancy's use of the preposition "to," it is the preposition "with" in *Being Singular Plural* that Hamacher follows after. As Hamacher points out, the "with" there is never "straightforward"; it even constitutes an incommensurability. In other words, whatever "communality" there is in Nancy "is not and is never capable of being consistent in itself and with itself." Put otherwise, what is constant of Nancy's "with" is its inconsistency, which but marks every existent's "historical mutation," marking (not just one but every) Being's *finite history*—to use Nancy's phrase—"as the aporetic consistency of the illimitably inconsistent." This "mutation" transpires furthermore before and beyond language, hence occurring through its own "mutism," which therefore also requires our attuned listening, a move Hamacher finds in Nancy's *Listening* (2002). In all, such reiteration of the "relation" of philosophy in terms of an inconsistent "with," for Hamacher, also demonstrates the generosity, if not the ethics, of thought, for the inconsistency of the "with" allows the "sharing . . . and dispensation . . . of the With to others" or the "giving-out of the With to others." And this would include others that do not (yet) exist, which leads Hamacher to supplement Nancy's ontology of coexistence with the thought of "co-inexistence" or "in-coexistence." Hamacher, therefore, is also already rewriting this relation, and he would go further by responding to Nancy's "Being-with" with an Aristotelian "Being-so," where the "so" gestures toward "an always indeterminate other" that is beyond name, concept, and definition, going beyond as well the universal and the particular. But to come back to the thought of Nancy among the philosophers, Hamacher's essay fittingly attests to the "communality" of philosophers Nancy's thinking of "being singular plural" follows after and influences: Heraclitus, Plato, Aristotle, Hegel, Nietzsche, Heidegger, Benjamin, Bataille, Blanchot, Agamben . . .

The collection closes with Nancy's "Infinitely Passing (or, Pascal Passes)." If there is one philosophical phrase that acts as a constant refrain in Nancy's mind, I would say that it is Pascal's "man infinitely transcends man" (*l'homme passe infiniment l'homme*). This phrase is always a reference, explicitly or otherwise, in Nancy's thinking of existence as passing or passage without Subject, freedom, community, sense, and art; undoubtedly so as well in his deconstruction of monotheistic religion and the thinking of the ineluctable relation between sex and ontology. It is with this in mind that I asked Nancy for a piece in which he would say more about his fascination with this phrase of Pascal. In his usual infinite generosity (never saying "no" to such requests of mine and surely of others as well), Nancy responded by writing "Infinitely Passing" specifically for this book. Here, one finds Nancy interestingly returning to close reading, as he focuses on §434 of Pascal's *Pensées*, wherein the phrase "man infinitely transcends man" is found, and explicates for us the idea of human transcendence that is freed from any sacred meaning, which we have already seen in the way Nancy talks about the transcendence of community or of the freedom of existence. If it is not already evident, the verb in Pascal's phrase in the original French is "to pass" rather than "to transcend." It is not surprising, then, that Nancy in this piece will return, as indicated by the piece's title, to the vocabulary of passing or passage, which he made the foreground of his essay "Passage" (1999), published almost twenty years ago.

To conclude this introduction, let me return to the mystery of Nancy's "art" of philosophy. As suggested earlier, this mystery could be constituted by Nancy's "art" of deftly and lucidly *passing between, passing alongside*, and sometimes *passing through or over* other thinkers. In a way, this is a mystery that undoubtedly confronts us pedagogically. For, given the reticulation of voices in Nancy's texts, those of us who love, or are enthusiastic, to teach Nancy in our curriculum would have surely wondered at some point: How do we begin illuminating for students the intricately complex philosophical backdrop to Nancy's thought? How do we begin teaching Nancy such that we, on our part, do not overlook or *pass over* the thoughts of the thinkers to whom Nancy makes reference? Consequently, and if we also want to illuminate for students the philosophical precedence of Nancy's thought, with which philosopher do we start? Do we proceed chronologically, starting with the earliest thinker Nancy has mentioned? Or do we jump into the middle of things and begin with the thinker or thinkers whose works seem more resonant with the topics closest to Nancy's concerns? In turning its attention to Descartes, Hegel, Marx, Heidegger, Weil, Lacan, Merleau-Ponty, and Lyotard, this book does offer a small sample of possible starting points. Yet I want to underscore that in doing so this book is not seeking to resolve the problems underlying the above questions. In fact, it should not; it would even be unapologetic in being representative, instead, of that very problematic. In other words, this book is not saying that the selected thinkers here are the ones to start with, or that the order presented here is the way things should be done when one teaches Nancy in one's curriculum. To the contrary: as much as it was up to the contributors, depending on their respective interest, to choose which thinker they wanted to write on in relation to Nancy, this book insists that the decision as to with which thinker to begin remains the prerogative or freedom of whoever teaches Nancy's writings or thought; it leaves the choice open to that person.

The selection of thinkers discussed here, to reiterate, is reflective of this book's casting its glance to the past. This does not mean, however, that the contributions here have no pertinence to contemporary concerns. Even though not explicitly stated, I believe that readers will be able to extrapolate from the essays here their implications for today's urgent questions on (1) the states of philosophy, particularly the legacy of Marxist thought, which seems to be increasingly marginalized, or that of Heideggerian thought in the wake of the publication of the incriminating *Black Notebooks*, or theory in general, which is very much a splintered field today; (2) how we think about touch and distance, made palpably problematic lately by the COVID-19 pandemic; (3) sexual relations and the future of feminism in our age of #MeToo; (4) questions of identity and/or subjectivity in light of gender *passing* and/or trans discourses; (5) questions of the aesthetic sublime amid the domination of contemporary digital technology that is driving our distracted attention economy of real-time scroll-downs, swipe-rights or swipe-lefts, and like-clicks; and (6) the possibility of thinking the infinite in our age of economic and existential precarity, on the one hand, and extravagant space travel, on the other. What the contributors in this book suggest is that a more critical reflection on these questions cannot proceed without *first* explicating the complex philosophical underpinnings that belie them. For such an explication, we will need to think, as this book does, Nancy in relation to another thinker: Nancy *and* Marx, or Nancy *and* Heidegger (*and* Weil), for the reflection on the states of philosophy; Nancy *and* Merleau-Ponty for touch and distance in a post-COVID world; Nancy *and* Lacan for a rethinking of sexual relations and feminism in the wake of #MeToo, or Nancy *and* Descartes for a continued "deconstruction" of the Subject that is attentive to gender *passing* today; Nancy *and* Lyotard for a contemporary sublime aesthetics; and Nancy *and* Hegel, or Nancy *and* Marx, for the thinking of a contemporary infinite in opposition to economic precarity and the colonization of outer space by the ultrarich or ultraprivileged.

In short, this book emphasizes a relational aspect of thinking (it is always the case of Nancy and X, and never Nancy alone), if not a certain paratactic thinking.[32] It explicates the commonalities Nancy's thought has with the selected philosophers or thinkers here; how it is from these commonalities that Nancy's thought will diverge and develop in its very singularity as his own "art" of philosophy delivered in a distinct "singular plural" voice. With regard to such a commonality that only signals differences, perhaps one should leave the last word to Nancy himself: Nancy's relation with other thinkers or philosophers can perhaps be captured by Nancy's other term of "being-in-common." As Nancy will caution us, the sense of commonality in "being-in-common" must not be confused with the idea of homogeneity among all beings. Each being is never common with another. There is always difference, which marks the singularity of each and every being, and this difference is the only "common" that is commonly shared among all beings. This is why Nancy does not rest with the phrase "being-in-common." For him, the real task or challenge for thought is to precisely think the preposition "in" in the phrase, "of exposing the inexposable 'in,'" through which the "in" will elucidate how an existent is first "received, perceived, felt, touched, managed, desired, rejected, called, named, informed [*communiqué*]" by the world as it presents itself in and to the world.[33] The relation of Nancy's thought with those of other philosophers—a relation that reaffirms a sharing of certain concepts that only sees to critical differences or disagreements—is the "being-in-common" that this book outlines. Finally, it remains to be said that this collection does not claim to have the last word on Nancy's "being-in-common" with other philosophers. Far from it. One can imagine expanding this book, or extending it to include several sequels, to think about Nancy's relation with other philosophers such as Kant, Schlegel, Schelling, Kierkegaard, Bergson, Sartre, Aron, Henry, Arendt, and many more. This book, in other words, is far from complete in covering Nancy's "being-in-common" with other thinkers. Yet, this book has no qualms about its incomplete status. In fact, it resists any totalizing will, gesture, or ambition. It recognizes that the endeavor of a project on Nancy's "being-in-common" with other philosophers does not, and cannot, have a definitive end, not especially with regard to Nancy, whose thought is so extensive that it stretches far, wide, and deep into both the history *and* future of philosophy. Indeed, his "art" of philosophy has *passed* us and many others before us. And it will *pass* others to come, without a doubt. Such a project, then, is always open to continuation, *passed on* to others, especially to those after us; it remains to be continually written and rewritten by them.

Notes

1. I note here that Nancy's affinity with "deconstruction" had previously lent him (as well as Philippe Lacoue-Labarthe, with whom Nancy worked closely and coauthored *The Title of the Letter* [1975] and *The Literary Absolute* [1978]) the derogatory label "second-generation Derrida" especially in the nineties. However, with an undeniable and enviable immense publication record that stretched from the seventies until his death in 2021, moreover one that, as mentioned above, covers an extensive range of critical topics, we have by now recognized that the label has been unfair to Nancy (and Lacoue-Labarthe). Nancy is clearly a philosopher in his own right, which Derrida himself also seconded in recognizing *Corpus* (1992), *The Sense of the World* (1993), *The Muses* (1994), and *Being Singular Plural* (1996) as Nancy's "most formidable works." Furthermore, when we think about community, touch, existence free from the sovereign Subject, or the deconstruction of Christianity, it is quite surely, more often than not, Nancy whom we refer to or consult *first*, if not primarily.

2. See of course Nancy's "Why Are There Several Arts?" in *The Muses*, trans. Peggy Kamuf (Stanford, CA: Stanford University Press, 1996).

3. See *Le partage des voix* (1982), translated as "Sharing Voices" in *Transforming the Hermeneutic Context: From Nietzsche to Nancy*, ed. Gayle Ormiston and Alan Schrift (Albany: State University of New York Press, 1990).

4. As Nancy argues in *The Experience of Freedom* (trans. Bridget McDonald [Stanford, CA: Stanford University Press, 1993]), a thinking that has freedom in mind is one that sees to a "*deliverance from foundation* in that it would withdraw existence from the necessity of foundation, but also in that it would be set free from foundation, and given over to unfounded 'freedom.'" He would add too that freedom itself is without foundation, or it resists all endeavors to found it: "freedom, if it is something, is the very thing that prevents itself from being founded" (12).

5. *Experience of Freedom*, 69.

6. *Experience of Freedom*, 54.

7. *Experience of Freedom*, 63. The question of freedom is clearly important to Nancy. This introduction is not the space to explicate Nancy's understanding of freedom, but let it be said that freedom, according to him, is not a philosophical concept, Idea, or object of inquiry to be claimed or explicated by a philosopher. Neither is it an object of jurisprudence, recognized by us only when it has been institutionalized and normalized, bearing a legal force. For Nancy, freedom is originary, announcing itself through the very existence of anyone, anything.

8. *Experience of Freedom*, 54.

9. Readers familiar with Nancy's philosophy will no doubt be taken aback by my choice of the word "operative" above, since Nancy, in following Blanchot's notion of *désœuvrement*, is more inclined to think the "inoperative" or "unworking" (which are the common translations of *désœuvrement*), and this is unequivocally announced in one of Nancy's more famous texts, *The Inoperative*

Community (1983). Yet, as I hope will become clear soon, I employ the word "operative" only to paradoxical ends.

10. Touch here, as Nancy would say himself, not only is a question of metaphor but also is material and vibratory (see his "*Rühren, Berühren, Aufruhr*," trans. Roxanne Lapidus, *SubStance* 40, no. 3, issue 126 [2011]).

11. Doing here must be understood as *not* in addition to the act of existing, *not* the putting into action of any conscious intention; it is coextensive, if not even synonymous, with existing. See Nancy's *Que faire?* (2016), translated by Charlotte Mandell as *Doing* (Kolkata: Seagull Books, 2021), on this.

12. "The Vestige of Art," in *The Muses*, trans. Peggy Kamuf (Stanford, CA: Stanford University Press, 1996), 86–87.

13. Or, in Nancy's own words, existence "has its essence in the *existence* it is, essentially in-essential" (*Experience of Freedom*, 70).

14. "Birth to presence" (*naître à présence*), of course, is the title of one of Nancy's essays.

On another note, in place of the Subject, Nancy would also prefer the term "passerby" to describe us all. According to Nancy, "The passerby passes, *is* in the passage: what is also called *existing*. Existing: the passing being of being itself. Coming, departure, succession, passing the limits, moving away, rhythm, and syncopated blackout of being. Thus not the demand for sense, but the passage as the whole *taking place* of sense, as its whole presence" ("Vestige of Art," 99).

15. Nancy, *The Inoperative Community*, ed. Peter Connor, trans. Peter Connor, Lisa Garbus, Michael Holland, and Simona Sawhney (Minneapolis: University of Minnesota Press, 1991), 35.

16. See Nancy's introduction to *Who Comes after the Subject?*, ed. Eduardo Cadava, Peter Connor, and Jean-Luc Nancy (New York: Routledge, 1991).

17. See Nancy's *Noli me tangere* (Paris: Bayard, 2003).

18. The title of this introduction, "Jean-Luc Nancy Passes," is actually a riff on Nancy's original title for his contribution to this book: "Pascal Passes." This was not my original intention; there was an altogether different title for this introduction. In the wake of Nancy's passing, however, the weight of the current title began to bear palpably, as if announcing itself necessarily in, or as, its title.

19. "Passage," in *Être, c'est être perçu* (Saint-Etienne: Cahiers intempestifs, 1999), 15. Translations from this text are mine.

20. As Nancy would argue, in the vein of materialist philosophy, bodies are always shedding imperceptible grams in their existence, and these grams nevertheless weigh on other bodies around them. See especially the chapter "The Miniscule Dispensation of a Few Grams" in *Corpus* (Paris: Métailié, 2000) for this.

21. "Passage," 20. Nancy would also go on to say that "singularity is the same thing as passage" (20).

22. "Passage," 15.

23. "Vestige of Art," 98, 95.

24. Since we have also spoken of Nancy's "art" of philosophy, Nancy in "The Vestige of Art" will also say that art, like existence, leaves behind a vestige. According to him, what remains of art is "the vestige [that] is man's, of man. Not of the man-image, not of the man subject to the law of being the image of his own Idea, or of the Idea of his 'own-ness' [*son propre*]. Thus of a man who fits the name 'man' only with difficulty, if indeed it is difficult to remove that name from the Idea, from humanist theology" (99). In other words, the vestige of art and/or the vestige of man say the same thing: common, finite (or rather in-finite) existence.

25. This book certainly does not seek to unravel the mystery of Nancy as a singular being (even though, without intending to do so, it might just reaffirm, if not deepen, this mystery). According to Nancy, no one can ever unravel the mystery of anyone.

26. "Vestige of Art," 95.

27. "Vestige of Art," 81, 97.

28. Nancy, *Being Singular Plural,* trans. Robert D. Richardson and Anne E. O'Byrne (Stanford, CA: Stanford University Press, 2000), 5. Nancy here is indeed speaking about the preposition "between," following his statement that claims "everything . . . passes *between us*."

29. *Being Singular Plural*, 5.

30. *Being Singular Plural*, 5.

31. Murray and I began our interest in the critical significance of prepositions in Nancy in the two volumes of the *diacritics* special issue on "The Prepositional Senses of Jean-Luc Nancy" (*diacritics* 42, no. 2 [2014] and 43, no. 4 [2015]). On my part, the development of that interest has taken on the form of the aforementioned *L'existence prépositionnelle*. Hamacher, on his part, had already explicated his thoughts on prepositions in *Premises*.

32. This paratactic no doubt has affinity with Deleuze's thinking of AND (see Deleuze and Claire Parnet, *Dialogues*, trans. Hugh Tomlinson and Barbara Habberjam [London: Athlone Press, 1997]). I also add that the relational thinking here breaks with the tendency in the field of continental thought for some scholars to be caught up with a particular philosophical figure or voice: to be "Derridean," "Agambenian," or "Lacanian," or even "Nancyean." In doing so, these scholars risk forgetting that a "Derridean" or "Agambenian" thought is not so singular but constituted by other voices such as Plato's, Aristotle's, Hegel's, Heidegger's, and Foucault's. To be fair, this happens quite a bit in the field of recent affect theory too, where there is the inclination to defer principally to either Sedgwick or Berlant while forgetting affect's philosophical history or genealogy from Spinoza to Deleuze.

33. *La communauté désœuvrée* (Paris: Christian Bourgois, 2004), 230, 226. My translation.

1

The Iterative Cogito, or the *Sum* of Each and Every Time (Reading Descartes with Jean-Luc Nancy)

GEORGES VAN DEN ABBEELE

All philosophers, at some point or other, must reckon with the work and legacy of René Descartes—and French philosophers, in particular, cannot forgo a determining encounter with the so-called father of modern philosophy. Jean-Luc Nancy is no exception, and his engagement with Descartes is both early and decisive in terms of the development of his own thinking. *Ego Sum,* first published in 1979, is the third and last of a series of monographs in which Nancy takes on first Hegel (*La remarque spéculative,* 1973), then Kant (*Le discours de la syncope,* 1976), before setting his sights on Descartes. One could view these three monographs spanning the decade of the 1970s, in fact Nancy's *first* three single-authored books, as a set of preparatory studies that enable his subsequent breakthrough works of the 1980s, none of which are monographs but rather problem-oriented studies: *Le partage des voix* (1982), *La communauté désœuvrée* (1983), *L'impératif catégorique* (1983), *L'oubli de la philosophie* (1986), *L'expérience de la liberté* (1988). While Nancy would occasionally return to the monograph in later years (Hegel, Derrida, Blanchot), the shift from the early monographical triptych to a broad-ranging set of philosophical interventions remains striking.

It is certainly tempting to view *Ego Sum,* then, as a kind of *oeuvre charnière* in the development of Nancy's philosophical corpus, including the very corporal theme of the body itself, as well as that of the "world," the whole question of how philosophy *presents* itself, the structural aporias of finitude, singularity, and interruption, and even the thought of "thought" itself. Curiously, and despite these promising qualities, *Ego Sum* has received remarkably little attention over the years. Although three chapters were translated early on (*Oxford Literary Review, MLN, Glyph*), the book as a whole appeared in English translation only in 2016, nearly forty years after its initial publication.[1]

My aim, then, is not simply to complete the pantheon of potential figures in the broader project of situating Nancy "among the philosophers." Of course, Kant, Hegel, and especially Heidegger loom large in any consideration of Nancy's philosophical inspiration. But the early monograph on Descartes should not be excluded simply because it would be absurd to claim a Cartesian dimension in Nancy's work. Rather, it is his powerfully critical and unconventional reading of the Cartesian text that should garner our attention to the extent that many of Nancy's signature terms, themes, and approaches find their earliest iteration in *Ego Sum*. No less an attentive reader than Jacques Derrida signals the importance of *Ego Sum* in Nancy's intellectual trajectory by starting his massive study, *On Touching—Jean-Luc Nancy*, with a sustained reading of Nancy's reading of Descartes.[2]

Ergo ego

Let's start with the title, *Ego Sum*, at once overstatement and understatement. The classic expectation would have been for the title to read, *Cogito ergo sum*, the Latin for the canonical "I think, therefore I am," that never actually appears per se in any Latin text by Descartes.[3] Instead, Nancy boldly draws the title explicitly from the following line of the Second Meditation, which he cites as an isolated epigraph following the title page: "denique statuendum sit hoc pronuntiatum, *Ego sum, ego existo,* quoties a me profertur, vel mente concipitur, necessario esse verum" (I must finally conclude that the proposition, *I am, I exist,* is necessarily true whenever it is put forward by me or conceived in my mind) (AT VII, 25; CSM II, 7). Nancy follows with his own expansive rendering to unpack Descartes's terse Latin: "finally one must rule, establish, decide, erect as a statue and ground as a statute the fact that this pronouncement, the utterance, this statement, *I am, I exist,* each time I proclaim, propose, or pronounce it, each time I conceive it in my mind or each time it is conceived by my mind, is necessarily true" (*Ego Sum*, xxvii). Nancy's unpacking of this sentence from the *Meditations* opens up the questions that guide the subsequent chapters of *Ego Sum*, all likewise given Latin titles,[4] each taken from a different text of Descartes. Before broaching the specific readings of the chapters, it is worth lingering a little longer over the choice of this sentence from the

Meditations, the implications of the title, and Nancy's gloss in the form of translation.

Ego Sum repositions the discussion of Descartes on ontological rather than merely epistemological grounds, following upon Heidegger's well-known critique.[5] It is the question of being rather than that of knowing that comes to the fore, with whatever we call "thinking" emerging as an outcome of being (and indeed, of our specific being as *Dasein*) rather than the other way around, which is the canonical approach of Cartesian scholarship.[6] Nancy nonetheless takes a determined distance from a strictly ontological reading by "interrogating not the essence, but the *proposing* or the *proposer* [le proposant], so to speak, of the proposition: *ego* uttering itself. Which amounts to the same thing as interrogating the 'essence' (if there is still one) of the *first* proposition: 'ego sum'" (13).

The *first* proposition of *first* philosophy (*Meditations on First Philosophy* being the full title of the work), "ego sum," already says too little, as evidenced by the longer sentence within which it is embedded, and too much, since the "ego" attached to "sum" is redundant in Latin, where the personal pronoun is *already* instantiated in the verb. The supplemental "ego" is, as Nancy states citing Nietzsche, already "an *interpretation* of the process and does not belong to the process itself" (15; Nancy's emphasis).[7] Latin grammarians, at this point, would probably retort that the "ego" of "ego sum" is less pleonastic per se than emphatic, as if to underscore the need to reaffirm the ego's stake in the issue, but that only further supports Nancy's fundamental argument in the book: "*the Cartesian establishment of the Subject corresponds,* through the most binding necessity of its own structure, *to the instantaneous exhaustion of its essential possibilities*" (16; Nancy's emphasis). This unraveling of the "subject" in its very constituting is, of course, classic deconstruction, and the emphasis on the subject is framed by Nancy's opening remarks about a certain "return of the subject" in "contemporary discourses" of the time (1ff.).[8] But it is now quite a while since 1979, and it seems on the one hand as though we have been subjected to countless and ongoing "returns of the subject," while on the other hand, Nancy's own truculent questioning in 1986 about "who comes after the subject?" still remains barely heard and with few attempts at an answer.[9] Unless, of course, we understand Nancy's whole trajectory past *Ego Sum* as his long and diligent attempt at an answer. Completing his early trio of philosophical monographs with a study of Descartes, the veritable poster child for the concept of the subject, Nancy goes on to engage a whole host of philosophical issues—community, world, the political, religion, art, the body—that require thinking past or at least through the deconstruction of the subject. But if the study of Descartes represents the very high point of this approach, its *nec plus ultra*, it is also the tipping point to something else. That something else is what remains to be explored.

Cogito interruptus

The *de trop* status of the "*ego*" in *ego sum* is the most evident sign of this tipping point, but even more glaring is the ego's ontological vulnerability in the sentence Nancy chooses as his point of departure and title of the first part of his preface, *quoties a me profertur*. The canonical reception of the statement *cogito ergo sum* seems to imply the permanence and selfsameness of the thinking subject, the singular prize of Descartes's method of hyperbolic doubt, the "indubitable foundation" on the basis of which the remaining task of philosophy is merely to deduce progressively the rest of knowledge (in his time, the existence of God and of the world; and later, the ongoing validity of scientific experimentation). But this sentence from the Second Meditation, arguably *the crucial* sentence of the *Meditations*, strikingly limits the applicable truth of the *cogito* to only as much as or as often as the subject reiterates it, as underscored by the Latin adverb *quoties*, which is typically and correctly rendered as "whenever," though I would like to emphasize the performative or iterative sense of the word, as qualifying the truth of the *cogito* as being dependent upon its actual use or utterance. *Ego Sum* is true, whenever I say or think it, that is, *every* time I "proffer" it, *each* time it is uttered, an implication corroborated by Nancy's French translation as "toutes les fois," an expression that also recalls the Latin ecclesiastical expression *toties quoties,* which applies to the granting of generalized indulgences whose effects can be called upon whenever they are needed. To underscore the weight of the word in this sentence from the *Meditations* and to emphasize its consequences, I am modifying the translation of *quoties* to "each and every time." This adjustment also underscores Nancy's interpretation of the *cogito* as an early version of the "à chaque fois" or "at each time" that marks his later reflections on time as the very *difference* that is time, to the very unexpectedness or surprise of time as event, as the incessant "coming to presence of another present," that is, in its very eventfulness *as* event.[10]

But if the ontological state of the subject is only "necessarily true" each and every time he "proffers" it, then what happens when "*ego sum*" is not being said or thought, whenever it is not "cogitated"? One is reminded of the old joke about Descartes in the bar: Noticing that the philosopher's glass is empty, the bartender asks him if he would like another drink. "I think not," Descartes responds, and instantly vanishes into nothingness. Do I have to keep thinking myself to be in order actually to be? The question is not trivial, given Descartes's explicit formulation of this crucial sentence as the "indubitable foundation" of his "first philosophy." If we are to follow Descartes here *à la lettre,* then the so-called *cogito,* or even just the expression "*ego sum,*" is no longer a constative utterance (or a statement of fact) but a performative one that must be repeated endlessly, "each and every time [*quoties*]," to secure the truth of the subject.[11] But then the *cogito* is also iterative in the sense Derrida gives to the stem, *iter,* whose Sanskrit root *itara* means "other"; hence an iteration or reiteration is a difference marked in/as repetition, a repetition marked in/as difference.[12] In Descartes's case, we need look no further than his reiterating the *cogito* first as *ego sum,* then as *ego existo.* What this implies is a discontinuous performance of subjectivity, a subject ceaselessly "inter-rupted" in its being, a being interrupted—to use still another term Nancy will mobilize to great effect in his subsequent work—as the essence of a distinctly finite subjectivity. If there is *cogito* with or without *ego sum,* it is a *cogito* radically interrupted, a *cogito interruptus.*[13]

This *cogito interruptus,* though, is not just some bathos of illogicality (by design or not) nor the tedium of distraction (whether constructive or not) but the very condition of subjective being, the chasm of the subject, *subjectum, hypo-keimonon,* the absence upon which its presence is staked: that "deep whirlpool" described by Descartes at the very beginning of the Second Meditation, "which tumbles me around so that I can neither stand on the bottom nor swim up to the top" (AT VII, 23–24; CSM II, 160). But it is that watery abyss *posited as itself*—ego sum!—which *posits* the subject on/as the sought-for Archimedean "firm and immovable point," that "certain and unshakable" foundation, from which all of "first philosophy" can be securely derived or deduced. Floundering, co-agitating (as per the etymological sense of *cogitare*), in boundlessly deep waters is where the subject always already finds itself, performing the solid ground of its being in the slippery, endlessly, ever-repeated iterations of its own *summation,* or *con-summation,* as being whenever or each and every time it is said or thought, *ego sum, ego existo, quoties a me profertur vel mente concipitur.* And complicating this self-positing of the *ego* that thinks itself *sum* is the passive voice of the verbs, *profertur* and *concipitur,* as if the very speaking and conceiving of the subject were something that happens to it, or befalls it, rather than the active work of a self-generating self.

This *interruption* of the subject per se is never named as such by Nancy in *Ego Sum,* even if it is repeatedly described. The word, as far as I can tell, never appears in *Ego Sum,* and certainly not as a conceptual operator of any kind. The concept of interruption does appear later in Nancy's work, and most notably with the chapter on "Myth Interrupted" in *The Inoperative*

Community.¹⁴ There, interruption is described neither as distraction nor as the kind of "disruption" that is synonymous in corporate environs with "innovation" (while surreptitiously belying new forms of performance enhancement, capitalist profitability, and exploitation). Rather, Nancy's interruption describes "the suspense and the 'difference' of sense in the very origin of sense" (178n), a formulation that explicitly recalls the Derridean notion of "writing" as well as, again, his concept of *iter* and *iteration* as the alterity of repetition. Interruption is the other of repetition, or repetition *as* other. Every interruption is different, but they are all the same *as* interruption. Interruption is not simply something that happens to an entity (sense, subject, myth, community, work); it is what constitutively suspends it in its claim to self-completion, what reveals the very lack of completion in its being, what reveals its finitude not just with relation to what stands outside of itself but in terms of its own inner constitution as such, the finitude by dint of which it shares being-in-common with others. Interruption is the structure of (in)completion that haunts the myth of self-sameness while enabling the supposed subject's ongoing reiteration, the finitude of its temporality or the temporality of its finitude. As such, interruption hearkens back to Nancy's second monograph, on the "discourse of syncope" in Kant, a.k.a. Logodaedelus, which a note in *Ego Sum* (120n) reveals to be the source for another word, more in line with "Cartesian premises," that appears not only in *Ego Sum* but frequently throughout Nancy's work and is to be construed in tandem with that of interruption, namely "areality." The careful definition of this term in fact closes the second and final section of *Ego Sum*'s "opening":

> What occurs to the subject, what befalls it—instead of supporting it with a sub-stance, and even instead of supporting it with a word—is, in the end, as we will see, its *areality*, . . . both lack of reality (which is not an absence, and makes it impossible to carry out a negative egology in the fashion of negative theology) and area—*area* in Latin—the quality of space and extension prior to any spatiality. Areality is not the transcendental form of space either; prior to the transcendental regime (but only thinkable on the basis of Kant), more "primitive," areality extends itself as the unascribable place of the formless experience the "subject" has of its "own" chaos. Precisely because it has thought the absolute subjectity of substance, Descartes's thought keeps, at every instant, seeing—without seeing anything—this experience befalling it unexpectedly. (19)

Areality plunges us back into Descartes's abyssal watery world, more of a sub-merging than a sub-jecting, a falling with no standing, and quintessentially the "unformed experience" of his "'own' chaos." Areality is both a nowhere and a distinct if "unascribable" place, a literal *u*-topia that appears as the spatial version of temporal interruption, the discontinuity of a spacing "prior to the transcendental regime," the marking of a prior or *a priori* difference before whatever can be said to constitute the subject, again a form of writing (*dum scribo*). But if areality is constitutive of subjectivity and of substance itself, then it cannot be simply something that "befalls" or happens to the subject "unexpectedly," since it would necessarily precede subjectivity and, for that matter, "experience." On the contrary, it would seem that the subjection or submersion into one's "own" chaos comes before the substance of experience—but how can a chaos be one's own? How can one "own" chaos unless it is through an appropriation that converts the chaos into form, submersion into substance, enabling a subject who can then experience that chaos as a mere accident of being, something that falls onto it or that it falls into with all the improvisational unexpectedness of a befalling? Areality is a happening before the subject, an a priori fall into being, the unexpectedness of a collapse prior to any erection, primordial castration, the (non)sum of *sum*. As such, the cogitation that proves the existence of that *sum* can itself only come after the ontological priority of being itself. Because I think, I know I am, but it is only because I am that I can think, and therefore know that I am. Areality, interruption, so many names for the retreat of thought itself. *Non cogito ergo ego sum interruptus.*

Singuli characteres in charta exprimuntur

Between areality/interruption, or between "between," we come across the scene of *"Dum scribo,"* the first full chapter of *Ego Sum,* whose very typography and narrative voice interrupt the conventions of academic discourse (tacitly respected until this point in the book), first by typesetting the entire chapter in italics (except for quotations, which then correspondingly appear in roman type), and second by seeming to speak in the very voice of Descartes in a most ironic adoption or adaptation of prosopopoeia. This chapter's very style thus figures an alternative space of visual, narrative, and conceptual disruption, a space in which Nancy appears to mimic Descartes's description of what happens "while I am writing" (*dum scribo*). This "scene" of writing, situated in the all-important Twelfth Rule, which resumes and concludes the first third of the *Regulae ad directionem ingenii,* also provides a foretaste of the famously reclusive philosopher's penchant for self-portraiture, later deployed on a grand scale in the *Discourse on Method.*

But this is not a simple moment of writerly self-reflection, a ready-to-hand pulling back of the curtain to reveal the writer in the privacy and retreat of his study. Rather the entire scene is presented within the larger context of an analogy about the way we understand sensory impression. While Descartes subsequently cautions that "this should be understood *merely* as an analogy, for nothing quite like this power is to be found in corporeal things" (AT X, 415; CSM I, 42; my emphasis), the so-called analogy works in a very imperfect and limited way. Cognition, or what Descartes here calls following the Aristotelian scholastic tradition, the "common sense," works for him in a manner utterly unlike that of a hand guiding a pen whose trail of ink cursively inscribes a set of letters and words. Rather, the tip of the pen instead of actively projecting ink is supposed to represent the body's passive reception of external stimuli, "when an external sense organ is stimulated by an object" and "receives" it as a "figure." Descartes proposes a schema that is both more and less than a "mere analogy." On the one hand, perception occurs as the "imprinting" upon our senses by external objects "in exactly the same way as" a seal imprints its image on wax. On the other hand, the understanding, which corresponds to the other end of the pen, the intellection that follows directly upon the writing of the sensory imprint (*dum scribo, intelligo*), can either follow from the senses or affect them in turn. The "airy" writing—another instance of areality—at the upper end of the pen in motion immediately communicates with the sense impressions of the lower but can direct these in ways that are different. Nancy brilliantly seizes upon the fluidity and inconsistencies of Descartes's extended analogy ("this pen is unimaginable" [37]) to underscore that the pen's movement again is not a cursive movement at all but is caught within a discontinuous structure of printing or imprinting: "While I am writing, at each instant, the distinctive mark of a phonematic unit of the language is imprinted: The printed whole of this phonography will not constitute a duration, since it will be a *sum* of characterological units. The *sum* will be characteristic: it will constitute the impression of the figure of thought expressed by language" (24; emphasis added). Like Descartes's metaphor of the wax and seal, the imprinting of each "unit" of language, each letter, corresponds to an instant, "at each instant while I am writing," or each and every time (*quoties*), but the instant, adds Nancy, "is not a chronological measure; it is quite evidently the achronic limit of such a measure" (23–24), again a certain areality. Note that Descartes speaks of individual letters being traced on the paper (*singuli characteres in charta exprimuntur*), or more properly, singular characters being "ex-pressed" or printed out (through a passivity not unlike in the earlier line from *Meditations* about the veracity of *ego* sum in the passive voice being put forward [*profertur*] or conceived [*conciptur*]). Writing is the metaphor of thinking being as imprinting/imprinted pen. As Nancy writing in the voice of Descartes specifies: "my model is a typographical one, like that of a printer—I am a writing machine, a typewriter [*Je suis moi-même une machine à écrire*]" (23). Or perhaps more like a film? Where the action of the "motion" picture happens through interruption and reprojection of *instantanés* or individual images (frames) and a projected areality: both lacking in substantial reality (even for so-called documentaries) and yet a recognizable space which is not itself spatially assignable. What appears as continuity is but a screen effect, with camera and projector functioning like the two ends of Descartes's pen. So too, the fragile sense of continuous subjectivity summed up by the iterative, interrupted, areal *cogito*, the work of understanding even as I write: *dum scribo, intelligo*. "My fundamental property lies in the immobility of my movement, in the death that in each instant interrupts and collects my writing gesture" (37). *Ego Sum* is but the "sum" or *ad-sum (da-sein)* of every instant in its endless interrupting, in its ever-repeated death, *quoties*, each and every time. Playing on the Latin word Descartes uses to describe this perilous pen, *calamo*, Nancy concludes still in mimicry of Descartes's voice, "I am a calamity" (37), only to reiterate a few lines later: "Truth is a calamity" (38).

Cogitationes publicae

This screen effect, but also (to try to respect Descartes's text) the effect of the seal's imprinting onto wax, is also the calamity of a certain appearance or mask, the scripted entrance of the philosopher falling out onto the world stage, the *larvatus prodeo*, "I come forward masked," recorded in Descartes's early *"cogitationes privatae"* (AT X, 213; CSM I, 2), and the point of departure for Nancy's second chapter: *"Larvatus pro deo."* What we could call Descartes's "coming out" will take place later and more dramatically in 1637 as the anonymously published self-portrait better known as the *Discourse on Method*, Descartes's first published book. But again as with the analogy of the writing pen, the trope of self-portrayal is not as simple as it seems and freights its own set of inconsistencies and contradictions, "this complex and artful device [*ce dispositif complexe et retors*]" (44), which Nancy carefully again unpacks at length. The self-portrait turns out to be more of a screen, or mask, by which the "anonymous" author can judge the reaction to his method while (not) revealing his identity:[15] "I shall be glad to reveal in this discourse what paths I have followed, and to represent my life in it as if in a picture, so that that everyone may judge it for oneself; and thus, learning from public response the opinions held of it, I shall add a new means of self-instruction to those I am accustomed to using" (AT VI, 3–4; CSM I, 112). It is again a question of showing something, of making something seen, namely the "paths" followed by the narrator in his intellectual itinerary and the *sum* of his life as if synoptically represented in a painting. In other words, a diachronic narrative of his ideas AND a synchronic self-portrait. It is not immediately clear, however, if there is any difference between these two. The problem is raised by the second moment in this pragmatic itinerary, when the addressee/spectator of the philosopher/addressor's self-representation is called upon to "judge" it. But what is being judged, the philosopher's thoughts or his life? The lack of distinction suggests that the judgment is the same on the one as on the other. This is where Nancy intervenes precisely to underscore the claim that "this method cannot be cloaked in an argument based on authority: It can be presented only according to what should be called an argument based on *authorship*: that of which *I* alone am the author can impose itself only upon the judgment that each *I* will be able to pass upon it" (40; Nancy's emphasis). But this authorial judgment in turn breaks down to the reader/spectator's recognition of the author's existence as such, to his self-presentation or de-monstration as author, to the mere verification of his ontological status as self-conceiving being: "Standing before the picture, then, and commenting on it, the viewer would perhaps verify not the resemblance, . . . but the very existence, the *sum* of the original. I am this thinking being that the other sees, or thinks she sees" (44; Nancy's emphasis). But what this means is that the very *sum* of the *cogito* depends upon a fundamental *mitsein,* or relation to otherness that both subtends (supports? subjects?) and undermines the very self-conception of the subject. The subject is literally ex-posed, or as Nancy puts it, "excogitated": "The *cogito*, insofar as it has or makes a figure, is excogitated; it is only thought by ex-posing itself, by feigning to expose itself and by exposing its feint, its fiction, its extravagance" (50). The philosopher's cogitative self-positing necessarily and simultaneously co-posits some other: "A fictive viewer is thus everywhere necessary for the exhibition of the portrait, that is, for the *conception* of the *subject* of the picture, or again, for *truth*" (58; Nancy's emphases), on the understanding that "'fictive' here does not mean 'imaginary' but designates a position or a *role* that is structurally indispensable in the production of the *theoretical* truth of the subject" (59; Nancy's emphases).

Nancy gives a further twist to this structural necessity of there being multiple subjectivities coterminous with any given subjectivity, underscoring Descartes's theological reasoning: "the resulting situation . . . is homologous to the recognition of the existence of God by means of the vision of his idea (faithful copy) within me. The viewer of the picture sees

Descartes as Descartes sees God . . . *larvatus pro deo*—I am masked in order to occupy God's place" (44), whence the wordplay that gives the chapter its title, from *prodeo* (to come forward, or proceed) to *pro deo* (for or on behalf of God). One is tempted to read out this structure in terms of Lacan's distinction between "other" and "Other," between the homologous other of mirrored spectatorship and the *sujet supposé savoir* of the paternal law.

One can see an entire line of Nancean thought emerge from this destructuring of subjectivity, from the very thesis of *The Inoperative Community* and the essays gathered in *The Birth to Presence* to the argument of *Being Singular Plural* as well as much of Nancy's political thought from *Rejouer le politique* and *The Experience of Freedom* up through *The Truth of Democracy*. Indeed, one of Nancy's key contributions is his insistent thinking of community, freedom, and the political not from the basis of subjectivity, or as some expansion of it that retains all the problems of the subject, but rather by thinking the "we" before and as the condition of the "I" as a kind of a priori *mitsein*. Ironic that the first germination of this critical approach comes from the reading of Descartes, the thinker most frequently accused of a kind of intellectual solipsism and as an early exemplar for the ideology of individualism. As Nancy recapitulates in *The Inoperative Community*,

> before recognition [*reconnaissance*], there is knowing [*connaissance*]: knowing without knowledge, and without "consciousness," that *I* am first of all exposed to the other, and exposed to the exposure of the other. *Ego sum expositus:* on closer inspection one might discern here a paradox, namely that behind Cartesian *évidence*—that *évidence* so certain that the subject cannot not have it and that it need not be proven in any way—there must lie not some nocturnal bedazzlement of the *ego,* not some existential immanence of a self-affection, but solely community—that community about which Descartes seems to know so little, or nothing at all. In this respect the Cartesian subject would form the inverse figure of the experience of community, of singularity. The Cartesian subject knows himself to be exposed, and he knows himself because his is exposed (does not Descartes present himself as his own portrait?). (31; translation modified)

But, as we saw earlier, Nancy also offers another narrative for the emergence, the coming out, the processional entrance of the thinking subject, one that begins not with a foundational otherness or an immersive *mitsein* but with the foundational experience of the world as chaos: "The radical or even the original nature of the Cartesian enterprise requires that it begin with Chaos—inseparably, indistinguishably with chaos and with the subject. The minimal condition is at once the creation of a chaos by a subject, and the conception of the subject evidenced by the matter of this chaos" (54). Nancy playfully terms this version of *cogito* the *chaogito:* "to know chaos is to know oneself as such." This copresencing of subject and chaos evokes that other great strand of Nancy's thought, regarding the sense of the world, whose roots begin here and in the title of Nancy's third chapter from *Ego Sum: "Mundus est fabula."*

Mundus facta est

How can we reconcile this apparent divergence between community and world, between the *cogito,* as structurally implicit but unavowed *mitsein,* and the *chaogito,* as unacknowledged copresence of self and world? What matters here is less some conceptual difference between world and community, both of which terms Nancy has consistently tried to keep both as rigorous and as open as possible. "Community" is certainly not limited to *dasein* or to human beings, or even just to living creatures, but also potentially inclusive of inanimate objects, to all beings in fact to the extent that we and they are all with one another, co-appearing as being-in-common.[16] "World" too is clearly not to be understood merely as the geophysical sphere of the planet we inhabit, nor even in some restricted regionalist sense (such as the "worlds" of Louis XIV, of sports, of Islam, or of popular culture), but simply as a totality or space of meaning (SW, 41, 120n), as "a differential articulation of singularities that make sense in articulating themselves" (SW, 78), "the being exposed of the ones to the others" (SW, 71). And just as community should be understood neither as an organic unity nor as an aggregation of preexisting individuals, so too does Nancy caution against "construing the relation between humanity and world as a relation between subject and object" (SW, 56). Just as community can only ever appear within the context of a specific world or worlds, so too does the differential structure of a world imply the fundamental *mitsein* or being-with of beings that defines a given community.

At issue, then, in Nancy's reading of Descartes appear to be two alternative ways of understanding the *cogito* that differ in significant ways from the traditional view of Descartes's grounding of philosophy in the subject's self-certainty, which *both* objectivizes the world *and* fails to think the reality of communal existence.[17] Nancy's careful reading instead argues the priority of both world and community in the very possibility of the *cogito*. Still, how are we to understand the relation between the *chaogito* of the metaphysician floundering in a bottomless watery world and the requisite enabling gaze of the other for the masked philosopher stepping out onto the stage or hiding behind his self-portrait? The "*Mundus est fabula*" chapter of *Ego Sum* articulates this bifurcated narrative, interestingly not as one might anticipate, by directly unpacking the concept of world or *mundus*, but by focusing on the workings of *fabula*: fable making, storytelling, fictionalizing, feigning, and so on. Presumably, if we can understand fabling, perhaps we can better understand world, which as the expression goes is itself a fable. Descartes, as Nancy details, does not hesitate to describe his own work as a kind of fable, most explicitly in the unpublished *Treatise on the World,* which he explicitly designates as a fable about an imaginary world whose properties can be systematically deduced from first principles. The validity of that philosophical fable is supported by the demonstrable coincidence of the properties deduced with the properties observed in our own, actual world. Even more dramatically, he applies the term *fable* to the very discourse of the *Discourse on Method*:

> My present aim, then, is not to teach the method which everyone must follow in order to direct his reason correctly, but only to reveal how I have tried to direct my own. . . . I am presenting this work only as a history or, if you prefer, a fable, in which, among certain examples worthy of imitation, you will perhaps also find many others that it would be right not to follow; and so I hope it will be useful for some without being harmful to any, and that everyone will be grateful to me for my frankness. (AT VII, 4; CSM I, 112)

As Nancy remarks, this is a most unusual fable, which aims not to teach in the classical sense—*fabula docet*—of an instructive "moral" that serves as the soul for the fable's narrative, or body,[18] but merely to present examples which can be followed or not according to the reader's whim. The examples given turn out to be nothing more than the tale of the author's life and search for truth, thus making of him an exemplary figure, the example of thought in action, that is of a thought or rather a thinking that in fact corroborates the existence of the thinking being itself, here redacted in the French text of the *Discourse* in the classically received formulation, "I think, therefore I am [*je pense donc je suis*]."[19] But as Nancy observes, this reduction of moralizing fable to exemplary narrative to ontological claim makes of the *Discourse* no longer a simple case of exemplarity which may or may not be imitated: "The passage to the limit of the example is what cannot be imitated; it is the original—an original than anyone can produce (perhaps), but that no one can reproduce. Such is the *cogito*" (78). Later in the chapter, Nancy invokes Benveniste's elaboration of the performative utterance to underscore *once again* the validity of the *cogito* only in its performative uttering, *quoties,* each and every time. No one can imitate this utterance or "reproduce" it: "The cogito cannot be said by an actor" (86). To utter the *cogito* is to produce it in and only in the actuality of its utterance. But if anyone can truthfully utter the *cogito,* can produce it as such, then the exemplarity of Descartes's fable is and is not "his," but the singular plural of any given being's being there, "that is, an ontology that blends with the invention of the discourse of my life, the invention of my life *as* discourse (or fable)" (83; Nancy's emphasis). Performing the *cogito,* like any other performance, is an event, but in the case of the *cogito,* "the event is here nothing other than the performance itself, or rather the *being* coextensive with this performance: *I am*" (85; Nancy's emphasis). The "performance" of the *cogito* is the event of being, the *(ego) sum* that happens each and every time it occurs, whether as "thinking," or more specifically in the course of the hypothetical doubting that leads to the advent of the *cogito,* as doubting, as feigning (to doubt), as fabling, or, gearing all the way down to the etymological antecedents, as *fari, for* (to speak). The *cogito* is, as Nancy puts it, the "self-performance, even the self-formation through the statement [*énoncé*] of the being of the one who utters [*énonciateur*] as being of truth" (85). This "true being [*l'être vrai*]," Nancy continues, "does not consist in a statement [*énoncé*], any more than in the substance who utters, or in the position of an utterance [*énonciation*], for substance, position, meaning of the statement are all performed in 'cogito' [one is tempted to add, "in-cognito"—GV]. Rather, it consists in an *uttering* [*énoncer*], in the *uttering* of utterance, of the one who utters, and the statement" (85; translation modified). And to the extent that, "as pragmatic linguistics asserts, all utterances are fundamentally performatives," *cogito* comes down to a "general or generalized 'for'" (85). "I am" cannot be distinguished from "I say," *sum* from *dico,* but at the same time that this *cogito/for* is only true each and every time I "proffer [*profertur*]" it, "bring it forward," whether by "pronouncing or conceiving" it, that is, each and every time I *perform* the event of the truth of being there, *da-sein, ad-sum.* Nancy describes this conundrum as a form of retrenchment (*retrancher*), another word that anticipates his more widespread and well-known use of the word, *retrait*: retreat, both re- and with-drawing. Retrenchment is a trenchant iteration that emphasizes the difference in the re-treat of repetition, literally a re-trenching which can mean excision, subtraction, or withdrawal as well as a "doubling down" or "digging in" that further entrenches whatever is trenched or trenchant but only at the cost of further diminution or withdrawal, literally digging out the ground from under one's feet, reemphasizing the subject by undoing the *sub-jectum,* in perhaps a slower, more arduous version of the plunge into bottomless waters. Each and every time

I "pronounce or conceive" *ego sum*, I mark and re-mark myself as irretrievably different from myself in the very repetitive act of uttering (the same). And that "I" need not be even the "same" utterer/being at different moments, as *cogito interruptus*, but also a completely other uttering being. Already, Nancy suggested this possibility when he earlier stated that this is "what cannot be imitated; it is the original—an original that anyone can produce (perhaps), but that no one can reproduce. Such is the *cogito*" (78). *Sum* is true for *whoever* says it, each and every time, as the iterative event of being there, regardless of who is the being there. This is why the *cogito* is both inimitable and performable by each and every one of us, each and every time.

Later, in *Being Singular Plural,* Nancy will further unpack the *cogito*'s implicit community: "the evidence for the *ego sum* comes down to, constitutively and co-originarily, its possibility in each one of Descartes's readers. The evidence as evidence owes its force, and its claim to truth, precisely to this possibility in each one of us—one could say, the copossibility. *Ego sum = ego cum*" (BSP, 31). The *sein* of *sum* equals the *mitsein* of *sum cum,* it consummates it (*cum sum*), and unexpectedly reveals the subjacent community of our being-in-common: "The truth of the *ego sum* is the *nos sumus*: this 'we' announces itself through humanity for all the beings 'we' are with, for existence in the sense of being-essentially-with, as a Being whose essence is the with" (BSP, 33). *Cogito*, therefore, would be the very "dis-enclosure" (ES, 80) of community,[20] of *mitsein*, as the iteration of singular plural being, a certain "sharing of voices" not just for other humans, but as Nancy specifies, "for all the beings 'we' are with." As Nancy further details in *Being Singular Plural*:

> critique absolutely needs . . . an ontology of being-with-one another, and this ontology must support both the sphere of "nature" and sphere of "history," as well as both the "human" and the "nonhuman"; it must be an ontology for the world, for everyone—and if I can be so bold, it has to be an ontology *for each and every one and for the world "as a totality,"* and nothing short of the whole world, since this is all there is (but, in this way, there is *all*). (51; emphasis added)

We come back, then, to the problem of the world, which is also the fable of a certain uttering, *mundus est fabula,* as Nancy tells us near the end of that chapter of *Ego Sum*: "the world is the uttering, the *pure* subject is I who utters itself uttering" (86).[21] But "everywhere in this world," this subject "at the height of purity" retrenches and withdraws itself in the very uttering of its utterance, "within and from its *for*" (87). We are back to the *chaogito* as the copresencing of *sum* and world, but Nancy adds some precious qualifications to the *chaogito* that offer a parallel to the *cogito senso stricto*, where as we remember the truth of the *sum* comes at the end of the process of hyperbolic doubt, as its extremity, where everything can be doubted, or feigned to be doubted, except for the I who feigns such a doubt: "you are, and you cannot not be, just as the chaos, from which the world—or its fable—can arise, cannot not be conceived" (83). The chaos from whence world can arise cannot not be "conceived." The *chaogito* "parallels" the *cogito* with I co-appearing in chiasmus with chaos: "*Chaos*—I am. I am—*chaos*" (83). And just as the content of feigned doubt at its extremity retrenches before the truth of the *cogito*, so too does the fiction or fable of the world find its truth in its very invention: "this truth is not only parallel or homologous to that of its content (the fictive creation): it functions only insofar as it invents itself—or invents itself as—the veritable creation, the unfictionable origin of a world in general. True or feigned, an invented world remains the invention of a world" (82–83). Nancy bases this startling conclusion upon his parallel reading of Descartes's *Treatise on the World* alongside the *Discourse on Method*, remembering that both announce themselves as "fables" whose pursuit in extremity leads to the retrenchment of their fictionality before a claim to truth. In the first case, the fable of an imaginary world leads to the summary description of the real world; in the second, the fiction of extreme doubt reveals the actuality of *sum*. Our previous questioning about the priority of world or community for the *cogito* seems to indicate the relation between *cogito* and *chaogito* as "parallel."

A further answer to the question regarding the relation between these unavowed encounters—*sum* and world, *sum* and community—can be found if we reconsider what happens between the end of the First Meditation and the beginning of the Second, where as we recall Descartes describes the result of his first meditation as a fall into a bottomless watery abyss. But how did he fall into this calamitous chaos, except through the final step in the hyperbolic doubt, which requires that he imagine some powerful entity able to deceive him in absolutely everything he might think to have been true, including "the sky, the air, the earth, colours, shapes, sounds, and all external things" or even whether he has "hands or eyes, or flesh, or blood or senses"? The enabling figure for this most extreme doubt is not "God, who is supremely good and the source of truth, but rather some malicious demon [*malin génie*] of the utmost power and cunning [who] has employed all his energies in order to deceive me" (AT VII, 22; CSM II, 15). Only this fictional malicious or evil demon can drown the philosopher in a sea of doubt so deep and boundless, so chaotic, that the truth of *sum* can emerge. While Nancy's book-length study of Descartes is remarkable in many ways, it is also remarkable that this very figure of the evil genius, the very height of Descartes's feigned doubting, receives scarcely a mention, appearing only in a brief footnote that reduces that fiction to a mere reversal (*revers*) of the strategy of feigning doubt, a passive reversal of that feint: "*I am tricked [feinté]*, and I am tricked by my *fiction of an Evil Genius*" (129n). A double (*diavolo*) to God, although one theologically empowered to do evil and wreak falsehood (a devil), the malicious genius not only enables the fiction of hyperbolic doubt to attain the extremity whereby the residue of what cannot be doubted comes to the fore, *ego sum, ego existo,* but also *personifies* the chaos of a world where nothing is sure and as the very *face* of otherness itself, be it the faceless face of the divine Other—*larvatus pro deo*. As such, the malicious genius articulates the convergence of *chaogito* and *cogito*, or between world and community, appearing first at the very end of the First Meditation and then reappearing near the beginning of the Second Meditation, right after the initial evocation of the chaotic watery abyss in which the philosopher finds himself after the encounter with the malicious genius and with no sure footing. This second appearance by the malicious genius leads straight to the sentence that is the starting point of Nancy's reading of Descartes:

> I have convinced myself that there is absolutely nothing in the world, no sky, no earth, no minds, no bodies. Does it now follow that I too do not exist? No: if I convinced myself of something [or thought anything at all—French translation] then I certainly existed. But there is a deceiver of supreme power and cunning who is deliberately and constantly deceiving me. In that case I too undoubtedly exist, if he is deceiving me; and let him deceive me as much as he can, he will never bring it about that I am nothing so long as I think I am something. So after considering everything very thoroughly, I must finally conclude that this proposition, *I am, I exist*, is necessarily true whenever [*quoties*: each and every time] it is put forward by me [*profertur*] or conceived in my mind. (AT VII, 25; CSM II, 16–17)

If "true or false, an invented world remains the invention of a world," wouldn't an invented other still be the invention of an other? The fiction of another—whether God or malicious genius—implies the other of fiction, not only for the "certain" existence of the *ego* that speaks *sum* and the truth of the utterance that says or thinks so, but also for the existence of others *tout court,* since the very positing of some other, whether "true or false," as heuristic ploy or as feigning fiction, reveals the structural necessity of there being some other or others in order for there to be *sum,* or stated otherwise, the necessary plurality of the singular.[22] The fiction of the malicious genius also forms the most minimal of communities, based here not on love (as per the Bataille of *The Inoperative Community*) but on mutual deception *and* presencing. But what do we make of the framing of the image of liquid chaos by the two evocations of the malicious genius? In fact, the resulting triptych articulates *cogito* with *chaogito*, the becoming community of or in the world with the becoming world of or through community, their mutual *iteration* and *retrenchment*: "the *self* becomes equivalent to *chaos*" (87). *Mundus est fabula* also means the coappearance of *sum* AND chaos, and of community AND world, where the face of the other is also the mask of the world in the etymological sense of Latin *mundus* and of Greek *cosmos*. Community and world join as the prosopopeia of each other, *self* in the place of *chaos* and vice versa, leading to the question of what we mean by face if not essentially the mouth, *os,* that internal cavity whose retrenchment nonetheless "makes up the very act of *ego*, its self-position in the form of: it retrenches *itself,* and this *happens* to it, at the extreme point of its fabulation—of its *saying*—, like an accident through which the *self* [*auto*] becomes equivalent to *chaos*. As soon as I open my mouth, I retrench myself. The place of this mouth does not let itself be circumscribed" (87; translation modified).

Quasi permixtum

Circumscribing the place of this mouth puts us awkwardly between mind and body, another irreconcilable duality supposedly imposed by Descartes according to the traditional reading. But where others claim a rigid distinction, Nancy sees "convulsion," as we move to the final chapter in *Ego Sum*: "*Unum quid.*" Although not as much a catchphrase as the other Latin titles, the importance of this odd expression comes buried in a key line from the Sixth Meditation: *"me non tantum adesse meo corpori ut nauta adest navigio, sed illi arctissime esse conjunctum et quasi permixtum, adeo ut unum quid cum illo componam* [I am not merely there in my body as a pilot is there in a ship, but that I am most closely conjoined and, as if all mixed in, with it, so that I compose one thing with it]" (AT VII, 81; CSM II, 56; translation modified). In the book's most audacious move, one that effectively wreaks havoc with any concept of Cartesian dualism, *unum quid* posits a *single something* that "I" would "compose" with my body. To be sure, the composition of this *unum quid* is not a claim to some monism over and against Descartes's reputed dualism, far from it, as the very fact of its composition attests. Nancy describes it as a "convulsion" in Descartes's thought, if not as the convulsion that is his thought, a "spasm of a system" that "tightens, ties, and contracts its parts as much as it disjoints or disarticulates them, . . . forcing the joint by tightening it rather than breaking it apart" (88). What brings together body and soul is what separates or distinguishes them, following the logic of retrenchment we've already seen at work. We can recall that *unum quid* is a legal term, by which is meant that various things are, for convenience or for some other reason, treated *as if* they were one. The oneness of body and soul is the act of treating them "*as* one" despite or because of the incommensurability of their difference, understood by Descartes as a radical gap between *res cogitans* and *res extensa*, or between the substance that "thinks" but has no extension in space and the one that extends in space but does not think.

Nancy contests the facility of this distinction while probing the instability of the *unum quid* as a com-position, or co-positing, co-appearing of what it brings together in difference. The "convulsion" in Descartes's thought will resound all throughout Nancy's subsequent thinking of the body, most notably in *Corpus* (whose textual corpus was itself published in various forms and editions from 1993 through 2006). For Descartes, as he stipulates in the passage from the Sixth Meditation, mind or soul is not something that is inserted into a body, like a boatswain in a boat, but rather body itself is conjoined or inextricably mixed in (*permixtum*) with mind. How does this work? To be sure, Nancy is not contesting that there is a difference for Descartes between mind and body, or between "thought" and extension, but what that difference is remains to be shown. Again rereading Descartes carefully and scrupulously, Nancy reveals that the difference between thought and extension is in fact the very condition for there to be a unity of mind and body, for there to be that *unum quid* that com-poses the two together, not as separate parts—*partes extra partes*—added to each other or the one inserted into the other, "like the pilot of a ship," which would imply some minimal "extension" for the thinking substance, be it the vanishing "point" of the pineal gland (as Descartes will later try to argue, less than convincingly).[23] Nor do these two substances—soul or mind and body, and I merely note the slippage between the two terms of *mind* and *soul* in Descartes and hence in whoever tries to explicate his thinking—form some new substance over and beyond the uneasy composition of this *unum quid*. The "union" of *unum quid* is no dialectic, no *Zauberkraft* of the negative. It is only because the two substances are *incommensurable* that they can come to occupy the same place in or as the living human being, as the *dasein* or "*adsum*" of its existence: "*adesse* meo corpori . . . ut unum quid," being there in my body as one with my mind. Nancy concludes: "the proof of the distinction opens the space for what could be called a *singularly double* status of 'me'—of a strange couple of forces, disjunction and conjunction at the same time, exerting themselves on me" (95; emphasis added).

To this "singular duality" is added a fundamental divergence in cognition: the thinking substance knows itself through the meditating feint of doubting everything resulting in the irrefutable evidence of its own feigning/thinking, but as Nancy recalls from Descartes's June 28, 1643, letter to Princess Elisabeth, the practice of meditation, or directed cogitation, may *a contrario* work to obscure the innate evidence of one's own bodily existence: "But it is the ordinary course of life and conversation, and *abstention from meditation* and from the study of the things which exercise the imagination, that teaches us how to conceive the union of the soul and the body" (AT III, 692; III, 227; Garnier III, 46; emphasis added). Despite this evident contrariety between the truth acquired through meditation and the truth acquired by the absence of meditation, both the apperception of self, of ego, *and* of the union between body and soul impose themselves not as logical or argumentative proof based on prior principles, but as the incontrovertible (self) evidence of experience. But this "experience" needs to be qualified. Nancy writes:

> The experience of the subject has nothing to do with the order of the empirical, nor with that of some existential intimacy. It builds the structure of the substance when the latter becomes the modern Subject. In this experience, the Subject apprehends its own *sub-stare* to the extent in which he does not grasp it as the *object* of an action, or a thought. . . . The evidence of the *cogito* stands underneath every faculty and every substantiality. Cartesian experience is the experience of the *sub* without stasis or stance. Up to the end and without reserve—*ex-perior*—the *sub* puts to the test what it can be. *Ego* is the proof of the *subex*. (107–8)

We seem to be back to the image of Descartes floundering in the depthless waters of uncertainty, the experience of being unsupported by anything below one's sinking self. As if afloat in a vast amniotic fluid prior to the birth to presence and/or calamitously drowning at the very point of absent expiration, the "antinomic" experiences of *sum* and of soul/body union, thinking and living, are the same "singularly double" experience of *unum quid*, "traversed by contrariety" and both "prior and subsequent to the distinction between substances" (108). Or, as Nancy will extrapolate in *Corpus*, which in many ways is an extended meditation on this final chapter of *Ego Sum*: "Experience is neither knowledge nor nonknowledge. Experience is a passage, a transport from border to border, an endless transport from shore to shore [I'm inclined to interpolate, from birth to death—GV], all along a tracing that develops and limits an areality" (C, 113).[24] This areality traced or retraced, retreated and retrenched, by experience is that of the "constitutive instability" (102) that is *unum quid*: "Unum quid: a something that makes up a One without having any thingness, and hence without having any one*ness*" (109).

Indeed, Nancy explains that beyond the distinction between *res cogitans* and *res extensa* there is also necessarily the distinction between the subject or "subex" and the distinction itself between the two substances: "There is thus the distinction between substances, and the distinction between the subject and the distinction between substances" (97). *Unum quid* might thus read *ego sum distinctus* (96), as it is distinction itself that distinguishes the *sum* of each and every time, beyond the question of that incommensurable distinction between thinking and extension:

> the distinction of *ego,* insofar as it is the distinction of what has, so to speak, no really substantial substantiality—but it is not a *what*, it is the *what* that is only *I*, that consists only in the *I* (who say I). This distinction, which is nothing other than the *distingo* of the *for*, raises (or, precisely, does not raise) the question of the existential status that *I* bestows upon itself, that *I* as such (or the *for* as such) consists in bestowing upon itself. Therefore it raises (or does not raise) the question of a non-substantial *status*, of a constitutive *instability*. The instability, in sum, of the *sum* that grasps itself in the *for*. Yet, the status of this insubstantial substance is precisely identical with its apprehension: *ego sum* is true "whenever [*quoties*] *I* pronounce it or whenever *I* conceive it in my mind" (it is *I* who underline *I*). This "status"—that of evidence—necessarily has the structure of immediacy as *self*-relation. To this extent, it is not distinguishable—with regard to its structure—from the immediate apprehension of the union of soul and body. (102; Nancy's emphases; translation modified)

The "constitutive instability" of the "*sum* which grasps itself in the *for*" is what we have been calling the "iterative cogito," the "punctual identity" (104) of an uttering or a proffering that articulates itself "each and every time" and *only* "each and every time" as the evidence of itself as uttering being, as *for*. This iteration (re)marks itself, retrenches and redraws itself, interrupts itself, withdraws itself, every time, in distinction from any previous iteration. Nancy again proposes the metaphor of photography:

> If *ego* sees itself in the snapshot [*l'instantané*] that allows the luminous trace of its unstable image to be inscribed (but is it an image? it is an utterance, an uttering, at most the opening of a mouth . . .), this vision and this inscription themselves depend on—in truth they do

> more than depend on it, they are "consubstantial" with—the instantaneous shuttering (the instant "is" also instability) of the diaphragm through which light passes. The evidence of the *cogito* has the nature of a *diaphragm*. It is what gets in the way of something, obstructing or obfuscating it. (103; Nancy's emphasis; translation modified)

Following this, we can see the cogito no longer as "interrupted" but *as* interruption, but perhaps again, as I suggested earlier, less the isolated flash of a given snapshot than the repetitive or iterative workings of that series of snapshots or "frames" that defines the *motion* picture or cinema, whose illusion of continuity, the "sum" of its *sum,* is as much a misprision as is the Cartesian subject's supposed sense of durable identity. Or, following Nancy (and Descartes) more closely in another register, the articulation/disarticulation of language in the proffering of *ego,* "each and every time I say it or conceive of it," be it most minimally the mere opening or closing of the mouth. And that is where we find the point of *unum quid,* where thought meets extension in the incommensurate *spacing* of the maw, the making space that is the internal cavity of the body, the *sum* of its *areality.*[25]

The overcoming of Cartesian dualism between mind and body does not mean the suppression of their difference but rather their indefinite and ongoing spacing and difference, the interruption of ceaseless (re)iterations, the stutterings of a vertiginous, invaginating exteriority: "the incommensurable extension of thought is the opening of the mouth. . . . But the human being is that which spaces itself out, and which perhaps only ever dwells in this spacing, in the *areality* of his mouth" (111–12).[26] But far from any comforting prosopopeia, this mouth has no face, only a hole or holes for mouth/eye,[27] the mask again of *larvatus pro deo* that stages the disenclosure of a necessarily absent God.[28]

Unum quid tells us that the Cartesian body is not an interiority sheltering an even more interiorized mind/soul but a radical, incontrovertible exteriority, further exteriorized by the elucubrations of a thinking being that operates only iteratively to further exteriorize, differentiate, space out the "I" whose *sum* is coterminous with an incessant withdrawal, retrenchment, or retreat not *from* itself (which would presuppose a priorly existing self from which something could be taken) but *as* the very sense of self the "I" can claim, that is, as sense sensing itself. Taking us back again to the philosopher's watery doubt, Nancy concludes:

> The subject ruins itself and collapses into this abyss [*s'abîme en ce gouffre*]. But *ego* utters itself there. It externalizes itself there, which does not mean that it carries to the outside the visible face of an in-

visible interiority. It means, literally, that *ego* makes or makes itself into *exteriority*, spacing of places, distancing and strangeness [*écartement et étrangeté*] that make up a place, and hence space itself, primordial spatiality of a true *outline* in which, and only in which, *ego* may come forth, trace itself out, and think itself.

   It is this thought—*ego, unum quid*—that can alone find out that it does not give rise to any recognition of its subject, of the human being. This thought is always in advance withdrawn from the possibility of recognizing itself, and hence from the possibility of thinking. (112)

"*Ego* contracts thought to the point where it is wrenched away from itself," writes Nancy on the very last page of *Ego Sum* (112). Thought's greatest "advance" brings its own retreat. This retreat of thought, or its "*convulsion*," that the thought of Descartes stages is nonetheless what is denied by the subsequent development of philosophical thought: "from Descartes onward, thought has refused to confront its own convulsion: violence is begotten in what one refuses to confront" (112).

Confusi cogitandi

We began by noticing the absence of the term *thinking*, or *cogitating*, from the title and theme of the book, the traditional *cogito ergo sum* reduced simply to *ego sum*. But now, at the end of the book, we are still left wondering what this "thought" actually is, or what this thinking is that can both tear itself asunder in its retreat and "refuse" to confront the convulsion that defines what it is, through a violence in denial of its retreat, of its retrenchment. Nancy, of course, will pursue the question of what thinking is elsewhere in his work (confirming again the importance of this reading of Descartes for Nancy's further philosophical development), although some intriguing hints already appear in *Ego Sum* itself. To begin with, the reduction of thinking and doubting to an activity of feigning (that there is no "sky, air, earth, colours, shapes, sounds, and all external things" or even that I have no "hands or eyes, or flesh, or blood or senses," that everything I sense is just the deceitful fabrications of a malicious genius) also paradoxically expands thinking to include sensory perception in general to the extent that what I *seem* to sense becomes indistinguishable from thinking and ipso facto from my being, as seen in this passage from the Second Meditation, cited by Nancy (*Ego Sum*, 46): "Nevertheless, at the very least, it is very certain that it seems to me that I see (*videre videor*), that I hear, that I feel hot, and that is properly what in me is called sensing, and that, taken precisely so, is nothing other than thinking" (AT VII, 29; CSM II,

19; my translation). Again, later in the Second Meditation: "But when I see, or think I see (I am not here distinguishing the two), it is simply not possible that I who am now thinking am not something" (AT VII, 33; CSM II, 22, cited by Nancy, 72). And in a striking passage just following the line about *unum quid* in the Sixth Meditation: "sensations of hunger, thirst, pain and so on are nothing but confused modes of thinking (*confusi cogitandi*) which arise (*exorti*) from the union and, as it were, intermingling (*quasi permixtione*) of the mind with the body" (AT VII, 81; CSM II, 56; Alquié II, 186, 492; *not* cited by Nancy).[29] The extremity of hyperbolic doubt ends up blurring the distinction between the two meanings of sense (as sensation and as meaning), that is, between the sensible and the intelligible, or between "body" and "mind." Sensations may be "confused modes of thinking," but they are *still* a form of thinking, one that testifies to the "intermingling of the mind with the body," the *unum quid*. Or even hearkening back to the "calamity" of *dum scribo*, where a typography of sensation seamlessly connects with the imprinting of intellection, or cognition, the actual writing with its airy counterpart at the other end of the pen. A convulsive cogitating or co-agitating of the pen, *unum quid*, that is also nothing less than an ex-cogitating that marks a thought that is outside or beside itself:

> Thinking is not about a subject placing an object in front of itself to examine and evaluate it. It is what finds itself only in what it thinks. So it is, for Descartes, everything takes place in such a way that I find myself in it, or I touch myself in it, at the same time that I come up against something, a representation, a sensation or an affection. This is what makes it so that *ego sum* becomes equivalent to *cogito*: far from being able to establish an intellectual subject, this thought of *sum* accedes to a being that gives *itself* or that finds *itself* in as much as, infinitely, it wraps and unwraps itself (*s'enrobe et se dérobe*) with everything in the world. This is indeed why, as we know, the self-evidence of this *ego* is identical with its eclipse, and it too, as *res cogitans* withdraws in its nakedness. . . .
>
> What a thought that is stripped away (*la pensée dérobée*) thinks, it thinks therefore only as what is taken away from itself (*ce qui la dérobe à elle-même*). This is how it is "still thought." . . . An ex-cogitated *cogito,* a thinking beside itself [*pensée hors de soi*]. (*La pensée dérobée*, 12, 38; my translation)[30]

These lines emerge from a discussion about the paradox of thinking nonknowledge as differently thought by Sartre and Bataille, and so all the more strange to see Descartes emerge here as the exemplar of deconstructed thought, or as the deconstruction of thought that is its unraveling or disrobing, its being taken away from itself, its exposure that exposes us all, its exscription and retreat. It offers a vision of thought in its finitude, or as finitude, a finite or finished thought (*une pensée finie*), which Nancy explains in *A Finite Thinking* as follows: "A finite thought is one that each time thinks the fact that it is unable to think what comes to it. Of course, it isn't a matter of refusing to see ahead or plan. Rather, a finite thinking is one that is surprised each time by its own freedom."[31] It is a thought that "has to think itself as what loses itself in thinking—necessarily, if that sense it thinks is the sense of innumerable finitudes, . . . a thinking that can no longer impose itself, nor even propose itself, but that must, with all its resources, *expose itself* to what is finite about sense. Multiple, and each time, singular" (30). Thinking too, whatever we conceive it to be, necessarily still follows the logic of being/sensing singular plural, each and every time inside itself, outside itself, beside itself: ex-cogitated in its very cogitation.

What all this comes down to is an *ethics* of thinking, which is as much inspired by Descartes as it is very different from the classical "Cartesian habits,"[32] very different from the innateness of what is clear and distinct, but very much a following out of the paths upon which we find ourselves, paths whose sense (in both the directional and the cognitive "senses") emerges only in its happening, in the openness toward what comes to it, each and every time.[33] The iterative cogito, the *sum* of each and every time, exposes us to ourselves and to each other in our finitudes, in our singularities, in our multitude, as the very sensing of our existence. Or, as Nancy will later conclude: "the act of sensing and the act of the sense are the same. Existence is the act internally differing from its own sense, its self-sensation as its own dehiscence. Nothing else is at stake, in the final analysis, in the *Ego sum, ego existo* of René Descartes, in the obscurity of its self-evidence and in the madness of its self-certainty" (SW, 28).

Nancy's Descartes therefore is "the founder neither of humanism nor of anthropology or the so-called human sciences" (109). Neither the hallowed source of rationalism nor the founder of some "idea of man," but rather, and dare I say, *simply,* the very interruption of thought, its finitude as its openness, its retreat that is at once withdrawal and reinscription—*dum scribo*—, as masked dis-enclosure, stepping forth, stepping back, setting forth (*profertur*), setting back (*refertur*)—*larvatus pro deo*—, as world creation and *chaogito—mundus est fabula*—, as the areality of *unum quid*. In *sum*, as the ever renewed (re)iterations of *ego sum*, whenever or each and every time I set it forth, whoever "I" may be . . .

Descartes, the reputedly solipsistic thinker of *res cogitans*, becomes the surprisingly radical locus for rethinking body, community, world, and thought itself. Nancy thus drives a durable wedge between the traditional "habits" of Cartesianism and the text of Descartes. Not that Nancy's critical interruption isn't also indebted to the examples of other key philosophers—Kant, Hegel, Nietzsche, Heidegger, and Derrida especially—and no doubt one could undertake an equally surprising journey through Nancy's readings of those philosophers, though I doubt any of them would emerge as irrevocably altered as Descartes, as exposing the areality of an iter marked by gaps, divergences, and interruptions, by *d'écartes*. I can only conclude in agreement with Antonia Birnbaum when she writes regarding Jean-Luc Nancy that "his passage through Descartes restores all its force to the strange method thanks to which a philosopher reinvented thought."[34] Perhaps it would be more apt, however, to speak of a mutual "being with," a dramatic compearance emerging from Nancy's *touching/reading* of Descartes that enjoins us—as they each in their own singular way explicitly invite us to do—to think thought anew, to "reinvent" thought *along with* them, that is, with the classically (un)masked philosopher of body, community, and world and the contemporary thinker of finitude, dis-enclosure, and being *with* or *to*. Imagine Nancy/Descartes as *unum quid*, where the unity is that of incommensurable differences, the perpetual reiteration of a *sum* whose interruptions define the areality of an existence where thought is always still to come, a thinking/sensing singular plural, each and every time . . .

Notes

1. Jean-Luc Nancy, *Ego sum* (Paris: Flammarion, 1979); *Ego Sum: Corpus, Anima, Fabula,* trans. Marie-Eve Morin (New York: Fordham University Press, 2016). The previously translated chapters are "Dum scribo," trans. Ian McLeod, *Oxford Literary Review* 3, no. 2 (1978): 6–21; "Larvatus pro Deo," trans. Daniel Brewer, in *Glyph* 2, ed. Samuel Weber and Henry Sussman (Baltimore, MD: Johns Hopkins University Press, 1977), 14–36; and "Mundus est fabula," trans. Daniel Brewer, *MLN* 93, no. 4 (1978): 635–53.

2. Jacques Derrida, *On Touching—Jean-Luc Nancy,* trans. Christine Irizarry (Stanford, CA: Stanford University Press, 2005), 20–35.

3. The actual expression, "I think, therefore I am," appears only in the French text of the *Discourse on Method*, and in the never published *Recherche de la vérité*. René Descartes, *The Philosophical Writings of Descartes,* trans. John Cottingham, Robert Stoothoff, and Dugald Murdoch (Cambridge, UK: Cambridge University Press, 1984), II, 417. Further references to this English translation will be indicated in the text only as CSM, followed by volume and page number. References to either Descartes's Latin or French will be to the standard eleven-volume *Oeuvres de Descartes,* ed. Charles Adam and Paul Tannery (Paris: Vrin, rev. ed., 1964–76), indicated as AT, followed by volume

and page number (in the current case: AT VI, 32); or to the three-volume *Oeuvres philosophiques,* ed. Ferdinand Alquié (Paris: Garnier, 1963–73), which Nancy prefers to cite. References to this edition will be indicated as Alquié, followed by volume and page number (in the current case: Alquié II, 1136).

4. Nancy's signature affection for giving Latin titles to his works, and well beyond those focused on Descartes, is worth reflection, especially given the following remarks from "Lapsus judicii," in *L'impératif catégorique* (Paris: Flammarion, 1983), where he questions the becoming juridical of philosophy when it moves from Athens to Rome: "If philosophy is Greek, then it is the *Latin* question of philosophy; if Rome is the dissolution of philosophy, then it is the *philosophical* question of Rome. . . . If Roman law substitutes itself for philosophy, or imposes its mask upon it, this is also perhaps because metaphysics, in Rome and since Rome, begins to speak through the law. There would thus be, intimately woven within the *Greek* discourse of metaphysics, a *Latin* discourse: juridical discourse" (36–37). Does Nancy's repeated use of Latin titles signal and thus *expose* an awareness of the implied juridical aspect of critical philosophy per se (and Kant figures well in this discussion as well), its embeddedness in or as a discourse of judgment and legitimation? And "Lapsus judicii" also closes with or opens up a strong line of discussion with the Jean-François Lyotard of *The Differend.*

5. The basic lineaments of Martin Heidegger's evolving critique of Descartes can be found in *Being and Time,* trans. Jane Stambaugh (Albany: State University of New York Press, 1996), 83–93; *Nietzsche, Volumes Three and Four,* ed. David Krell, trans. F. A. Capuzzi (New York: Harper and Row, 1982), passim; *What Is a Thing?,* trans. W. B. Barton Jr. and V. Deutsch (South Bend, IN: Gateway, 1967), 98–108.

6. But even as traditional a Descartes scholar as Ferdinand Alquié recognizes the problem in his critical edition of the *Meditations:* "There is certainly, in this sense, at the point of departure, an ontological experience of the self as existent (*ego sum, ego existo,* says the Latin text) . . . experience [that] positions us far away from idealist interpretations, which would like to see Descartes begin with thinking in general, or with a properly cognizant subject" (Alquié II, 416n).

7. In the preface to the translation of *Ego Sum,* Nancy himself concedes that the expression *ego sum* "tautologizes its 'I' since the Latin word *sum* already contains the first person pronoun and has no need of *ego*" (xii). I tend to see the line less as a clean tautology that would close and totalize the utterance than as the striking excess of pleonasm, and as such, a harbinger of the iterative, non-identitarian work of what we too readily call "the" cogito.

8. Nancy's philosophical work, among other notable features, has been marked by an insistent foregrounding of contemporary actuality, which is not at all seen as diverging from a rigorous philosophical praxis, on the contrary. Nancy deftly evades the pitfalls, on the one hand, of a fashionable taking of positions at the expense of an openly critical thinking, and on the other hand, of an abstract detachment that fails to rise to the level of comprehending the

sense of the world in which we live. See my "Monograms: Then and 'Now,'" in *Nancy Now*, ed. Verena Andermatt Conley and Irving Goh (Cambridge, UK: Polity, 2014), 59–89; and "Lost Horizons and Uncommon Grounds: For a Poetics of Finitude in the Work of Jean-Luc Nancy," in *On Jean-Luc Nancy: The Sense of Philosophy*, ed. Darren Sheppard, Simon Sparks, and Colin Thomas (London: Routledge, 1997), 12–18.

9. Irving Goh is a major exception. See his *The Reject: Community, Politics, and Religion after the Subject* (New York: Fordham University Press, 2014). Nancy's query about "who comes after the subject" dates back to at least 1991 with the publication of the volume by that same title edited by Eduardo Cadava, Peter Connor, and Jean-Luc Nancy (New York: Routledge, 1991).

10. See especially "The Surprise of the Event," in *Being Singular Plural*, trans. Robert D. Robertson and Anne E. O'Byrne (Stanford, CA: Stanford University Press, 2000), 159–76; and also Irving Goh and Verena Andermatt Conley's perceptive remarks in their introduction to *Nancy Now*, 10–11.

11. Nancy, it should be said, is neither the first nor the only one to note this performative aspect of the *cogito*. See especially Jaako Hintikka, "Cogito, Ergo Sum as an Inference and a Performance," *Philosophical Review* 72, no. 4 (1963): 487–96.

12. Jacques Derrida, *Limited Inc*, trans. Samuel Weber and Jeffrey Mehlman (Evanston, IL: Northwestern University Press, 1988), 7. What does it mean to read Nancy under the sign of a key concept developed by his mentor, Jacques Derrida, but which as far as I can tell he never has used himself? On the other hand, *iter* and iterability and their derivatives do seem to intersect in all kinds of unanticipated ways with much of Nancy's critical vocabulary: interruption, areality, experience, exposition, and even the sense of his deployment of the word *sense*.

13. Now, this term, *cogito* (or *cogitus*) *interruptus*, seems easy enough to accept in our post-Freudian, post-Lacanian, post-Althusserian, post-Deleuzian world where unconscious processes are freely acknowledged to determine and inform what consciousness we think we have, but the expression also has a separate history dating to Umberto Eco's devastating review in 1967 of books by Sedlmayr and McLuhan (reprinted in *Travels in Hyperreality*). For Eco, the illogicality and misguided belief of these two authors in a "world inhabited by symbols or symptoms" represents a deliberate failure of thought or "cogito interruptus" (Umberto Eco, *Travels in Hyperreality* [San Diego: Harcourt, 1986], 222). More recently, Eco's idea has been explicitly deployed by Kyoo Lee in her astute and challenging reading of the correspondence between Descartes and the Princess Palatine Elisabeth, yet her concept of *cogito interruptus* is more focused on the literal interruptions of thought in the course of embodied life and the "intersubjectivity" of dialogue (Kyoo Lee, "*Cogito Interruptus*: The Epistolary Body in the Elisabeth-Descartes Correspondence, June 22, 1645–November 3, 1645," *philoSOPHIA* 1, no. 2 (2011): 173–94. More colloquially, as evidenced by even a quick googling of the term, *cogitus*

interruptus seems to have cropped up as an explanatory concept in all kinds of business and corporate thinking regarding ways to overcome the constant interruptions and distractions workers experience in the contemporary digital or wired environment that would result in countless amounts of lost time, productivity, and profits. See, for example, Dan Markovitz, "Cogitus interruptus: The Case for Focus," which begins: "Cogitus Interruptus is the disease of the modern workplace. Its symptoms are familiar to any executive: the inability to complete a thought or a task without losing focus under the onslaught of relentless interruptions. It results in a lack of efficiency, a loss of time to solve problems, to think strategically, to plan, to dream—to get your company from here to there. But there's hope: there are techniques to help you regain the opportunity to think without interruption"; https://www.socialmediatoday.com/content/cogitus-interruptus-case-focus. The author is identified as the president of something called TimeBackManagement.

14. *The Inoperative Community*, ed. Peter Connor, trans. Peter Connor, Lisa Garbus, Michael Holland, and Simona Sawhney (Minneapolis: University of Minnesota Press, 1991), 43–70.

15. One can only reflect on the irony of the strikingly conflicted or even duplicitous "anonymity" of the *Discourse on Method*, whose princeps edition amounted to a mere two hundred copies printed without the author's name but each then individually signed by Descartes and mailed to his interlocutors. See Adrien Baillet, *La Vie de Monsieur Des-Cartes* (Paris, 1691), 275–79; Etienne Gilson, *René Descartes: Discours de la méthode; Texte et commentaire* (Paris: Vrin, 1947).

16. See especially his critical rejection of Heidegger's statement that "the stone is without world," arguing instead that the stone is "nonetheless toward or in the world," and concluding that "all bodies, each outside the others, make up the inorganic body of sense. The stone does not 'have' any sense. But sense touches the stone." *The Sense of the World*, trans. Jeffrey S. Librett (Minneapolis: University of Minnesota Press, 1997), 59–63. Further references to this work will be indicated by the initials SW and the page number.

17. Perhaps nothing speaks Descartes's reputed solipsism louder than his questioning whether the people he sees outside his window are "any more than hats and coats which could conceal automatons" (CSM II, 21), yet this line from the Second Meditation following right upon the discussion of the piece of wax emphasizes rather the perils of relying *solely* on the evidence of the senses in favor of critical intellection. The lines here make it clear that while what I *see* is nothing more than ambulatory "hats and coats," I do *judge* them to be people rather than automatons underneath the outerwear.

18. See my "Fabel," in *Historisch-Kritisches Wörterbuch der Marxismus*, ed. Wolfgang Fritz Haug (Berlin: Argument-Verlag, 1999); English translation, in *Historical Materialism* 16, no. 4 (2008): 233–38; and *A World of Fables*, ed. Brenda Schildgen and Georges Van Den Abbeele (Berkeley, CA: Pacific View, 2003).

19. As Nancy notes elsewhere, this more famous reiteration of the *ego sum* supplies both a *content*, "thought," and a *logical sequencing*, "therefore," that are not otherwise justified: "Between *The World* and the *Meditations,* the *Discourse* represents . . . the weakest model in that the extremity of the withdrawal [*retranchement*] is immediately covered over, saturated, and guaranteed by the name of thought and by the formal mark of reasoning (*therefore,* I am). But the 'concept' of this name and its demonstrative 'reason' reside in fact . . . in their impossible articulation" (*Ego Sum,* 83; Nancy's emphasis).

20. It is tempting, of course, to read in this early use of the word *dis-enclosure* an anticipation of Nancy's much later work on Christian theology (*Dis-enclosure: The Deconstruction of Christianity,* trans. Bettina Bergo, Gabriel Malenfant, and Michael B. Smith [New York: Fordham University Press, 2008]; and *Adoration: The Deconstruction of Christianity II,* trans. John McKeane [New York: Fordham University Press, 2012]), a temptation at least somewhat justified by the "pro deo" revealed here to underlie Cartesian discourse, and also by the fact that the term was already in use, specifically by Emmanuel Martineau to render the term *Entdeckung* in his translation of Rudolf Boehm, *La Métaphysique d'Aristote, le Fondamental et l'Essential* (Paris: Gallimard, 1976).

21. The intrusion of purity here reflects again the meaning of *mundus,* as Nancy explains it: "This is no word play. It is the same word, *mundus,* pure, clean, proper, well-disposed, well-ordered, world. This is what, according to Plutarch, Pythagoras meant by the word *kosmos.* The world is nice arrangement, clear, clean, pure, and proper. The world is that which is not impure [*immonde*]" (*Ego Sum,* 66–67).

22. Cf. SW, 156: "without this coming toward the world that the world in turn spatializes, an 'ego' purely present there would not properly speaking be (this is what Descartes cannot see) or it would be immediately all of given sense (and this is what philosophy desires from Descartes to Husserl)."

23. See Antonia Birnbaum, "To Exist Is to Exit a Point," in *Corpus,* 145–49.

24. And much more recently, in *An All-Too-Human Virus,* trans. Cory Stockwell, Sarah Clift, and David Fernbach (Cambridge, UK: Polity, 2022), Nancy with reference to Descartes returns to the uncertainty of experience itself:

> Every experience is an experience of uncertainty. Certainty—knowledge that is sure of itself and by means of itself—is the distinctive mark of Cartesian truth. Far from being exclusively French, this certainty structures all our representations of knowledge: scientific, technological, social, political and virtually cultural. It is therefore the entire order of our guarantees and convictions that is being put to the test. For this reason, we really are having an experience: we are being pushed beyond our programming. . . . To have an experience is always to be lost. We lose mastery. In one sense, we are never really the subject of our experience. Rather, experience gives rise to a new subject. (69–70)

25. See *Corpus,* 131, where Nancy completes this rethinking of Descartes: "For Descartes, thought is sensing, and as sensing, it touches upon the extended thing, it's touching extension. . . . For Descartes, the *res cogitans* is a body."

26. The critique of any historical concept of "man" pursued by Nancy in the closing pages of *Ego Sum* also reveals his intervention within the famous polemics between Derrida and Foucault regarding the latter's argument that Descartes's rejection of the possibility of his being mad also inaugurates a certain idea of "man" whose legacy lies in the subsequent development of the human sciences. See Michel Foucault, *History of Madness*, ed. Jean Khalfa; trans. Jonathan Murphy and Jean Khalfa (New York: Routledge, 2006); the only complete English translation of Foucault's *Folie et déraison: Histoire de le folie à l'âge classique* (Paris: Plon, 1961); and Jacques Derrida, "Cogito and the History of Madness," in *Writing and Difference*, trans. Alan Bass (London: Routledge, 1978), 36–76.

27. On this mouth without a face, see Sara Guyer, "Buccality," in *Derrida, Deleuze, Psychoanalysis*, ed. Gabriele Schwab (New York: Columbia University Press, 2007), 77–104; and Derrida, *On Touching—Jean-Luc Nancy,* 20–25.

28. Or are we giving too much credit to the mouth as the privileged opening of the body, and the areality of the space between or as body and soul, but why not the vagina, for instance, the very locus of birth as the spacing of bodies, of human beings who "space themselves out" and "only ever dwell in this spacing" (112), as the very locus of our birth to presence in the particular "being with" of mother and child? Or, we could go even further, imaging a kind of vaginal mouth, as in Magritte's famous painting of a face with the features of a naked woman, where breasts stand in the place of eyes and a vagina for a mouth. Might we pursue *unum quid*'s "convulsion of thought" as orgasm or ecstasy, as the non-*sum* of passionate being with one another? Or, alternatively, as the violence of violation and intrusion?

29. The rapprochement between thinking and sensing might occasion a rereading of Pierre Gassendi's defense of sense-based knowledge and concomitant critique of the mind-body split as well as Descartes's response in the "Fifth Set of Objections" to the *Meditations* (AT VII, 256–412; CSM II, 179–277).

30. The French word *dérober* means to steal or rob, but Nancy in this passage and in others also plays upon the buried sense of disrobement, hence my translating it variously as to strip or take away.

31. "A Finite Thinking," trans. Edward Bullard, Jonathan Derbyshire, and Simon Sparks, in *A Finite Thinking*, ed. Simon Sparks (Stanford, CA: Stanford University Press, 2003), 15.

32. *Le poids d'une pensée, l'approche* (Strasbourg: Le Phocide, 2008), 13.

33. One can see Nancy's conceptualization of what thinking is as a radicalization of Heidegger's notion of *gelassenheit* (*What Is Called Thinking?*, trans. J. Glenn Gray [New York: Harper and Row, 1968]). For Nancy, it is not just a question of being "open" but of thought "always surprised by its own freedom" (*A Finite Thinking*, 15).

34. Birnbaum, "To Exist," 149.

Nancy with Hegel
The Restless Pleasures of Calculus and the Infinite Opening in Finitude

JOHN H. SMITH

> An alterity that one ought to try to read in Hegel's text.
> —Jean-Luc Nancy, *The Speculative Remark*[1]

> It is indeed this unrest that gives Hegel's text its greatness and its strength.
> —Nancy, *Speculative Remark*, 148

> And what are these Fluxions [infinitesimals]? The Velocities of evanescent Increments? And what are these same evanescent Increments? They are neither finite Quantities nor Quantities infinitely small, nor yet nothing. May we not call them the ghosts of departed quantities?
> —George Berkeley, *The Analyst*[2]

> We can enjoy a differential equation.
> —Alain Badiou and Jean-Luc Nancy, *German Philosophy: A Dialogue*[3]

The concept of the infinite has been a, if not *the*, hot topic in French thought for the past few decades. In his 1998 study of Leibniz and the Baroque, *The Fold*, Gilles Deleuze turns his attention to the metaphysics of calculus, which makes it possible to envision the world as a continuum of an infinity of infinitely small entities and thereby to perform mathematical operations using "infinitesimals." He is also one of the few contemporary thinkers to take seriously Salomon Maimon, an insightful, if occasionally opaque, post-Kantian, who had the idea to introduce differentials and the "mathematical infinite" into epistemology to help explain the infinite gradations of consciousness.[4] In 2003, two volumes of translated essays appeared in English, one by Alain Badiou, *Infinite Thought* (translated by Oliver Feltham and Justin Clemens) and one by Jean-Luc Nancy, *A Finite Thinking* (edited by Simon Sparks). And Quentin Meillassoux's *After Finitude* appeared in French in 2006, followed by an English translation in 2009. There's something going on here. Alain Badiou has based his entire philosophical enterprise on the postulate that "mathematics is ontology," whereby he strives to modify such tools as Georg Cantor's set theory and Abraham Robinson's form of calculus ("nonstandard analysis") in order to grasp the "actual infinite."[5] Badiou's student Quentin Meillassoux has argued that only a thinking of the infinite, "after finitude," can liberate us from the restrictions of a post-Kantian philosophical paradigm that limits human knowledge to phenomena, that is, to what can appear to us, and thereby puts "things in themselves" out of the reach of our reason.[6] What is at stake for Badiou and Meillassoux is an insistence that "everything can be known absolutely" (in principle) and the infinite manifold of being grasped mathematically, since without these core axioms we open the door to irrationalisms, faith-based mysticism, and obscurantism in the face of that which would remain "the unknowable" or absolutely Other.[7]

In this chapter, I shall argue that the stakes are equally high for Jean-Luc Nancy.[8] In the section entitled "Infinite Finitude" from *The Sense of the World*, Nancy makes a dramatic statement about what he sees as the central issue confronting philosophical thought:

> *Finitude is not privation.* There is perhaps no proposition more necessary to articulate today, to scrutinize and test in all ways. Everything at stake at the end of philosophy comes together there: in the need of having to open the thought of finitude, that is, to reopen to itself this thought, which haunts and mesmerizes our entire tradition.[9]

Although one can find other places in his *oeuvre* that highlight important tasks for philosophy, my goal here is to take him at his word in this near hyperbolic claim, to scrutinize his non-privative concept of finitude, to explore how he constantly circles around an infinite opening within finitude, and to test it by looking at where it has haunted and mesmerized that thinker from "our entire tradition" who is such an important source of Nancy's thinking, namely, Hegel. Nancy's creative and largely positive reception of Hegel makes him a preeminent philosopher of the infinite within the finite today. The reason for Hegel's significance to Nancy's project, I am arguing, is Hegel's own deep engagement with the (mathematical) infinite.[10] To show this, along the way we will have to do some calculus, explore the pleasure of speculative writing, and tolerate restlessness. We will spend time reading Hegel with Nancy.

Let us begin with a passage from one of Nancy's two books explicitly on Hegel, *The Speculative Remark (One of Hegel's Bons Mots)*. The book offers a close reading of the "remark" in Hegel's *Science of Logic* at the end of the opening dialectic of Being. In that remark, Hegel discusses the concept of *"Aufheben"* (sublation) and what he sees as the inherently philosophical nature of the German language, which contains terms like *"Aufheben"* that have multiple, even contradictory meanings (to cancel out, to preserve, and to elevate). Nancy's book offers in general an example of how to read Hegel, namely, to search for the internal "alterity" within his thought (see the epigraph above), an alterity that will make possible an infinitesimal, but nonetheless still infinite, opening within finitude. In discussing the passage just before the "remark," Nancy writes:

> The whole necessity of the *aufheben* has, up until now, been held in this discretion; it has kept itself in these slidings, these imperceptible displacements, in the play of vanishing apparitions, which will have, in fact, constituted the entire text in the manner of an infinitesimal calculus, whose example Hegel has precisely invoked. For infinitesimal magnitudes constitute this "pure concept," whose determination or whose being merges with the "vanishing." (*Speculative Remark*, 40)

Nancy raises the issue of the paradoxical nature of infinitesimal or differential calculus as a mode of (or perhaps within) representation: "As a concept, sublation will at least have . . . been illustrated through infinitesimal magnitude; but from the strictly conceptual point of view, the illustration is itself only a 'vanishing magnitude'" (*Speculative Remark*, 40). That is, Nancy picks up on the way Hegel uses the illustration of the infinitesimal, but the illustration is also a vanishing quantity. That is, "the discourse of the *aufheben* is justified only by comparison with another discourse, and very precisely, with the discourse of a calculus; discreetly, the *aufheben* appears to liken itself or to become analogous to this series of magnitudes, whose infinite decreasing diminishes the (mathematical) discretion without, however, canceling it out" (41).

To this section Nancy appends three interesting footnotes:

> n. 14 reads: "Infinitesimal calculus is moreover, through a sort of exorbitant privilege, the only particular object whose ulterior analysis Hegel announces in the first chapter of the *Science of Logic*" (*Speculative Remark*, 169).

n. 15 refers to two works by Jean-Joseph Goux, "Dérivable et in-dérivable," *Critique* 26 (1970) and *Symbolic Economies: After Marx and Freud* (Ithaca, NY: Cornell University Press, 1990). Nancy says he's taking a different course from Goux, but does not deny his relevance, for he (Goux) "gathers together derivative [the mathematical notion taken from calculus—JHS] and *aufheben* in the same economy of meaning" (*Speculative Remark,* 169).

n. 16 reads: "We are thus touching . . . on what could form the general question of the functioning of the mathematical in philosophy, a question that might itself be accompanied by the singular conjunction of the mathematical and the metaphorical, which would necessitate at least a detour through Kant" (*Speculative Remark,* 170). And a bit later: "the rapprochement between the process of becoming and differential calculus is carried out in a rather equivocal manner. It is not an identity, and it is not a comparison: Hegel states that the one and the other are exposed to the 'same dialectic' (in the Aristotelian-Kantian sense, then), which the understanding opposes (*SL* 104–05). Their proximity, which is neither conceptual nor rhetorical, entails at least the identity of an effect." (*Speculative Remark,* 170)

It is important to emphasize the way Nancy is connecting the two parts of the *Logic* here because in doing so he gets to the real essence of Hegel's thinking and lays his claim to Hegel's approach to the infinite via the speculative relationship between calculus and dialectics. The truly beautiful section and comment on *becoming* (*Werden*) and *Aufhebung* in Book 1 of Hegel's *Science of Logic* captures the metaphysics of a world of change.[11] And Hegel is absolutely right that precisely this metaphysics is what the mathematical infinite of his day—calculus—can measure with an unprecedented power and extensiveness. If we carefully trace the lines of thought contained in this one passage by Nancy on Hegel, including the footnotes, we will be at the heart of Nancy's contribution to contemporary discussions of finitude and infinity. Or, we can consider that although Hegel takes up a finite place in Nancy's oeuvre, that place opens up an infinite thinking. So here we need a longer discussion that covers all the aspects of the quote and footnotes.

Although the relationship between finitude and infinity (*die Endlichkeit* or *das Endliche*, and *die Unendlichkeit* or *das Unendliche*) cuts across his entire philosophy like other major dialectical pairs—the immediate and the mediated, the negative and the affirmative, identity and difference—there are three specific places in the *Science of Logic* where Hegel addresses the infinite explicitly and at length.[12]

1. *The infinitesimal and becoming*

The *Science of Logic* begins with the famous dialectic of being and nothing. If Hegel wants to provide a systematic analysis or development of all the concepts (categories) that can be applied to being, it makes sense for him to begin with the very concept of "pure being" *before* (logically) there are any categories, that is, before it is determined in any way. But, he concludes, such a pure notion of being is empty and thus the same as *nothing*. After all, "pure being," without any determinations or qualities by definition could not be distinguished from nothingness, which is equally blank. Or, as Hegel says, "in absolute light one sees just as much and as little as in absolute darkness. . . . Absolute light and absolute darkness are two voids that amount to the same thing" (*SL*, 69). With this paradoxical—or dialectical—opening he can establish the first and fundamental category that makes up determinate being or *Dasein*: the identity of being and nothing, that is, *becoming*. In Hegel's world, everything that *is* finds itself at the same time transitioning to *nothing* and from *nothing* to *being* (something else): "Their [being and nothing's] truth is therefore this *movement* of the immediate vanishing of the one into the other; *becoming*, a movement in which the two are distinguished, but by a distinction which has just as immediately dissolved itself" (*SL*, 60).

Hegel clearly knows the resistance that this dialectical reasoning will encounter, for the three paragraphs on "Being," "Nothing," and "Becoming" take up about a page, but they are followed by four "Remarks" that extend for some twenty pages explicating what it can mean that "being *is* nothing," and hence that only *becoming* really *is*. Here, I am interested in the fourth remark, where Hegel introduces the limited thinking of the "understanding" (*Verstand*) or "reflexive thought" that would *separate* being from nothing—for what could be more different (in its eyes)? But in doing so, such thinking must deny the possibility of beginning or ceasing-to-be or becoming or motion (think here of Zeno and the Eleatics), or simply find those phenomena *incomprehensible*. The understanding thus runs up against a dialectic in the formulations "being is nothing" and "nothing is being," which it experiences in a Kantian sense of an unsolvable antinomy (indeed, for Hegel, Kant's philosophy largely stays at the level of *Verstand*). And Hegel adds:

> The dialectic just cited is also the same as the understanding deploys against the concept of *infinitesimal* magnitude given by higher analysis. . . . These magnitudes are so determined that they *are in their vanishing*—not *before* this vanishing, for they would then be finite

magnitudes; not *after* it, for then they would be nothing. Against this pure thought, it is objected and endlessly repeated that these magnitudes are *either* something *or nothing*; that there is no *intermediary state* between being and nothing ("state" is here an inappropriate barbaric expression).—Assumed here is again the absolute separation of being and nothing. But we have shown against this that being and nothing are in fact the same, or to speak in the language cited, that there *is* nothing which is not an *intermediary state between being and nothing*. Mathematics owes its most brilliant successes to precisely that determination which the understanding rejects. (*SL*, 79–80)

This is a remarkable passage that may be playing off the quip by Bishop Berkeley (cited as an epigraph above), who likewise had no grasp of the reality of infinitesimals. The very nature of existence, determinate being (*Dasein*), needs to be grasped conceptually, beyond the understanding, as *infinitesimal*, as the vanishing of being—and we'll see, also the vanishing of nothing—the moment of becoming playing itself out infinitely at the heart of finitude.

2. *True infinity as the truth of existence*

Armed with this fundamental conception of determinate being as becoming, Hegel proceeds in Book 1 to unfold some of the determinations, qualities, or categories that follow logically out of it, such as "something" and "(its) other," "limit," "ought" (by which he means the transgression of a limit which is already implied in the very notion of a limit), and "finitude" itself (for all being, as becoming, comes to an end). And at this point Hegel turns to the notion of infinity in one of the most well-known explications of the *Science of Logic*. For if it is the nature of the finite to cease to be (by definition, come to an end), that "ceasing-to-be" also yields to a new being. This cycle of finitude, or becoming, thus continues without end, *ad infinitum*. However, Hegel famously relegates his "and *so forth to infinity*" (*SL*, 112) to the status of "bad infinity":

This alternating determination of self-negating and of negating the negating is what passes as the *progress to infinity*, which is accepted in so many shapes and applications as the unsurpassable *ultimate* at which thought, having reached this "*and so on to infinity*," has usually achieved its end. (*SL*, 113)

It is "bad" the way all determinations formed by the understanding are "bad," not morally so but dialectically inadequate. It does not think the alternating determinations *together*. In Hegel's terminology, to separate being and nothing is to think ab-stractly, rather than con-cretely (taken in their etymological senses). Not that they are merely identical or put into a "*formula* of a *unity*" (*SL*, 118), which would negate them. But now we can say that determinate being, insofar as it is the ceaseless becoming, is itself a manifestation of the infinite, which in turn is no longer the distant, unreachable *other* of the finite. He writes:

> This infinite, as being-turned-back-unto-itself, as reference of itself to itself, is *being*—but not indeterminate, abstract being, for it is posited as negating the negation; consequently, it is also *existence* or "*thereness*" [*Dasein*], for it contains negation in general and consequently determinateness. It *is*, and *is there*, present, before us. Only the bad infinite is the *beyond*. (*SL*, 118–19)

We have, therefore, a finitude that, to speak with Nancy, is no longer "privative," no longer "lacking" compared to the infinite. For the infinite is infinitely "breaking out" or "negating the negation" within the finite, keeping it in motion. And, we will see, this quality of being makes it *calculable* in a unique way.

3. *The mathematical infinite (calculus)*

In the logical progression of the *Science of Logic*, Hegel takes the next step of abstracting from this rich world of becoming by disregarding the particular determinations that constitute being as *Dasein*. Having established the infinity of finitude, he can step back and say, in effect: "So, it's all the same, one thing becoming another."[13] But if we abstract from the particular qualities of things we flip over into a different conception of them as *quantities*, for insofar as we are only interested in the *number* (of things), determinate qualities or differences become irrelevant (comparing five things to five different things, their quantities are equal regardless of what they are). While Hegel often either casts his discussion in terms that are peculiar (the way the "one" "repels itself" into the many and the many "attracts itself" back into the "one") or addresses familiar topics (like continuity and discreteness) in unfamiliar ways, the crucial aspect of this section is the analysis of "quantitative infinity" and the two extended "remarks" on calculus, which are of an order of magnitude longer than any other in the work (some fifty-six pages). Nancy, as we will see, emphasizes that Hegel grants calculus "exorbitant privilege."[14] Why?

We saw above that the concept of the *infinitesimal* came to Hegel's mind in his early remark on *Aufheben* when attempting to clarify the essential feature of being as becoming. But that was not the place for a discussion because he had not yet unfolded even the broad categories of infinity (bad and true) or quantity, under which the *mathematical* infinite would be subsumed. But now he can pursue a two-sided analysis: On the one hand, his logical categories can provide a philosophical grounding that was lacking in mathematics (and led mathematicians to mistaken conceptions of infinitesimals, seeing them as *either* finite magnitudes *or* the equivalent of zero; addressed in *SL,* 219–21);[15] on the other, the "exorbitant privilege" afforded to calculus here indicates the significance of this mathematical tool that can truly map onto his metaphysics of becoming.

Hegel has in mind throughout his discussion one of the main problems that calculus came to solve, namely, the determination of the slope of a line tangent at a given point on any curve defined by a continuous function. This geometrical problem had tremendous significance and applicability because if the curve mapped a change over time (like the flight of an object through the air) then the slope of the tangent line indicates the rate of change at an instantaneous moment in time. We might want to know what its rate of change is, that is, its velocity at any given point (in time), *p*. On a graph, that change would be captured by the change along the y-axis divided by the change along the x-axis, represented by $\Delta y/\Delta x$ (the Greek letter delta symbolizing difference). As that difference approaches zero we have the rate of change at a particular point, we have a ratio of two infinitesimal *differentials, dy/dx*. While it might seem as if we are approaching the undefined ratio dividing zero by zero (0/0) the remarkable thing is that as the differences approach zero or become infinitesimal, their *ratio (dy/dx)* approaches a definite number, which is what we are seeking.[16] In this sense, we can "zoom in" with an "infinitesimal microscope" to imagine what is happening at that point where the line is tangent to the curve.[17]

It is precisely here that Hegel located the "infinity" that, in his image, would require a "telescope" (and, of course, would still be "beyond" vision), but note that with the infinitesimal we have an infinite that is not "out there" beyond our reach but always already *within* a given finite interval.[18] Hegel had such an extensive note on calculus because he saw in, or "behind," it a conception of being as becoming. Nancy seizes upon the "exorbitant privilege" assigned to calculus in Hegel's *Logic* precisely because it captures the movement of the infinite within the infinitesimal gaps of the finite.

Although Hegel discusses the Newtonian version of calculus (fluxions), he, like most of the mathematical community, focuses largely on Leibniz's theory of differentials. There are two fundamental statements Hegel makes. In the first, we have the mathematical formulation of the statement from the opening section on becoming:

> But there is still another stage where the mathematical infinite manifests its peculiar character. In an equation in which x and y are first

posited as determined by a power-relation [like the parabola in my discussion above—JHS], *x* and *y* as such are still supposed to signify quanta; now this whole significance is entirely lost in the so-called *infinitesimal differences. dx, dy*, are no longer quanta, nor should they signify quanta, but have meaning only in connection, *the meaning of mere moments*. They no longer are a *something*, the something taken as quantum, nor are they finite differences; but *neither* are they *nothing*, not a null void of determination. Outside their relation they are pure nullities; but they are to be taken only as moments of the relation, as *determinations* of the differential coefficient *dx/dy*. (*SL*, 215)

Note that here he is *not* rejecting the *concept* or category of infinitesimal or differential as such (as Badiou and Pinkard would claim he does). Nor is he denigrating mathematics as such in relationship to philosophy (as the former "manifests its peculiar—ontological?—character"). Rather, he does provide an alternative to the twin misunderstandings of them as either finite or zero. As "moments of the relation" they *are*, as he said, *in their vanishing*. For Hegel, this means that the quantitative relation, when the individual components are viewed within the mathematics of the infinite, now takes on a *qualitative* and thereby finite value. As he says: "The infinite magnitudes of calculus are, therefore, not only comparable, but exist only as terms of comparison, in relation" (*SL*, 216). Or in other terms: "the mathematics of the infinite . . . treats any determination which it takes from pure mathematics [finite quanta] by converting it into an *identity with its opposite*—as when, for instance, it converts a curved line into a straight one, the circle into a polygon, and so on" (216).[19] This identity of contradiction, or *coincidentia oppositorum*, or flipping of quantity into a qualitative relation, captures the moments inherent in becoming. That is, he wants "to show that the infinitely small which in the differential calculus occurs as *dx* and *dy* does not have the merely negative, empty meaning of a non-finite, non-given magnitude (as when one speaks of an 'infinite multitude,' of an '*ad infinitum*,' and the like), but has the specific meaning of a qualitative determinateness of the quantitative, of a relational moment as such" (228).

In combining the qualitative and the quantitative dialectically, Hegel is, in my view, hardly offering a "poisoned chalice" (Badiou). Rather, he is addressing *avant la lettre* Badiou's call to see "mathematics as ontology." That is, Hegel argues here for the inseparability of the mathematics of calculus, which can work with the infinite and infinitesimal, and the very nature of being. True, Hegel calls for a philosophical or conceptual clarification of mathematics, but he still recognizes that the mathematics captures something essential about being itself, namely, its nature as *becoming*. We will see that Nancy points us in this direction by reminding us of a crucial passage from the beginning of the *Science of Logic* where Hegel characterizes determined, qualified existence as "becoming" and reminds us that this is the key insight of the mathematical infinite.

And it is at this point that we can also appreciate Nancy's reference to Jean-Joseph Goux, who turns to a later development in the mathematical field of analysis.[20] It is worth exploring Jean-Joseph Goux's essay because it points to ideas connecting mathematics (calculus), Hegelian dialectics (*aufheben*), and the deconstruction of logocentrism (economy of meaning). The step Goux is taking beyond Hegel is one that both he and Nancy seem to see inherent within the dialectic. True to the spirit of the journal *Critique*, which had been founded as an organ for reviews in 1948 by Georges Bataille and published all the major up-and-coming "poststructuralists," Goux takes as his point of departure a book on mathematics, *Leçons d'analyse fonctionelle* (*Lessons in Functional Analysis*) by Riesz and Nagy. He barely cites this text but focuses on one remarkable "paradox" that they mention at the opening of their book, an interesting set of functions that are a kind of footnote in the field of analysis (which studies functions) but that, according to Goux, create a kind of opening or gap in the center of traditional mathematics; they leave "an open reservoir for the indefinite and for non-sense" ("une réserve ouverte sur l'indéfini et le non-sens"; Goux, 51).

The mathematics and definition of these functions can get complicated, but Goux simply gets to what is at stake. Calculus assumes that any *continuous* function—a term that is defined rigorously in terms of limits but which basically means that the "space" between two numbers on the function can be made as small as possible and there will still be a number in between; that is, there are no "gaps"—is derivable (the derivative or line tangent to the curve at any point can be found, as above). However, in the second half of the nineteenth century, some functions were discovered that are *continuous* but *not derivable*. One of the most famous, named after its discoverer, the brilliant mathematician Karl Weierstrass, is a kind of highly erratic wave function that has the property that at each point the wave pattern is repeated.[21] That is, if one "zoomed in" with a kind of infinite microscope, one would see, "all the way down" as the spaces between the numbers got smaller and smaller, not the limit of a point but merely "smaller and smaller" versions of the wave function itself. Thus, although it is continuous, there is no possibility of finding its rate of change at a particular point. According to Goux, the discovery of these functions was an affront to mathematics—and he cites the way they were treated as "distasteful," "horrifying," and "pathological" (Goux, 43–45). Why? Because the dominant (and powerful) mathematics of calculus rests on the principle that any curve can be analyzed and represented in terms of the infinite number of straight lines that are its rate of change at any particular point—but these non-derivable functions undermine that principle:

> [Traditional—JHS] curves had been conceived on the scale of the rectilinear economy.... The underivable [on the other hand—JHS] remains unintelligible to an economy of the traced line, to a thought of the moving point. This is an untraceable function from a reservoir that cannot be raised up.[22] No examination, neither microscopic nor telescopic, will get to the bottom of its form. It escapes from all schematics, from the formalizing economy of visible tracing. (Goux, 51)

> Les courbes ont été conçues *à l'échelle* de l'économie rectiligne.... L'indérivable reste inintelligible à une économie du tracé, à une pensée du trajet. C'est une fonction intraçable de la resérve non relievable. Aucun examen, ni microscopique, ni télescopique, ne viendra à bout de sa forme. Elle échappe à tout schématisme, à l'économie formalisante du tracement visible. (Goux, 51)

From here Goux draws parallels to the structural linguistics of Saussure, and one can feel the excitement of those early heady days of deconstruction (not surprisingly, Derrida is the single most cited author of this essay).

For Goux, the discovery of continuous undifferentiatable functions at the heart of analysis furthermore means that the very principle of *Aufheben*, the emergence of meaning, knowledge, Spirit (*sens*) out of the disappearance of the particular and material (which are reduced to moments) has, likewise, at its heart a non-sublatable (Goux, 57–64). We are, according to Goux, thanks to the discovery of these functions, at the limits of idealism: "What these functions without derivations prove is that we are therefore at the limits of *spirit*. What the existence of these continuous yet underivable functions proves are the 'economic' limitations of idealism" (64). And this challenge posed by these functions demands, he writes at the conclusion of his essay, a thinking that has as its task "to raise/sublate what is not, in principle, sublatable by consciousness, and which, consequently, can only function dialectically with that which consciousness sublates" (64). And with this we are at the heart of *Nancy's* task of thinking with Hegel, thinking the infinite rupture within the finite, the opening that *is* (within) *Aufheben* itself. In the sense of calculus and going beyond it, Nancy takes Hegel to the infinitesimal limit where he becomes his other. To see this task in Nancy—and thus to grasp the way he takes up Hegel—we can return to the passage in the *Speculative Remark*, to which this necessary detour through Goux and calculus was a footnote, and ask about the relation between the "mathematical" and the metaphorical. We will be turning to the infinite pleasures of a kind of writing.

Let us begin, then, by turning attention to the early work that Nancy published with Philippe Lacoue-Labarthe in 1977, *The Literary Absolute*. This study of the famous journal, *Athenäum*, published briefly from 1798 to 1800 in Jena, was one of the first to take seriously the thought of Early German Romanticism, in particular the "symphilosophy" of Friedrich Schlegel and Friedrich von Hardenberg (who wrote under the pen name "Novalis"), as well as others like the brother August Wilhelm Schlegel and the theologian Friedrich Schleiermacher.[23] They undertook the study of this journal for reasons not just "archeological" and "historical" but "related to our situation and interests today," since "we still belong to the era that [romantic critique as theory] opened up" (*Literary Absolute*, 15). In particular, in the wake of Derrida's writing on *écriture* they see especially in the "fragments" published in *Athenäum* the "extreme limit of romantic writing" (14), which characterizes the "literary Absolute." What would this "Absolute" for our own time be? By analyzing romantic writing they can bring into view the essence of critique, a practice they describe as follows:

> For the literary Absolute aggravates and radicalizes the thinking of totality and the Subject. It *infinitizes* [emphasis in original] this thinking, and therein, precisely, rests its ambiguity. Not that romanticism itself did not begin to perturb this Absolute, or proceed, despite itself, to undermine its Work [*Oeuvre*]. But it is important to carefully distinguish the signs of this small and complex fissuring and consequently to know how to read these signs. (*Literary Absolute*, 15)

My argument is that the essence of Nancy's philosophical project lies in "reading the signs" of such "infinitization," exploring how writing—of others as well as his own—can "perturb," open up "fissures" within the finite.

So what defines the "fragment," that "extreme limit" of writing, a writing that is at the limit? (The notion of "limit," also central to calculus, will emerge below as central to Nancy's understanding of the relation between the finite and the infinite.) Lacoue-Labarthe and Nancy begin their analysis by pointing to an apparent contradiction or paradox: On the one hand, by definition, a fragment is incomplete; on the other, in the famous *Athenäum Fragment* 206, Friedrich Schlegel humorously states that each fragment "has to be . . . complete in itself like a hedgehog" (cited in *Literary Absolute*, 43). But precisely this dual feature, plus the fact that there is always a multiplicity of published fragments ("inherent to the genre" [43]), make up its essence: "Fragments are definitions of the fragment; this is what installs the totality of the fragment as a plurality and its completion as the incompletion of its infinity" (44). That is, the totality contains the fragmentary and the "complete" or finite, self-contained fragment opens up to infinity. But "the truth of the fragment is not, therefore, entirely in the infinite 'progressivity' of 'romantic poetry' [as Schlegel defined it in fragment 116], but in the actual infinity, by means of the fragmentary apparatus, of the very process of truth" (*Literary Absolute*, 45). Here romantic writing takes a step from the "dialogical to the *dialectical* [emphasis in original]" (46) and, indeed, Lacoue-Labarthe and Nancy interject parenthetically, "we are very close to Hegel" (47). But we are not quite there. Why not?

In their discussion of Schlegel's fragment collection called *Ideen*, Lacoue-Labarthe and Nancy take up the question: What is an idea? They cite one fragment by Schlegel himself: "Ideas are infinite, autonomous, continuously moving in themselves, divine thoughts" (*Ideen*, 10; *Literary Absolute*, 63); and a definition of "thoughts" from an earlier letter by Schlegel, *On Philosophy*: "A thought is a representation that is perfected for itself, fully formed [*ausgebildet*], total, and infinite within its limits. It is the most divine element in the human spirit" (*Literary Absolute*, 63–64). They gloss these two definitions by putting them in relation to both Kant and Hegel: The definitions indicate

> That if the "thought" is the infinitization of representation (in the Kantian sense), this infinitization operates within a philosophy of understanding, that is, intentionally or not, within the limit of a philosophy of finitude. The idealistic "step" has been effected (in the motif of infinitization), but not without a kind of obscure resistance to idealism itself, or more precisely, not without a sort of (quite unexpected) folding back of idealism into Kant, and of the transgression of finitude into the finite itself. Here is something that, once more, seems to double the movement of Hegelian dialectics—but that is nonetheless separated from it by an abyss. (*Literary Absolute*, 64)

If the aim for Nancy in "our situation" is to find a way to "infinitize finitude," to open it up to a form of the Absolute, romanticism offers a powerful example that continues with us today. But it has its limits insofar as it follows the path of drawing the infinite *down* into the finite, thereby repeating the ultimate trope of Christology. But, the implication is, we're close to Hegel still and need to make the leap across the abyss to grasp *his* infinitization of the finite. We will look at the conclusion of the *Phenomenology of Spirit* (1807), with its *reversal* of the flow of the infinite.

At the conclusion of the essay *Faith and Knowledge,* Hegel reformulates the conception of a "true infinity" that emerges out of a double negation, this loss of privation, the absorption of limited finitude, in more Baroque and religious terms. By "Baroque" I mean the seventeenth-century sensibility that would see the loss of this sphere of opposition with the "infinite grief" in response to the realization that "God himself is dead."[24] It is not by chance that he quotes Pascal: "la nature est telle qu'elle *marque* partout un Dieu *perdu* et dans l'homme et hors de l'homme [Nature is such that it *signifies* everywhere a *lost* God both within and outside man]" (*Faith and Knowledge,* 190). But this loss is to be reconceived as a "speculative Good Friday . . . in the whole truth and harshness of its God-forsakenness" so that the "highest totality" can reemerge (191).

The image of Good Friday returns at the conclusion of the *Phenomenology of Spirit,* but here with a slightly different and less Baroque valence.[25] Having followed throughout the book all the different images and shapes (*Bilder, Gestalten*) of Spirit, Hegel looks back over them in the last chapter. The recognition that they have all contributed to the transformative education and cultivation of Spirit, even as each of them has given way to others or become "but a trace" (Preface to the *Phenomenology,* 16), leads to the image of Golgatha, the place of the skull and the biblical site of the crucifixion. The place of absolute knowing is the place of "comprehended History" (*Phenomenology,* 493; as well as following quotations), where forms from the past are remembered and buried in the "Schädelstätte des absoluten Geistes" ("the Calvary of the absolute Spirit"). But it is here, where we might have that Baroque sense of transitoriness, that Hegel makes a remarkable turn. For these preserved remains are the source of a kind of infinite consolation for absolute Spirit, which, without them, would languish in a solitary isolation: "das leblose Einsame" ("lifeless solitude"). Loosely citing Schiller, he ends with the word: "infinitude" (or "infinity"; *Unendlichkeit*): "Aus dem Kelche dieses Geisterreiches / schäumt ihm seine Unendlichkeit" ("From the chalice of this realm of spirits / foams forth for Him [absolute Spirit] his own infinitude"). Nancy cites this passage in his dialogue with Badiou and cheekily poses the question (in German!): "Is there not here a bit of Badiou?" ("Gibt es nicht darin auch ein bißchen Badiou?") (*Dialogue,* 22). Indeed, what we see in this passage, and what Nancy finds so central in it for his own conception, is, on the one hand, the directionality: infinity flows *out of the finite world toward God/Spirit,* thereby reversing the "privative" notion of finitude; and, on the other hand, the *pure movement,* the "evanescent overflowing" (foaming, frothing; *Schäumen*) that Nancy emphasizes and associates with an absolute abundance and/of pleasure.

That is, as opposed to the romantic concern with a Christological "transition from the infinite to the finite"—a formulation that occurs with slight modification in the writings of all the German romantics and idealists (Friedrich Schlegel, Novalis, Schelling, Hegel, Hölderlin)—we have here the conception of a finite world *out of which* the infinite emerges. Spirit is the glass of champagne that never goes flat, issuing forth endless bubbles from the infinite abyss of the finite flute. It is a view of finitude, of existence (*Dasein*) as in constant movement because it *is* only insofar as it is *becoming*. And that *becoming* of finitude, which can be grasped with the help of the mathematical infinite, is a source of evanescent pleasure.

The goal of thinking is to attend to this abundant movement of/within the world, its "pleasure" (*jouissance, Genießen, Genuß*). Although Nancy does not demand, as does Badiou, that this ontology be identified with a mathematics of the multiple (derived from Cantor's set theory of actual infinities), he nonetheless has derived from Hegel an identification of pleasure, mathematics, and affirmative dialectics. He says:

> Hegel is perhaps the first thinker of infinite *jouissance*.... Now *jouissance* in Hegel is precisely that which cannot cease, that which never exhausts itself.... I would say that the *jouissance* of which Hegel speaks is his way of naming the relation to the outside of a spirit—to use his terms—that precisely cannot exhaust itself by itself, that cannot arrive at its own end. But unable to arrive at one's own end is at the same time to be infinitely fulfilled. (*Dialogue*, 28)

And with Hegel (even if he never said it as such although he *showed* it in his extra-long comment from the *Science of Logic*), our relation to this being is likewise one of pleasure, for Nancy says near the end of the dialogue, only half in jest, "we can enjoy a differential equation" (*Dialogue*, 60).

But the pleasure, as we saw above with the romantics, emerges also in *writing*, that is, the nature of (philosophical or speculative) language.[26] Céline Surprenant, the translator of Nancy's *Speculative Remark*, comments in her introduction on the prevalence and deep significance of the phrase *à même* in the book (*Speculative Remark*, x). Although generally rendered as something like "(right) at the level of . . ."—as in such expressions as "à même le texte de Kant," "right at the level of Kant's text"—it is closely associated with the German phrase, *an sich* (in itself), injected into the heart of philosophy thanks to Kant's understanding of the *Ding an sich* (the thing in itself). For Nancy, the preposition *an* in German, however, is not captured by the English "in" because he considers the *an* as in a crucial sense *distancing*, even if infinitesimally, the thing *from* itself. After all, *an* in German is used when something is next to or touching (like a painting hanging on a wall or a seat at a table). And here we are at the heart of Hegel's thinking as well. The very movement of the dialectic, which Hegel described as the process of experience (*Erfahrung*) in the "Introduction" to the *Phenomenology of Spirit*, takes consciousness, *and its objects*, from an initial encounter with an object itself (*an sich*), through the (often painful, negative) recognition that what was thought to be *an sich* is, in fact, only *für sich*, only *for consciousness*, to a new and more complex understanding of the object now as *an und für sich* (see *Phenomenology*, 55–56). Through this process, what was at first simple and abstract (in the etymological sense of isolated and drawn away from other things) is revealed to be (to have always already have been) double and concrete (also in the etymological sense). Or, in Hegel's use of German, what was thought to be *einfach* (simple, singular) is now experienced as *zweideutig* (ambiguous, of two meanings), that is, a combination of its past and now present senses. This, of course, is the famous *Aufhebung*, and it forms the core of Nancy's notion of *sense*.

In this regard, this could match Nancy's view of speculative and figurative language (see *Speculative Remark*, 121–22): it is the gap that exists within language and thus is a kind of "infinite approximation" in the heart of all (philosophical) language.

What he likes most about Hegel is his "infinite pleasure," which he qualifies as follows: "The infinite pleasure is finite. The finite opens itself infinitely" (*Dialogue*, 28). This means first that despite any appearance of closure, totalization, or "exhaustion" (Badiou's term), Hegel's system is always open to history and contingency. Hence Nancy's interest in the "*Schaum*" (froth, foam) that emerges anew at the end of the *Phenomenology of Spirit*. Another (Hegelian) term for this infinite opening of the finite is "restlessness" (*Unruhe, inquiétude*).

Nancy engages and thinks *with* Hegel, or perhaps *touches* on his thought, most intimately in *Hegel: The Restlessness of the Negative*.[27] At the heart of the Hegelian dialectic he finds an Absolute that is without end. The process or progress of the absolute is an infinite process or progress, but

> an infinite process does not go on "to infinity," as if to the always postponed term of a progression (Hegel calls this "bad infinity"): it is the instability of every finite determination, the bearing away of presence and of the given in the movement of presentation and the gift. Such is the first and fundamental signification of absolute negativity: the negative is the prefix of the *in*-finite, as the affirmation that all finitude (and every being *is* finite) is, in itself, in excess of its determinacy. It is in infinite relation. (*Restlessness*, 12)

For this reason, "[philosophy] even does nothing, initially at least, other than expose the finite as finite—the infinite finitude of every 'form of life'" (*Restlessness*, 26).

Nancy recognizes that "spirit" for Hegel is not some "metaphysical" entity beyond the realm of the real, but the internal unrest within being itself by means of which it is exposed: "How spirit is the finite that finds itself to be infinite in the exposition of its finitude, this is what is to be thought—which is to say, this is what it is to 'think'" (*Restlessness*, 31). Thus, if so many contemporary (French) thinkers express the need to get "beyond" Hegel, Nancy embraces the negativity that opens up a space of the "in-between" *within* Hegel, making him both finite and without end, inescapable and self-negating:

> Hegel neither begins nor ends; he is the first philosopher for whom there is, explicitly, neither beginning nor end, but only the full and complete actuality of the infinite that traverses, works, and transforms the finite. Which means: negativity, hollow, gap, the difference of being that relates to itself through this very difference, and which *is* thus, in all its essence and all its energy, the infinite act of relating itself to itself, and thus the power of the negative. It is this power of the negative that inhabits the gap where relation opens, and that hollows out the passage from presence to presence [= becoming!—JHS]: the infinite negativity of the present. (*Restlessness*, 9)

Thus, the "reader of Hegel" must understand the nature of the subject as it appears in Hegel, which is not "subjectivity" that could be reduced to a "metaphysics of presence." Rather:

> The *subject* is what it *does*, it is its act, and its doing is the experience of the consciousness of the negativity of substance, as the concrete experience and consciousness of the modern history of the world. . . . It is in this way, in the restlessness of immanence, that the spirit of the world becomes. [Think here of the generation of a curve out of dx/dy—JHS.] It neither seeks itself (as if it were for itself an exterior end [a bad infinity—JHS]) nor finds itself (as if it were a thing here or there), but it effectuates itself: it is the living restlessness of its own concrete effectivity. (*Restlessness*, 5)

In fact, this subject, Nancy rightly sees, is the will that can only "exist" by willing beyond itself, for there is no such thing as "pure willing": "But the condition of the decision is the subject itself insofar as it is undetermined, or insofar as it is 'abstract will, infinite for itself in its immediate singularity'" (*Restlessness*, 9).[28]

In Nancy's explanation of "finite thinking" we can hear the (Hegelian and romantic) tradition that haunts and mesmerizes his thought.[29] At first it seems that Nancy might be part of the "problem" as he stresses that the problems of the day, the decisions that need to be made across all the fields of the sciences and humanities, demand "a finite thinking," indeed "a thinking of *absolute finitude*" (*Finite Thinking*, 27). It would be "absolutely detached from all infinite and senseless completion or achievement" (27). This formulation sounds as if he is calling for two separate realms, the finite and the infinite. But, as we know from Hegel, such an opposition of the finite and the infinite leads to the dialectical collapse of each of the supposedly opposed poles, for an infinity that is *opposed* to the finite is thereby limited, and a supposed finite that can exist in isolation, for itself, without reference to any other, attains the infinite quality of relating only to itself. As Hegel says, the task must be otherwise for "it will be found that in the very act of keeping the infinite pure and aloof from the finite, the infinite is only made finite." Thus, Nancy also restates and clarifies the notion of thinking *absolute finitude*, which would really be the attending to the infinite/infinitesimal opening that constitutes becoming at the limit of being and nothing: "Not a thinking of limitation, which implies the unlimitedness of a beyond, but a thinking of the limit as that on which, infinitely finite, existence arises, and to which it is exposed" (*Finite Thinking*, 27). It is here, at the heart of existence, that thinking, or language, "*touches* its limit" (28). Without any explicit mention, the mathematical infinite, the field of calculus, has entered into finite thinking, for what is "touch[ing] its limit" except for that unrepresentable yet calculable point where a tangent line "touches" (*tangere*) a curve, giving us the rate of change, the rate of the curve's *becoming*, at one instantaneous moment, the vanishing point between being and nothing.

This non-privative notion of the finite coincides with what Nancy wants to say about world and sense and atheism. Rejecting the idea that sense is given to the world by some creator, Nancy also wants to avoid the view that we have, therefore, a senseless world. Rather, by being in the world (and that means being-with others) is to be in sense. There is no need of an outside or painful loss of the outside. The finite world is not lacking. However, our exposure to its sense can be blocked. Reason must therefore have the resources to think through the infinite, and the infinite must be reconceived not as a transcendent beyond but in relation to immanence. Of course, the differences will be played out over just what "think through" and "in relation to" mean in the previous sentence, lest the dangers of religion be simply replaced by the dangers of a hubristic humanism, with "mastery" of the infinite our ultimate goal and the abandonment of all humility vis-à-vis otherness. Nancy explores, deconstructs, Christianity not as a return but as a means of opening up reason to a new limitless field. Thus, he opens *La Déclosion*: "It is not a question of reviving religion, not even the one that Kant wanted to hold 'within the bounds of reason alone.' It is, however, a question of opening mere reason up to the limitless that constitutes its truth."[30] That opening can take place only after the "death of God," that is, after Christianity has fulfilled its own historical fate such that "sense" now becomes a question for us, not a given.

Hegel figures large for Nancy (and, as we know, for all contemporary Continental philosophers) because, if this condition is our "modernity," he is the philosopher of modernity. Indeed, the decision to philosophize, to think, is the decision to explore this condition without end. Nancy writes: "Philosophical decision thus clearly signifies that it decides neither for faith nor for knowledge, but that its decision consists precisely in separating itself from both. What Hegel calls 'knowing' or 'science,' and 'absolute knowing,' opens modernity as the age of the world that can no longer posit the relation to sense or truth as either immediate or mediate" (*Restlessness*, 14).

Here we have to do with ethics and sense after the "death of God." Near the end of their dialogue in Berlin, Badiou and Nancy address the topic of the "question of Being." They both agree that Heidegger's singular significance for modern philosophy lies in the fact that he posed this question anew. But the issue that seems to divide them is that Badiou insists on the absolute "indifference" of Being—it has no direction, no meaning, no special (God-given) relation to mankind—whereas Nancy introduces precisely the notion of meaning (*sens*, also direction). In what strikes Badiou as an odd formulation, Nancy seems to say they are not as far apart as it might seem: "sense/meaning" and "indifference" could be interchangeable (*Dialogue*, 63). Nancy's position is explicable only if one recalls his formulation: "The world doesn't *have* sense, it *is* sense" (*Sense,* 8). By this he means that, indeed, no transcendence confers meaning *onto* the world, it simply unfolds. However, within that unfolding, or, with Hegel, "becoming," each moment, each transition, contains or is generated by an infinitesimal difference, an opening where being flips into nothing and nothing flips into being, where quantity flips into quality and into quantity. Within the finitude of being, therefore, there is an infinity of such openings. They give being its ceaseless movement from within being itself. Being is the restless pleasure, the "foaming forth," the differential "directions" or *sens* of that movement.

Notes

1. Jean-Luc Nancy, *The Speculative Remark (One of Hegel's Bons Mots)*, trans. Céline Surprenant (Minneapolis: University of Minnesota Press, 2001), 165n17. Hereafter cited as *Speculative Remark* in the text.

2. George Berkeley, *The Analyst* [1734], §35, in *From Kant to Hilbert: A Source Book in the Foundations of Mathematics*, ed. William Ewald, vol. 1 (Oxford: Clarendon Press, 1996), 81.

3. Alain Badiou and Jean-Luc Nancy, *German Philosophy: A Dialogue*, trans. Richard Lambert (Cambridge, MA: MIT Press, 2018), 60. Hereafter cited as *Dialogue* in the text.

4. Gilles Deleuze, *The Fold: Leibniz and the Baroque*, trans. Tom Conley (Minneapolis: University of Minnesota Press, 1992; Fr. 1988), esp. chapter 5, "Perception in the Folds" (85–99). Maimon could be seen as extending Leibniz's notion of "petites perceptions," which were intended as a way to challenge Descartes's dualism, and giving them a mathematical foundation.

5. Badiou's breakthrough insight was formulated in his early essay, "La subversion infinitésimal" ("Infinitesimal Subversion"), *Cahiers pour analyse* 9.0 (Summer 1968): 118–37. There he addresses the importance of Robinson for introducing the concept of infinitesimal in a rigorous way after its centuries-long "banishment" and ideological suppression. The rhetoric of what he's trying to undo ("the annulment of the infinitely small as such" [124]; "excluding every infinitesimal composition" [125]; "the story . . . of the effacement of this trace" [125]; and elsewhere) indicates how it gave the fundamental direction to his work. He works out the significance of set theory in *Being and Event*, trans. Oliver Feltham (London: Continuum, 2005; Fr. 1988). See also the essays in *Badiou and Hegel: Infinity, Dialectics, Subjectivity*, ed. Jim Vernon and Antonio Calgagno (Lanham, MD: Lexington Books, 2015).

6. Quentin Meillassoux, *After Finitude. An Essay on the Necessity of Contingency*, trans. Ray Brassier (London: Continuum, 2008; Fr. 2006).

7. Badiou states these stakes most clearly in the dialogue with Jean-Luc Nancy, *Dialogue*, 10, 17–19.

8. It is not by chance that Nancy figures prominently in a number of papers from a conference on "Finitude" (which always includes its infinite other), gathered in an issue of *Centennial Review* from 2017. Three essays are of note: Rodolphe Gasché, "'Infinitely Finite': Jean-Luc Nancy on History and Thinking," *CR: The New Centennial Review* 17, no. 3 (2017): 1–19, accessed July 21, 2021, doi:10.14321/crnewcentrevi.17.3.0001; María Del Rosario Acosta López, "'An Infinite Task at the Heart of Finitude': Jean-Luc Nancy on Community and History," *CR: The New Centennial Review* 17, no. 3 (2017): 21–42, accessed July 21, 2021, doi:10.14321/crnewcentrevi.17.3.0021; and Francesco Vitale, "Finite Infinity: Reading Gasché Reading Derrida Reading Hegel . . . 'and so on without an End,'" *CR: The New Centennial Review* 17, no. 3 (2017): 43–61, accessed July 21, 2021, doi:10.14321/crnewcentrevi.17.3 .0043. They all begin with references to Hegel. However, none of them pursues the mathematical infinite, as I will here, even though it is both a touchstone for Nancy's reading of Hegel and a central concern of contemporary (French) philosophy.

9. Jean-Luc Nancy, *The Sense of the World*, trans. Jeffrey S. Librett (Minneapolis: University of Minnesota Press, 1997), 29. Hereafter cited as *Sense* in the text.

10. Precisely on this point we see a fundamental difference between Badiou, who vehemently rejects Hegel on infinity, and Nancy, who puts Hegel's infinite to use for him.

11. G. W. F. Hegel, *The Science of Logic*, trans. George di Giovanni (Cambridge, UK: Cambridge University Press, 2010). Hereafter cited as *SL* in the text.

12. A fuller discussion of finitude and infinity in Hegel would have to begin with one of Hegel's earliest published essays, *Faith and Knowledge* (1802). There he makes the case for the first time that a "true" infinite cannot be *opposed* to the finite. It is interesting that Hegel's motivation is not unlike that of contemporary French thinkers, namely, a critique of any philosophies that would limit reason and thereby open up a realm of uncognizable faith.

13. In his commentary on Hegel's *Logic*, Andy Blunden refers to this movement as "It's just one damn thing after another." See his "Non-Linear Processes and the Dialectic," accessed July 21, 2021, https://www.ethicalpolitics.org/ablunden/pdfs/Non-linear%20processes%20and%20the%20dialectic.pdf. Or one can think of Mephistopheles's more poetic version of the cycle of life and death in Goethe's *Faust*: "How many have I buried now! / Yet always fresh new blood will circulate again. / Thus it goes on—I could rage in despair!" (ll. 1371–73). *Goethe's Faust*, trans. Walter Kaufmann (New York: Anchor Books, 1963).

14. Badiou returns to this section again and again in order to differentiate himself from Hegel. See, for example, "The Infinitesimal Subversion," where he says Hegel's discussion introduced into the analysis of infinity the "poisoned chalice of 'qualitative' relation" ("Infinitesimal Subversion," trans. Robin Mackay with Ray Brassier, accessed July 20, 2022, http://cahiers.kingston.ac.uk/pdf/cpa9.8.badiou.translation.pdf, 135); *Being and Event*, esp. 161–70; *The Century*, trans. Alberto Toscano (Cambridge, UK: Polity, 2007), 157–59. However, I think precisely this dialectic of quantity and quality around the infinite and infinitesimal is Hegel's greatest insight—and I argue that Nancy would agree. The fact that Badiou needed to think beyond his *Being and Event* to account for the *appearing* of *Dasein* could be seen as his way of reconceiving this "poisoned chalice," even if he does so with the utterly different mathematics of categorical theory. See Badiou, *Mathematics of the Transcendental*, ed. and trans. A. J. Bartlett and Alex Ling (London: Bloomsbury, 2014), esp. the introduction, 6–7.

15. Terry Pinkard tries to make sense of Hegel by reconstructing his argument in more contemporary terms (category theory), but makes some errors by exaggeration, especially by claiming Hegel has nothing but disdain for the infinitesimals. "Hegel's Philosophy of Mathematics," *Philosophy and Phenomenological Research* 41, no. 4 (June 1981): 452–64.

16. Strictly speaking, dy/dx is not a quotient, but I use the term *ratio* because that is how Hegel viewed it. It is, rather, another function, the "derivative." If a

function is "derivable" it means this relation between *dx* and *dy* is a number and the function is continuous. For a complication of this aspect of functions, see below on Goux.

17. Here I am borrowing from Abraham Robinson's "nonstandard analysis," an effort beginning in the 1960s to reintroduce the notion of the infinitesimal. Robinson's approach was crucial for Badiou's early philosophical turn to the infinite. For a rethinking of calculus (and textbooks) that uses the visual aid of "zooming in," see H. Jerome Keisler, *Elementary Calculus. An Infinitesimal Approach* (Mineola, NY: Dover, 2012).

18. Hegel was aware that mathematicians like Cauchy were working toward an approach to calculus that would use the concept of a "limit" and would thus do away with the notion of "infinitesimal" (which was notoriously contradictory—again, see Berkeley's quip cited as an epigraph above), and he welcomed this approach. But conceptually he was focused on the way "vanishing" quantities could yield a value through their pure relationality.

19. Here one finds an interesting echo of Nicholas of Cusa (1401–1464). It is thanks to this embrace of the unity of these opposites as moments that he can rethink the Kantian mathematical and dynamic antinomies. This is why Nancy says that a full discussion of Hegel on the mathematical infinite would take us through Kant. On the "coincidentia oppositorum," see Nicholas of Cusa, *On Learned Ignorance: A Translation and Appraisal of* De docta ignorantia), trans. Jasper Hopkins (Minneapolis, MN: Arthur J. Banning, 1981).

20. Jean-Joseph Goux, "Dérivable et indérivable," *Critique* 26, no. 272 (1970): 43–64. Hereafter cited as "Goux" in the text.

21. This function would be the beginning point for the mathematics of fractals that comes to underlie chaos theory.

22. The French—"la reserve non relevable"—points to Hegel, since "non relevable" could be translated "that cannot be sublated."

23. Philippe Lacoue-Labarthe and Jean-Luc Nancy, *The Literary Absolute: The Theory of Literature in German Romanticism*, trans. Philip Barnard and Cheryl Lester (Albany: State University of New York Press, 1988). Hereafter cited as *Literary Absolute* in the text.

24. Georg Wilhelm Friedrich Hegel, *Faith and Knowledge*, trans. William Cerf and H. S. Harris (Albany: State University of New York Press, 1977), 190. Hereafter cited as *Faith and Knowledge* in the text.

25. Georg Wilhelm Friedrich Hegel, *Phenomenology of Spirit*, trans. A. V. Miller (Oxford: Oxford University Press, 1977). Hereafter cited as *Phenomenology* in the text.

26. Nancy associates this pleasure with art as well: "Art is a fragment because it borders on pleasure it *gives* pleasure [*il* fait *plaisir*]. It is made both out of and for the pleasure it gives, the pleasure thanks to which it touches—and with a touch that comprises its essence" (*Sense*, 133–34). From a different perspective, the other contemporary French philosopher who has written powerfully on Hegel's language is Catherine Malabou, *The Future of Hegel:*

Plasticity, Temporality, and Dialectic, trans. Lisabeth During (New York: Routledge, 2005).

27. Jean-Luc Nancy, *Hegel: The Restlessness of the Negative*, trans. Steven Miller and Jason Smith (Minneapolis: University of Minnesota Press, 2002). Hereafter cited as *Restlessness* in the text.

28. See the translator's introduction to *Restlessness*. Also Jean-Luc Nancy, *The Experience of Freedom*, trans. Bridget McDonald (Stanford, CA: Stanford University Press, 1994), and *The Inoperative Community*, ed. Peter Connor, trans. Peter Connor, Lisa Garbus, Michael Holland, and Simona Sawhney (Minneapolis: University of Minnesota Press, 1991). Also my *Dialectics of the Will: Freedom, Power, and Understanding in Modern French and German Thought* (Detroit: Wayne State University Press, 2000).

29. Jean-Luc Nancy, *A Finite Thinking*, ed. Simon Sparks (Stanford, CA: Stanford University Press, 2003). Hereafter cited as *Finite Thinking* in the text.

30. Jean-Luc Nancy, *La Déclosion (Déconstruction du christianisme, 1)* (Paris: Galilée, 2012), 1.

The World, Absolutely
On Jean-Luc Nancy (and Karl Marx)

RODOLPHE GASCHÉ

While attempting to demonstrate in the essay "Finite History" that history is something that happens in the form of being-*in*-common constitutive of community, Nancy remarks that history thus understood, that is, as a happening, or an event, is without "the directional and teleological path" that it has been considered to be.[1] He writes: "History no longer *has* a goal or a purpose, and therefore, history no longer *is* determined by the individual (the general or the generic individual) or the autonomous person that Marx frequently criticized in the speculative, post-Hegelian way of thinking."[2] In a note appended to this statement, Nancy submits that "Marx never accepted the representation of history as a subject. He always insisted that history is 'the activity of man.'" And, significantly enough, Nancy adds, "In this sense—not to mention the additional analysis of Marx that would be necessary—I am attempting here [in the essay "Finite History"] nothing other than a reelaboration, in a quite different historico-philosophical context [than that of Marx] of this indication."[3] In other words, Nancy confides that his reconception in the essay of history as finite history, and as the fundamental trait of being-in-common, that is, of community, is not only indebted to Marx's thought, but, at bottom, a "reelaboration" of Marx's thesis that history is "the activity of man." It follows from this that Marx is of pivotal importance—the starting point, as it were—for Nancy's rethinking of being-together, or community, and the finite historicity that it implies. If this is indeed the case, the surprisingly frequent references to Marx throughout Nancy's work are anything but fortuitous. Marx seems to play an eminent and crucial role for Nancy's thought, a role, of course, that does not exclude, but demands a sustained critical debate with him. Needless to say, I cannot in order to substantiate this point address the totality of Nancy's references to Marx. However, by limiting myself to a specific concern in Nancy's writings, I will be able to make a case that rather than "a dead dog," Marx is very much alive for Nancy.[4] This concern is that of the sense of "world."

As a response to the contemporary loss of world, Marx's assumption that in its final stage the worldwide interconnection accomplished by the capitalist global market economy that so far has been destructive of the world could be reappropriated by humanity in an act through which it would thus come to enjoy itself in its self-production, is, Nancy argues in "*Urbi et Orbi*" (the first essay in *The Creation of the World or Globalization*), problematic in several respects. Determinative concepts such as "process, consciousness, the possibility of uncovering a value and an end in itself," which among others subtend Marx's conception of world history, are no longer self-evident (37).[5] And yet, Nancy adds, apart from everything that has become doubtful in Marx, "something [of him] remains nonetheless, in spite of everything, something resists and insists" (37). Nancy highlights two issues in particular that in Marx continue to be topical in the present. What remains of Marx is, first, the insight that what he analyzed under the name of the "worldwide expansion of capital," which since then underwent an exponential expansion, but also the increasing fragility of all representations of belonging, and identity resulting from globalization, rather than being something to be fought, is, on the contrary, the very condition of possibility for creating a world worthy of its name. What insists with Marx, is the insight that "world" is only what it is if it is truly worldwide, or universal. Second, what remains of Marx's conception is that since he linked all value to that of a self-creating humanity, it has become increasingly clear "that the place of sense, of value, and of truth is the world" (37).[6] By making the world the exclusive creation or production of the human being by the human being, Marx also made the world into something that is not determined by something different from it such as a prior given principle. Differently put, since Marx, sense, truth, and value are no longer to be looked for in another world; the world, that is, *this* world is the sole setting for any possible sense or value. Nancy avers that "from now on, whoever speaks of 'the world' denounces any appeal to 'another world' or a 'beyond-the-world.' 'World-forming' [*mondialisation*] also means, as it does in . . . Marx, that it is in 'this' world, or as 'this' world—and thus as the world, absolutely—that what Marx calls production and/or creation of humanity, is being played out" (37; translation modified). Since Marx, sense, truth, and value not only make sense solely in relation to this world, they are also only ontological (and at the same time, perhaps, also ethical) modalities, that is, manners or modes in which the "world" itself exists. In short, whatever the anachronisms of the conceptual framework of Marx's analysis may be, his recognition that the "place" where humanity's self-creation, and absolute value, are to take place is the world, and nowhere else—that is, this world, the world freed not merely from all theological secondarity, but also detached from all secular meaning—in other words, the world in an absolute sense, remains more than ever intact. And this entirely worldly world which for Marx coincides with humanity's self-emancipation and self-creation is also from now on the sole "place" with respect to which it is possible to speak of meaning, value, and truth, and which rather than intimating a transcendent beyond of the world, are thus exclusively world-immanent.

Yet, even though Marx sought to detach the world from any outside cause, and thus to leave behind representations of the world to which it has to conform itself, by conceiving of the world as the unfolding of a production of men by themselves, the theme of humanity creating itself surreptitiously turns the world again into a representation. However paradoxical it may sound, a world constituted by a self-producing humanity could still be an otherworldly world. It is, therefore, that Nancy takes issue with Marx's identification of world and self-created humanity, suggesting that such an identification is an inherent limit of his conception. Nancy not only relinquishes most of Marx's determinative concepts for thinking "world" in a radical mundane sense, he also departs from the role that the latter attributes to humanity as a subject fashioning such a world. More precisely, Nancy objects to Marx's conception of the human being as an *archae,* and as a *telos* and/or *eschaton* that would drive the process of world history, and which at the end of history would have realized itself without a remainder in the shape of a world, that is, as a world that would be the fully spread-out realization of human being's essence. As a result of this metaphysical conception, it is also only at the end of history that world in a wholly worldly sense would have been created as the full actualization of the thus purported human essence. Furthermore, according to Marx's metaphysical humanism, and its construal of the "human" as a "figure," or *Gestalt* of sense, that is, as a representation of sense, that as such faces the world from the outside, as it were, rather than being immanent to it, the accomplished world would be a realization of this figure, a process in which the world would have been replaced with an external figure of it. Not only that, with the complete execution of this figure of the world, the world would have come at the end to its end. Humanity's enjoyment of itself as its own product—an end after which world history would have come to a perfect standstill—would in principle not be different from that of the Aristotelian God's gazing at himself in blissful ecstasy.[7] By contrast, for Nancy, sense, value, and truth are not things that qua representation come to the world from outside, and that could be imposed upon the world so as to ply it, say, to more human values, but are what they are only if they are intrinsic to the world as such, that is, to the world in an absolute, radically "secular" (because beyond the secular) sense.

Given that Marx already implicitly attributed a concept of absolute value to humanity's self-emancipation and self-creation through the power of labor (and the simultaneous inversion that it brings about of the order of the circulation of commodity value and all the relations implied by this order), and, hence, to the world as one of self-producing humanity, I will be interested, hereafter, in understanding how Nancy conceives of "value," or rather "absolute value," as a world-immanent category, and as pertaining to the world in a radical worldly sense, once it has been severed from Marx's identification of the world with humanity's self-creation. For, indeed, in spite of Marx's continued significance for understanding both the disastrous effects and the potential of globalization, and for a conception of the world in exclusively worldly terms, one cannot follow him any longer as regards his assumption that a fully worldly world would be that of self-produced humanity. As is well known, Marx's concept of labor, or production, is inseparable from the human subject. It entertains an essential relation to the human as the subject of labor, and hence is humanist in nature. Now, if in spite of this metaphysical and humanist heritage Marx's thought can still be relevant today, it is also because this very heritage becomes already problematic in Marx himself. Nancy holds that it is "not certain that with Marx the teleo-eschatological logic is so strictly geared toward the accomplishment of a final value. Quite the contrary! In a sense, it is even the determination of such a finality that remains lacking in Marx. . . . In Marx's entire text, nothing determines, in the end, any accomplishment except as, essentially open and without end, a freedom ('free labor') and an 'individual property' (that which is proper to each in the exchange of all)" (38; translation modified).[8] What Nancy offers here is that Marx's characterization of the end of the teleo-eschatological process of world history as freedom and individual property is, in the end, not an end, but the necessarily open-ended "world of the proper freedom and singularity of each and of all without claim to a world beyond-the-world or to a surplus-property" (38). In other words, rather than a conclusive end, what the communist revolution brings about is an infinitely open-ended state. Furthermore, such an "opening without finality is never a work nor any product," in other words, not of the making of a humanity making itself through labor, but the "enjoyment by human beings of what opens their humanity beyond all humanism" (54), that is, of a richness of the world made by the difference of the singularities that constitute it.

World history, it follows, is a process driven not only without any extra-worldly principle such as the idea of humanity which in the end would become conscious of itself in a final dialectical actualization, but also of a radically "secular" nature. This is an argument that Nancy makes probably with the late Marx in view. But if the process of history is not "the accomplishment of a final value," it will also be necessary to rethink the notion of absolute value itself because within Marx it is entirely determined in terms of the human. Not only that, what since Marx has also remained unresolved is how to grasp a world of freedom and individual property in a concrete sense, for, indeed, "the infinity in act of proper ends," which, for Marx, "could [still] be the space of the play of freedom and of its common/singular appropriation," appears to us today only as "a bad infinity, if not as the imminence of a finishing [*finition*] that would be the implosion of the world and of all of us in it" (38). A further task follows from this, namely that of conceiving of a finishing that is neither teleo-eschatological nor spuriously infinite, but that in the end [*pour finir*] is finite, or more precisely, infinitely finite.

Before further focusing on these tasks of contemporary thought, I return, first, to the issue of value, for it is, precisely, at this turn of his argument in "*Urbi et Orbi*" that Nancy picks this issue up again. If he holds that "at this point, it is necessary to clarify the nature [*l'essence*] of *value* in itself, or absolute value: the one that Marx designates as 'value' pure and simple, not as use-value of which exchange-value is the phenomenal mask and social extortion or exploitation," it is certainly because he wishes to uncouple that notion of value itself, which, in Marx, is that of laboring humanity, from humanity (38). According to Marx, "value," that is, value itself, or abstract value, is "a congelation [*Gallerte*] of labour."[9] Value is the jellied vital force of humanity, that is, abstract and homogeneous social labor become cold. Labor, as what all commodities (including labor as a commodity) have in common, is what makes it possible to consider them as equivalent (in certain quantities), and hence what allows for their exchange. By understanding labor as the expression of the essence of what humanity is, namely, self-producing humanity, however, will not per se transform the nature of "value itself" inasmuch as it subtends the exchange on the basis of the form of equivalence, that is, of a form of value into which everything can be converted at all moments. As a result, it becomes necessary to go beyond value, that is, to absolute value in another sense, to a value that is no longer measurable in terms of equivalence. To accomplish this, value has to be disjoined from humanity as a laboring force.

The aim of such uncoupling of world and laboring humanity is, of course, to link absolute value with a conception of "world" that is "the infinity in act of proper ends," of a world that is entirely worldly in that the constituting finite and plural ends of the singularities that make it up are immanent to it (38). In a footnote, Nancy explains that the "clearest text" by Marx regarding the distinction of value and value pure and simple, or absolute value, "is perhaps the one of 'Marginal Notes on Adolph Wagner's *Lehrbuch der politischen Ökonomie*'" from 1879–80 (118n7). It is true that in these notes, Marx, while quoting regularly from *The Capital*, highlights the need to consider value as that which is the common substrate of all exchange values in and for itself, that is, independently of its phenomenal form (*Erscheinungsform*). This distinction of value in itself from both use and exchange value is necessitated by the need to recognize both of them as concrete products of labor. Rather than something "abstract" that lends itself to all sorts of hairsplitting, value or "value itself" has as an "economic category" a very concrete and determinable meaning.[10] In the context of an analysis of the historically concrete economic period of bourgeois capitalism "value itself" refers to the human power of labor, more precisely, to the "*'social' labor-power*" contained in both use and exchange value.[11] What Marx distinguishes as "value itself" thus refers to the power of labor, but that is also, of course, the power of laboring humanity in its entirety not only under specific historical and social conditions, but also of humanity as such, and, therefore, no longer simply an economic category. Now, as mentioned, Nancy's question concerns "the nature [*l'essence*] of *value* in itself, or absolute value: the one that Marx designates as 'value' pure and simple" (38), independently of the metaphysical figure of "humanity" that Marx confers on it, and which as such is reductive of this value in that the figure in question shapes it into a representation no longer immanent to the world. Indeed, the task is to conceive of absolute value as "the 'thing in itself' behind the phenomenon" (38), that is, beyond representation, and no longer as a *Gestalt* anymore to be realized in the shape of an instrumentalized world, as it were, at the hands of humanity as a whole, but in a way that the absolute value becomes constitutive in act of the world itself, of the world as inherently worldly, and whose worldliness imparts on it its absoluteness.[12]

According to Marx, the value behind the relative value of a commodity, be it an object, or labor, is the totality of social labor, a part of which is incorporated in a given commodity. In other words, humanity itself, in the shape of social labor or work, is the absolute value objectified in its products. But that also means that by producing commodities humanity produces itself in an objective form, as a work (that as such calls to be reappropriated). Thus with, undoubtedly, the passage from *The German Ideology* previously alluded to in mind, Nancy writes:

> Absolute value is, in fact, humanity incorporated in the product through work as human work. It is thus humanity producing itself by producing objects (or . . . creating itself by producing). But what is humanity? What is the world as the product *of human beings*, and what is the human being insofar as it is *in the world* and as it *works* this world? What is the "spiritual wealth" of which Marx speaks, which is nothing other than the value or meaning of human labor as human, that is to say, also "free," but free to the extent that it is to itself its own end and that therefore it is neither value measured according to its use value giving itself as general equivalency . . . ? What is a value that is neither finalized nor simply equivalent to itself? What is a "human value" toward which the work refers, or whose trace it bears, without however signifying it and without covering it with a mystical veil? (This question, we note, amounts to asking: What is human value considered at a level beyond the reach of "humanism"?) (39; translation modified)

All these questions concerning humanity as absolute value aim at uncoupling absolute value from a humanist conception of the human and the world, the one of Marx included. Undoubtedly, if the absolute value is the sum total of social labor, the humanity that produces itself while producing commodities is a humanity that produces itself as a social whole, or historical world, and, if understood as a life force, a social vital force in, and of, this world.[13] But precisely because a self-producing humanity is one that produces in the same breath a social world, Nancy can immediately raise the questions of what kind of a world it is that humanity thus engenders, and what the human being is, in turn, if he, or she, dwells in it, and works the world it has produced. These questions are not only intended to clarify the nature of the immanence of such a world if it is brought about by those who inhabit it, but also what humanity as absolute value must be if it is not to be a transcendent world creator however immanent it may be to this world.

From what we have seen so far, for Marx, the absolute value is that of a humanity producing itself through labor—as the labor force in capitalism, and, after the revolution, in free labor. If the issue is to disconnect absolute value from humanity and to link it to the world itself, two issues, at least, need to be addressed. Supposing that, indeed, the humanist heritage becomes already problematic in Marx himself, what is it then, precisely, that allows, or even necessitates, passing from humanity to "world," and what is it that allows, or necessitates, the passage from labor as the essence of humanity to an absolute value associated with the infinite acts of singularities that by holding themselves in the world constitute this world?

Prior to sketching an answer to this question, I wish to make the seemingly counterintuitive claim that in rethinking the sense of the world, Nancy may, indeed, be more indebted to Marx than to Heidegger. This declaration is preposterous in that all evidence suggests the contrary. Quantitatively speaking, the debate with Heidegger in Nancy's developments about "world" far outstrip the overall very limited engagement with Marx. More specifically, Nancy's elaborations on being-singular-plural and being-with are not conceivable without the existential analytic of *Dasein*. They do not only presuppose the analytic in question, but are clearly the result of a critical transformation, and radicalization, of it. Furthermore, Nancy's reading in "*Urbi et Orbi*" of Marx's conception of the "social," or more precisely, of the reciprocal and mutual production of humanity after the overthrow of the existing order, is hardly imaginable without a theory of being-with for which Heidegger unmistakably provided the guidelines. It thus seems to be utterly implausible to hold that Nancy's analysis of world as a place of infinities in act draws first on Marx before drawing on Heidegger's analyses.

However, in "*Urbi et Orbi*," it is said not only that, after Kant, Marx is *the* thinker who, "by his insistence on the world," performed a "decisive advance of the self-deconstructive gesture" that undermined the onto-theology in the great transcendent accounts of Western rationalism, but also that, "however paradoxical it may seem," "it is indeed in Husserl and Heidegger . . . as well as, albeit differently, in Bergson and Wittgenstein" that this Marxian gesture finds its continuation and consequences ("*ses prolongements*") (41). In short, Heidegger, to restrict myself to the latter, is thus to be seen as further developing and extending the problematic of the world that in Marx erupts into full view in thinking. But the point Nancy makes here is not just that Heidegger is indebted to Marx.[14] In order to glimpse the significance of Marx's thought in evaluating Heidegger, let's first ask why in *The Creation of the World* Nancy when he raises the question of the value of the world—in addition to its truth and sense—turns to Marx in the first place, rather than to Heidegger? It is not simply because one finds, as we have seen already, in Marx a first scientific theory of value, and, hence, a first rigorous concept of value. If a turn to Marx occurs here in the first place in order to develop a notion of value that once the latter's metaphysical humanism has been overcome can be linked to the world as the space of human interaction, it is also because Nancy aims at a kind of relation between singular existents that is not found like that in Heidegger, but only in Marx, and that reveals a sense of social and political engagement and concern that is wholly absent from *Being and Time*. Heidegger's primary emphasis is on the authenticity of the singular (*Einzelne*), in spite (or because) of his or her entanglement with others, who as the They are struck with inauthenticity. In *Being Singular Plural*, Heidegger's fundamental existential ontology is held to have to be redone in its entirety, starting from the outset with the co-originarity of every *Dasein*, in other words, on the basis of "*the plural singular of origins*, [that is] from *being-with*."[15] If Nancy proceeds in such a way, is this not because of a sense of the social and of justice that is only present in Marx but not at all in Heidegger? My point, then, is that without Nancy's profound social and political commitment that takes its inspiration from Marx—an inspiration that may go as far back as his reading of Jean-Yves Calvez's *La pensée de Karl Marx* (1956)[16]—and motivates the concern with the world as a space opened by the infinite acts of singular existents, Nancy's recourse to Heidegger, and the specific way in which he resolutely transforms the latter's analysis of world as the place of being together, would not be conceivable.

I add that the postulated priority of Marx over Heidegger in Nancy's reflections on the world should not at all be that surprising considering the essential gesture that characterizes Nancy's style of thinking, and which is most clearly manifest in what he calls the "deconstruction of Christianity." Indeed, in a way similar to the great systems of rationalism of Western metaphysical thought which under the cover of a concern with a transcendent God make a case for the world in an absolute sense, and in all its immanence, Marx is held to be not only underway to Heidegger's analytic of *Dasein*, but even to contain an intuition of an understanding of being-with that in many regards is more radical than that of Heidegger.

In order to further substantiate the seemingly counterintuitive assertion, I return to the claim made in *Being Singular Plural* that Marx's correct intuitions remain buried in his work. Nancy's repeated assertion here is that everything that Marx developed with respect to the social nature of labor, and the realization, by way of an inversion of the capitalist order, of free labor, reveals an insight, or rather, a "knowledge [*savoir*]" for which we have to "find a language that is *ours*."[17] The language needed to properly articulate Marx's intuitions is that of an ontology of being-with, which Nancy, rather than borrowing in full from *Being and Time*, redoes again so as to become an ontology of being-singular-plural. To give some examples of the buried intuitions in question: when demanding "the dissolution of politics in all spheres of existence (which is the 'realization of philosophy')," in order to accomplish the very essence of community, Marx, according to Nancy, is still unaware of the fact that the separation thus overcome is not in fact that of politics and existence, but of the constitutive separation of existence and the essence of community, that is, of "being-in-common *as the dis-position* (dispersal and disparity) of the community."[18] Or, second example, what in Marx is called "society" in "the broadest and most diffuse sense of the word," is, according to Nancy, "the figure [*chiffre*] of an ontology yet to be put into place," but that Marx anticipated "when he qualified humanity as social in its very origin, production, and destination, and when the entire movement and posture of his thinking assigned Being itself to this social being."[19] The last example leads us already to seek a response to what it is in Marx that makes a transition possible from labor as constitutive of humanity to understanding it as being shaped by being-with. Indeed, Nancy writes that "by leaving open the question of what must be understood as 'free labor' . . . this suspense opened onto the demand for another ontology of the 'generic being' of humanity as 'essentially social': a co-ontology."[20]

To begin responding to the question of what necessitates leaving behind "humanity" for the benefit of "world," and what is it that allows, or necessitates, the passage from labor as the essence of humanity to an absolute value associated with the infinite acts of singularities, if, indeed, the humanist heritage has already become problematic in Marx himself, I take my departure in Marx's observation in "Critique of the Gotha Programme" (1875):

> In a higher phase of communist society, after the enslaving subordination of the individual to the division of labour, and thereby also the antithesis between mental and physical labour, has vanished; after labour has become not only a means of life but life's prime want [*das erste Lebensbedürfnis*]; after the productive forces have also increased with the all-round development of the individual, and all the springs of common wealth flow more abundantly—only then can the narrow horizon of bourgeois right be crossed in its entirety and society inscribe on its banners: From each according to his abilities, to each according to his needs![21]

What Marx describes here as pertaining to "a higher phase of communist society," namely, a stage where labor is no longer a necessity dictated by nature, but has become "life's prime want," and where instead of a means labor has become an end, corresponds, no doubt, to the final stage of humanity's self-production. This final stage is that of the realm of freedom. It is not a realm free of labor but one in which labor not only has become free, but has become "life's prime want." What this seems to mean is that for

Marx free labor is not only the sense of the process of the liberation from alienated labor in that it concludes the self-production of humanity which the latter made possible, but also the condition from thereon of thus liberated humanity itself. In other words, "labor," whether alienated or not, designates the prime ontological mode of human relations to what is, humans included. Now, as Nancy remarks, if the revolution consists in a passage on the basis of labor as the organic exchange with nature, that is, of labor as a means of life, to labor as the power of humanity that is its own end, then labor is still both labor in its common sense, but, perhaps, also something completely different. Does this mean, he asks, that "labor labor[s] on labor?," and that "labor makes itself free."[22] And does this mean that both forms of labor share the same essence, or that the essence of free labor is radically distinct from that of alienated labor? The assumption is that if this dialectical passage from one kind of labor to another implies "a complete change of sphere . . . accompanied by the conservation of something whose identity would be indicated by the name of 'labor,'" the question arises whether it is "possible to tear from 'labor' the secret of a transmutation of necessity into freedom."[23] With this the fundamental question arises whether "to pass from necessity to freedom *while holding onto labor* means to pass from production to creation," or whether "in terms that are more rigorous (more Aristotelian and more Marxist) to pass from *poiesis* to *praxis*, from the activity that produces something to the activity through which the agent of the action 'produces' or 'realizes' him/herself."[24] For Nancy, the stakes of this difference are considerable: even if it is through an act of *praxis* rather than *poiesis*, the agent's self-production is still an actualization in the shape of a work of labor as the purported essence of the human, whereas freedom understood as creation is the mode of being itself in being-with-others. But as an act of praxis the act in question might also already be in Marx the intuition of creation as the act, not of a self-sufficient and autotelic self, but of a being-singular-plural of the relations that make up the world as the space of being-with. From what we have seen so far, this, then, also implies the passage from the value associated with humanity that realizes itself through free labor, to a value of a different kind involved with the creation of the world. Rephrasing the alternative of passing from production to creation, Nancy suggests that this can also be put in the following way: "it is a question of the passage from 'surplus value' determinable as extortion of added value, 'surplus value' measurable in terms of labor force and/or labor time, to 'surplus value' no longer determinable as 'value,' and thus to a beyond of value, to the absolute value—not measurable in terms of any other thing (as Kant said of 'dignity')—of an end-in-itself or a pure autoteleology (which is, moreover, each time singular and incomparable)."[25]

After recalling that for Marx the absolute value is that of humanity producing itself by producing objects, Nancy explains in a footnote that "no doubt it is possible, and perhaps necessary, to understand 'value' in Marx according to what Louis Gernet" in *The Anthropology of Ancient Greece* explains regarding the mythical idea of value in Greece (119n11). A note of caution is warranted at this point: the digression through Gernet is not intended to demonstrate that there is a more archaic form of value to which Marx's conception of value itself could be retraced, but to prepare a different understanding of value in Marx himself. In his study of the notion of value in prehistoric Greek civilization, more precisely, at its still premonetary stage, Gernet observes that at the moment one speaks of economic value one "tends to eliminate the very idea of value by substituting the idea of 'measure,' elsewhere an essential ingredient of the concept of the measured thing. But [in speaking of value itself] we are not concerned with value as something 'banal' or abstract. We are dealing with a preferential value embodied in certain objects, a value that not only predates economic value but is its very precondition."[26] Gernet thus clearly distinguishes value from "value itself." Even though Marx's conception of "value itself" is primarily economic, Gernet's distinction serves Nancy to open value itself to a beyond of the merely economic. This archaic notion of value antecedent to monetary value, and whose apprehension "presupposes or signifies a psychological tone [*tonus*] more elevated, more diffused, than the one in contemporary humanity," is associated with certain manmade objects that are "endowed with a special power," and pass from hand to hand, as when, for example, they are given as a prize for some extraordinary achievement.[27] If these precious objects convey "an idea of wealth," it is in the sense that they carry qualifications of formidable, magical power, religious awe, and danger.[28] For what we are interested in here, it is important to stress that the idea of value carried by these objects is largely linked to the fact that they are made from precious metals, such as gold, which, as Gernet remarks, is associated with the sun, its brilliance, its beauty. Richness, wealth as "value itself," is in archaic and premonetary mythical or symbolic representation intimately associated with brilliance, with a certain shining—that is, even though Gernet does not use the term, with a definite éclat.

Gernet's study of an archaic notion of value serves Nancy to further detach the concept of absolute value from "value itself," and its economic understanding, that, in Marx, still dominates the conception of a humanity that through its power of labor produces itself as its own work. Indeed, in order to elaborate on a world that would be truly immanent to itself, and to establish it as absolute value, the latter has to be uncoupled from an understanding of value that views it exclusively in terms of labor. After having pointed out that "mythical" in Gernet's talk of the mythical idea of value in archaic Greece "designates here the reality of the 'virtue of symbols,'" Nancy notes that if "the value of the valorous [for example] who measure themselves in the athletic *agon*" is compensated before the invention of currency by a "'pricey' object," the wealth it represents is not capitalized wealth. Rather, "it makes the brilliance [*l'éclat*] of what 'shows its worth' shine in gold, which we might risk translating into a 'to produce oneself,'" in the sense of a "to show oneself" (119n11). But even though Nancy admits that with the distinction he has made in Marx between commodity value and absolute value, the relation that he has sketched out "between Marx and the 'mythical' world, between abstract value and symbolic value" (119n11), would need to be elaborated, his further developments in "*Urbi et Orbi*" on absolute value definitely cast the latter in terms of brilliance, luminosity, radiance—of éclat, in short. Such value will be attributed to the world, to the world being world throughout. *Mondialité*, or throughout worldhood, is, Nancy holds, "the *symbolization* of the world, the way in which the world symbolizes in itself with itself, in which it articulates itself by making a circulation of meaning possible without reference to another world" (53). Worldhood is the world's immanent and absolute value. Let us remind ourselves that the becoming "mondial" of the world does not simply suggest that the space of the world "has spread out over the entire surface of the planet and beyond, but that it has [also] emerged as the surface of what is at play in the depths: the essence of being-with."[29] It is the wealth of this essence of being-with that comes to light in a world that is throughout world, and that shines forth in all its éclat. If Nancy adds that "our task today is nothing less than the task of creating a form or a symbolization of the world" (53), the task, then, is clearly one of creating a world whose wealth and value is not primarily economic (or in which being-with is not primarily dominated by labor relations), but symbolic in the sense of the shining, or of the éclat, of the infinite richness and "originality" of the modes in which the singularities that make it up relate to one another. The "absolute value" of such a world is no longer a value that underlies all relative values as is still the case with "value itself," but a value that forms the surface of a world without depth (and vertical transcendence).[30]

Notes

This essay is part of a book entitled *De l'éclat du monde: La 'valeur' chez Marx et Nancy*, trans. Cécile Dutheil de la Rochère (Paris: Hermann, 2019).

    1. Jean-Luc Nancy, "Finite History," in *The Birth to Presence*, trans. Brian Holmes et al. (Stanford, CA: Stanford University Press, 1993), 144.

2. Nancy, "Finite History," 144.

3. Nancy, "Finite History," 409.

4. In the "Afterword to the Second German Edition" of *The Capital*, Marx writes: "The mystifying side of Hegelian dialectic I criticized nearly thirty years ago, at a time when it was still in fashion. But just as I was working at the first volume of *Das Kapital*, it was the good pleasure of the peevish, arrogant, mediocre *epigonoi* [Epigonen—Büchner, Dühring, and others] who now talk large in cultured Germany, to treat Hegel in the same way as the brave Moses Mendelsohn in Lessing's time treated Spinoza, i.e., as a 'dead dog.' I therefore openly avowed myself the pupil of that mighty thinker, and even here and there, in the chapter on the theory of value, coquetted with the modes of expression peculiar to him" (Karl Marx and Frederick Engels, *Collected Works*, vol. 35, Karl Marx, *Capital*, vol. 1 [New York: International, 1996], 19). Being in quotation marks, the expression "dead dog" is a citation, most probably from Samuel, most likely, 2 Samuel 9:8. For a more extensive review of the expression in the Scriptures, see *Handwörterbuch des biblischen Altertums für gebildete Bibelleser*, ed. E. C. A. Riehm and F. Baethgen, vol. 1 (Bielefeld: Velhagen and Klasing, 1893), 666.

5. All page references in the text and in the endnotes as well refer to Jean-Luc Nancy, *The Creation of the World or Globalization*, trans. François Raffoul and David Pettigrew (Albany: State University of New York Press, 2007).

6. Nancy writes: "there remains, on the one hand, precisely what happens to us and sweeps over us by the name of 'globalization' [*mondialisation*], namely, the exponential growth of the globality . . . of the market—of the circulation of everything in the form of commodity—and with it of the increasingly concentrated interdependency that ceaselessly weakens independencies and sovereignties, thus weakening the entire order of representations of belonging . . . ; and there remains, on the other hand, the fact that the experience undergone since Marx has increasingly been the experience that the place of meaning [*sens*] of value, and of truth is the world" (37).

7. Nancy submits: "Our difference with him . . . reappears on this very point: with him 'human' implicitly remains a teleological or eschatological term, if we understand by that a logic where the *telos* and/or the *eschaton* take the position and the role of an accomplishment without remainder. For Marx, the human being, as source and accomplishment of value in itself, comes at the end of history when it produces itself: the source must therefore end entirely spread out and accomplished. For us, on the contrary, 'the human being' is reduced to a given principle, relatively abstract ('person,' 'dignity') and as such distinct from an actual creation. In truth, it is the figure of 'the human being' and with it the configuration of 'humanism' that are erased or blurred while we have, at the same time, the most compelling reasons not to replace them with (the figure of) 'the overman' or 'God'" (37–38).

8. See also the following passage: "it is also possible—and it is even in some respect necessary—to interpret it [the final and total accomplishment of humanity's self-production] differently: indeed, if the production of total humanity—that is

global [*mondial*] humanity, or the production of the humanized world—is nothing other than the production of the 'sphere of freedom,' a freedom that has no other exercise than the 'enjoyment of the multimorphic production of the entire world,' then this final production determines no genuine end, nor *telos* or *eschaton*" (45).

9. Marx, *Capital*, 1:68.

10. Karl Marx, "Marginal Notes on Adolph Wagner's '*Lehrbuch der politischen Ökonomie*,'" in Karl Marx and Frederick Engels, *Collected Works*, vol. 24 (New York: International, 1975), 549.

11. Marx, "Marginal Notes," 551.

12. It might perhaps be interesting to compare Nancy's concept of the world to Hermann Broch's notion of "das irdisch Absolute" in his later work. See Hermann Broch, "Politik: Ein Kondensat," in *Gesammelte Werke*, vol. 7, *Essays*, vol. 2, *Erkennen und Handeln* (Zurich: Rhein-Verlag, 1955), 203–18.

13. The reason for putting metaphysical humanism into question is not merely because it testifies, as Georg Simmel has pointed, to a delusion of grandeur (*Grössenwahn*) on the part of the human as regards the end of the world, but also because such humanism does not do justice to the "social," that is, to the specific relations among human beings.

14. Undoubtedly, Heidegger's critical, but, at the same time, positive reference to Marx in "Letter on Humanism" is one of the explicit places that can be construed in support of Nancy's argument. Heidegger writes, for example: "Because Marx by experiencing estrangement attains an essential dimension of history, the Marxist view of history is superior to that of other historical accounts" (Martin Heidegger, *Basic Writings*, trans. David Farrell Krell [New York: Harper and Row, 1977], 219). Yet although Marx's understanding of Being in terms of alienated labor does not yet allow him to grasp the essential historicity of Being, which would have required a questioning of the relation of labor to technology, Marx's insight paves the way for Heidegger's radicalization of the question of historicity and Being.

15. Jean-Luc Nancy, *Being Singular Plural*, trans. Robert D. Richardson and Anne E. O'Byrne (Stanford, CA: Stanford University Press, 2000), 26.

16. See Jean-Luc Nancy, *La possibilité d'un monde* (Paris: Les petits Platons, 2013), 19. But the point that I am making here is not merely biographical. Yet, in order to account for Nancy's overwhelming concern in his writings with the social, ethical, and political issues associated with a loss of "world" in contemporary life, the reference to Heidegger alone will certainly not do.

17. Nancy, *Being Singular Plural*, 70. The knowledge in question is one that "makes its way from Rousseau to Bataille, or from Marx to Heidegger," but that needs to find a language that is not only ours in the sense of us today, but also in the sense of being a language that is truly that of being-in-common.

18. Nancy, *Being Singular Plural*, 23–24.

19. Nancy, *Being Singular Plural*, 34.

20. Nancy, *Being Singular Plural*, 42.

21. Karl Marx, "Critique of the Gotha Programme," in Karl Marx and Friedrich Engels, *Collected Works* (New York: International, 1989), vol. 24, 87.

22. Jean-Luc Nancy, *The Sense of the World*, trans. Jeffrey S. Librett (Minneapolis: University of Minnesota Press, 1997), 98. Nancy wonders whether there is, in a general way, something like "non alienated labor." This question "can be described as follows: what does 'self-production' mean? Does it mean *poiesis*, *praxis*, or some other, unheard-of thing?" (100).

23. Nancy, *Sense of the World*, 96.

24. Nancy, *Sense of the World*, 97 (translation modified).

25. Nancy, *Sense of the World*, 97.

26. Louis Gernet, "The Mythical Idea of Value in Greece," in *The Anthropology of Ancient Greece*, trans. John Hamilton and Blaise Nagy (Baltimore, MD: Johns Hopkins University Press, 1981), 76–77.

27. Gernet, "Mythical Idea of Value in Greece," 73 (translation modified), 78.

28. Gernet, "Mythical Idea of Value in Greece," 83.

29. Nancy, *Being Singular Plural*, 45.

30. Is this concern with the éclat of worldliness, which is not a brilliance that shines from underneath the phenomena, and is thus distinct from the (economic) form of value itself underneath the phenomena of commodity and labor value, not also part of Nancy's attempts to overcome phenomenology?

4

Worldless
Heidegger, Simone Weil, and Anti-Judaism via Nancy

ELEANOR KAUFMAN

> I had come to the end of a life which, surely, the pebbles on the road would want to tell. But who talks or listens to a stone? Only a Jew.
> —Edmond Jabès, *The Book of Questions: El, or the Last Book*

Though roughly contemporaries, and each in their way a philosophical icon of the modern period, Martin Heidegger and Simone Weil are put into conversation with notable infrequency.[1] Jean-Luc Nancy, both in his cumulative work on the question of the "world" and more elliptically in his recent *The Banality of Heidegger*, gestures to a terrain where the posthumously published musings of the two thinkers both clash and resonate. On the one hand, Heidegger affirms if not inaugurates the modern sense of "world" as a realm of plenitude, strength, and active formation—a sense resonant with Nancy's sustained treatment of this term throughout his oeuvre. By contrast, Weil's thought, and particularly her notions of detachment and decreation, gestures affirmatively to the world's weakness, something Heidegger also does in his lectures from the early 1920s. However, in the *Black Notebooks*, the figure of the Jew signals poverty in world yet also a pejorative affinity with "the gigantic"; for Weil, Judaism's great sin is its strength, that it is too much *of* the world and not weak enough to prostrate itself before God. Whereas their thought aligns on a number of counts and both Heidegger and Weil voice if not enact unsettling expressions of anti-Judaism, the latter is accomplished by mobilizing the notion of the "world" to somewhat different ends, and Nancy's *The Banality of Heidegger* (in resonance with his larger oeuvre) helps elucidate that difference. Weil is part of a recognizable lineage of Jewish apostasy

91

that veers into heretical Christianity, whereas Heidegger is less categorizable, which opens his anti-Judaism to other lines of questioning.

Although it is not the goal of this essay to provide a full consideration of Heidegger's concept of world, something others have ably done, it is critical to highlight the way Heidegger contextualizes his concept of world in his 1929–30 course lecture *The Fundamental Concepts of Metaphysics: World, Finitude, Solitude*. Bracketing as it were the phenomenological and everyday world highlighted in *Being and Time* (1927), in the course lecture Heidegger begins by situating the world-problem theologically: "Here I would just like to give a very general indication of the context in which, from an external point of view, the problem of world initially arises. The most familiar aspect of the problem reveals itself in the distinction between God and world. The world is the totality of beings outside of and other than God. Expressed in Christian terms, such beings thus also represent the realm of created being as distinct from uncreated being. And man in turn is also a part of the world understood in this sense."[2] This is a distinction Heidegger would have known well given his early theological orientation, one that shifted to a philosophical one by the beginning of the 1920s.[3] And this Christian suspicion of the world is one he proceeds to turn on its head, without exactly signaling the extent to which he is doing so: "Yet man is not simply regarded as part of the world in which he appears and which he makes up in part. Man also stands over and against the world. This standing-over-against (*Gegenüberstehen*) is a '*having*' of world" (177). Heidegger nowhere says this as such, but to stand over and against the world is effectively to stand in the place of a god. With a sleight of hand, Heidegger thus overturns the Christian insistence on an unbridgeable distinction between God and world, uncreated and created being, before launching into the set of distinctions around having or not having world for which this lecture seminar is best known: the tripartite distinction between human, animal, and rock that are differentiated by their relative amount of world. While the human has world or is world-forming (*weltbildend*), the lizard is poor in world (*weltarm*), and the rock it sits on is worldless (*weltlos*). Like Aristotle's three levels of soul, the highest level excludes all but the human. However, also like Aristotle, Heidegger spends a great deal of time defining the parameters of what constitutes the other two categories, poverty in world and worldlessness. The former intermediary level, like Aristotle's sensate being, has limited access to world, what Heidegger characterizes as open but not openable (*offen* not *offenbar*), and Giorgio Agamben following him will gloss as an "openness to a closedness."[4]

What is generally less emphasized in the extensive critical literature on *The Fundamental Concepts of Metaphysics* is the extent to which Heidegger himself qualifies the hierarchy he would seem to be incontrovertibly erecting. Regarding the apparent distinction of human and animal to the favor of the former, Heidegger writes:

> Certainly the relation we have described above between the animal's poverty in world and the world-formation of man has a suspiciously self-evident clarity that actually disappears as soon as we come to grips with the issue. . . . Yet even a little reflection soon renders it questionable whether in fact poverty is necessarily and intrinsically of lesser significance with respect to richness. The reverse might well be true. . . . However ready we are to rank man as a higher being with respect to the animal, such an assessment is deeply questionable, especially when we consider that man can sink lower than any animal. . . . May we talk of a "higher" and a "lower" at all in the realm of what is essential? Is the essence of man higher than the essence of the animal? All this is questionable even as a question.[5] (194)

If Heidegger at the outset questions the human-animal hierarchy his tripartite schema would seem to support, the reflections that follow on the difference between "poverty in world" and "worldlessness" only underscore the inherent problems of hierarchizing. Whereas poverty signals a state of deprivation, being worldless for Heidegger means not even being deprived, hence paradoxically more fully itself. It follows then that this seemingly lowest state is not without its own ontological character, which Heidegger defines with a strikingly realist characterization: "[The stone] is—but is essentially *without access* to those beings amongst which it is in its own way (presence at hand), and this belongs to its being. . . . The *worldlessness* of a being can now be defined as its having no access to those beings (*as* beings) amongst which this particular being with this specific manner of being is. . . . For having no access is precisely what makes possible its specific kind of being" (197). There is thus an antinomy inherent in the very concept of worldlessness. While the worldless entity has no access to beings *as* beings, the very purity of its lack of access (something the animal lacks!) allows for the predication of its *own* manner of being. If one takes Medieval logic as any kind of model, God is distinctive for ontological simplicity. And so, too, is the rock. As Sartre writes in *The Critique of Dialectical Reason*, "if [man] could encounter pure matter in experience, he would have to be either a god or a stone."[6] Insofar as Heidegger, like Sartre, is generally thought to be engaged in a phenomenological project with a thinking, perceiving human as its perspectival focal point, how do we situate the rock ontology that is effectively produced?[7]

Jean-Luc Nancy evokes the richness of this ontology in *The Birth to Presence* in his meditation on "the heart of things." This timely conjoining of the heart and the thing, a topic which will have continued personal and philosophical import, brings together in seamless fashion the animate and the inanimate—and anticipates the sustained reflections on "being with" in *Being Singular Plural* that have resonated far beyond the French philosophical milieu.[8] With respect to stone, Nancy writes that "the heart of the stone consists in exposing the stone to the elements: pebble on the road, in a torrent, underground, in the fusion of magma. 'Pure essence'—or 'simple existence'—involves a mineralogy and meteorology of being."[9] Stone ontology here gets its bearings and is effectively enlivened by other less inert elements. It partakes of another form of plenitude that is not fundamentally constituted by lack or being without. The stone is not so much *without* world but rather pulsing *with* other elements. The stone may not "have" world, but for Nancy it is effectively touched by world, just as in *The Sense of the World* he writes that "the stone does not 'have' any sense. But sense touches the stone."[10] At an earlier point, Nancy insists that "sense" and "world" are so mutually embedded as to make "the sense of the world" something of a tautological expression.[11] This effectively echoes and anticipates formulations in Nancy's extended meditation on Heidegger in *Finite Thinking* in which he reiterates that "being *is* sense," and that "the sense of being is the being of sense."[12] In this essay on "Originary Ethics," he defines sense parenthetically as "the sense of human existence, but also, and along with it, the sense of the world."[13] While Nancy's later work on Heidegger will provide a crucial point of connection between Heidegger and Weil, at this juncture Nancy conjoins Heidegger's human-centered notion of *Dasein* from *Being and Time* along with aspects of the poor-in-world sensate being to portray a rather enworlded vision of the rock, and indeed of sense and of being. It is the contention here that, in thinking to its limit the purity of worldlessness, Heidegger is at least gesturing to something less relational and propositional than what we find in Nancy. This will have important ramifications for the concept of worldlessness, which is in some sense the unthought of Nancy's oeuvre.

Whereas the animal in *The Fundamental Concepts of Metaphysics* maintains a capacity for "relation to . . ." (253), it is precisely this capacity that distinguishes it from the human capacity to access beings as such (269). Because of its openness, a "*not-having of world*" (270) can be ascribed to the animal whereas, curiously, the stone does not have the same type of restriction: "we cannot even ascribe such not-having to the stone, because its specific manner of being is not determined by the being-open of behavior, let alone by the manifesting character of comportment" (270). Although it is counterintuitive to do so, if we take seriously Heidegger's claim that these are not hierarchical categories (194), then the nonrelational ontology of the rock that is without world is not to be dismissed out of hand, and ostensibly might be something good to think with.[14]

To complicate matters, being without world is not the seemingly demoted category for Heidegger at the beginning of the 1920s that it is by the time of *The Fundamental Concepts of Metaphysics* at the end of the decade. The earlier moment finds Heidegger moving in quick succession from a Catholic to a Protestant and then to a more secular philosophical orientation in a fashion worthy of Rousseau. His 1920–21 lectures on *The Phenomenology of Religious Life* underscore his newfound philosophical orientation though simultaneously rehearse rather standard negative monotheistic assessments of the world, all while considering the original way the Apostle Paul evokes nonrelation. In lengthy readings of Paul's letters to the Galatians and the Thessalonians, Heidegger delimits how the Pauline notion of *parousia* (παρουσία) is distinctive in that "Paul does not answer . . . in worldly reasoning," despite being saddled with his Rabbinical training.[15] Indeed, Paul's originality stems from his emphasis on personal enactment apart from the conditioned perceptions of time and social relation (73). Those who forgo self-authenticity to put their trust in the established order of the world risk ruination: "Those who find rest and security in this world are those who cling to this world because it provides peace and security. 'Peace and security' characterizes the mode of this relation to those who speak this way" (72).[16] The preferred approach that Paul epitomizes is one apart from the security of the world and the security of relation. This form of detachment is not unlike the state enjoyed by the rock in the *The Fundamental Concepts of Metaphysics*. Moreover, it derives from the notion of phenomenon and phenomenology with which Heidegger begins the 1920–21 lectures. Arguing that the history of philosophy has been dominated by the biases of such a relational approach, he advises that "a phenomenon must be so stipulated, that its relational meaning is held in abeyance" (44). What would it mean to hold relation in abeyance? Whereas a thinker like Nancy arguably develops a Heideggerian thought of abeyance (for example when he considers finitude not as a limitation but a "power to leave . . . open"[17]), his whole oeuvre also puts forward a strong thought of relation. Heidegger's early work, at the least, would seem to interrogate the primacy of relation, particularly in reference to theological examples.

Paul, then, is an exemplary phenomenologist for the way that he makes a "complete break with the earlier past, with every non-Christian view of life." (48) Specifically and pointedly for Heidegger, this is a break, constituted in struggle, not only with the Jews but also with the Jewish Christians, one of whom was Jesus himself: "Paul wants to say further that he has come to Christianity not through a historical tradition, but through an original experience. . . . Rather he has grounded a new Christian religion, a new primordial Christianity which dominates the future: the Pauline religion, not the religion of Jesus. One thus does not need to refer back to a historical Jesus. The life of Jesus is entirely indifferent" (49).[18] For Heidegger it appears not simply as a matter of the well-known supplanting of Jewish law by Christian faith, controversially described in Paul's letter to the Romans, but something more extreme and thereby, at least from most Christian vantage points, more heretical. In question is a phenomenological and otherworldly grounding in a primitive Pauline Christianity that does away entirely with the relation to the Jewish past. Though not presented in sustained fashion, undergirding Heidegger's *Phenomenology of Religious Life* is an affirmation of the nonworldly, the nonrelational, and the non-Jewish.

A final and fourth term to add to the mix is one that might seem out of keeping with the sequence but is crucial to what follows, namely the related affirmation of weakness. For it is Paul's weakness that is the measure of his authenticity: "The extraordinary in his life plays no role for him. Only when he is weak, when he withstands the anguish of his life, can he enter into a close connection with God. This fundamental requirement of having-God is the opposite of all bad mysticism. Not mystical absorption and special exertion; rather withstanding the weakness of life is decisive" (70). It is in becoming nothing and worldless for God that the Christian in some sense "has" God. While such a "having" arguably could be aligned with the relational quality of the animal which is poor in world, it seems far more proximate to the rock's particular constitution, that of something traversed by forces it does not control and whose history and composition it does not recognize, but able to withstand things that other entities who are more relationally grounded to their environment might not (what Deleuze will call a "larval subject"). This is resonant with though not fully proximate to what Nancy will formulate in *The Birth to Presence* as the tension between the mobility of thought and the immobile heaviness of things: "It is in the thought of the thing that thought finds its true gravity, it is there that it recognizes itself, and there that it collapses under its own weight."[19] Clearly there is a hardness and a fortitude that comes directly from a willed or constitutional weakness and opacity, both a gravity and a grace of things.

Before addressing the vexed and contradictory import of this subterranean current of Heidegger's thought to his distinctive form of anti-Judaism, it bears stating what is likely apparent to those versed in the work of Simone

Weil, namely, the striking degree to which her thought overlaps with Heidegger's. Though Weil does not employ anything approaching Heidegger's phenomenological methodology, she outlines a form of detachment so extreme that it not only translates the rock's nonrelational worldlessness to the human condition, but it pushes the limits of the Christian framework, something more central to her work and life than it was to Heidegger's. Weil's notion of detachment takes the form of a desire without an object, and a devotion to God with no compensation, a "fidelity in the void."[20] Unlike Christ's message in the gospels, which promises the inheritance of the earth to the meek, Weil insists on enduring suffering in the absence of any reward: "Those who wish for their salvation," she writes, "do not truly believe in the reality of the joy within God" (37). In the section of *Gravity and Grace* entitled "Detachment," Weil prefaces her concluding exhortation to "love God while thinking he does not exist" (15) with an injunction "to empty ourselves of the world," (12) something deceptively real only because of our unfounded attachment to it (14). For Weil, nothingness is what is real, and "unconsoled affliction is necessary" (12). In the section on "Decreation," she espouses an "acceptance of not being" (32) and a "go[ing] down to the vegetative level" (36). Like Heidegger's worldless mineral realm, the vegetative dimension is superior to that of worldly relation: "The vegetative and the social are the two realms where the good does not enter. Christ redeemed the vegetative, not the social. He did not pray for the world" (165). If Weil's unqualified insistence on detachment, nothingness, and especially her antagonism toward the world exceed anything that can be distilled from the juxtaposition of Heidegger's early and middle writings, her more absolute version of these positions is itself one of the refractory lenses that makes this submerged tendency in Heidegger discernible at all, since clearly his concept of world had shifted substantially by the time of the 1927 publication of *Being and Time*.[21]

Equally more pronounced in Weil is the dramatic dialectic of strength and weakness that pervades her thought, which is hard to separate from her life. Fragile by constitution, Weil from an early age tried incessantly to place herself outside her bourgeois assimilated Jewish upbringing and into direct contact with those less fortunate than she. This often took the form of inflicting severe depravations on herself, ones deemed commensurate with workers, soldiers on the front, or the fighters in the French Resistance, which she tried unsuccessfully to join early in 1943. Later in 1943, Weil died in England of tuberculosis, a death likely hastened by her extreme self-imposed alimentary restrictions. One sees in her an extraordinary pairing of fierce "intellectual honesty" (her own term for what she aspired to)[22] and persistent physical weakness—to the point that she was unable to sustain work in a factory where she placed herself, or alongside the Spanish Republican army, where she also placed herself, and was clumsy to the point of injuring herself so that she had to be rescued (more than once) by her parents. This combination of strength of character and physical fragility, the latter leading to her early death at age thirty-four, drew critical admiration from the likes of Susan Sontag, Leslie Fiedler, and a score of others.[23]

Notwithstanding her profound turning toward Christianity starting with a quasi-conversion experience at Assisi in 1937 (though she never formally converted to the Roman Catholic Church), certain aspects of Weil's Christian orientation, such as her dismissal of salvific goals, are markedly heretical from the perspective of Christian orthodoxy, and none more than her pronouncements about Judaism. Yet it is these painful statements that touch most pointedly on the thematic of weakness and strength, and which in turn expose a powerful tension if not incoherence in Heidegger's anti-Judaism. Excised from most collections of Weil's work, the passages that follow are objectionable particularly in the way they emphasize Judaism's strength.[24] Weil's essay "The Three Sons of Noah" is rarely anthologized in English collections, though it is included in the 1950 edition of *Waiting for God*; however, the paragraph in question was nevertheless still excised, and is here rendered from the French. Weil writes: "We don't realize that if the ancient Hebrews were revived among us, their first thought would be to massacre us all, including the infants in their cradles, to raze our villages, for crimes of idolatry."[25] In the equally incendiary essay "Israel," which she also calls the second Great Beast (Rome being the first), she writes: "Jacob's struggle with the angel—is not this the great blemish? . . . Isn't this the great tragedy, to battle against God and not to be vanquished?" She condemns Israel for having the strength to stand up to Rome, though this damnable strength nonetheless produces something quite anathema: "Israel stood up to Rome because its God, even though immaterial, was a temporal sovereign on a par with the Emperor, and thanks to this Christianity could be born. The religion of Israel was not noble enough to be fragile, and due to its solidity could protect belief in the most elevated."[26] In this scathing critique of Israel and its strength to stand up to Rome, the only redemptive outcome is that Hebrew unvanquishability at least allowed Christianity to be born and a new form of monotheism to continue. Much in the fashion of Hegel's lord and bondsman, the weak position enacts something of a dialectical reversal and itself gains a greater strength.

Roberto Esposito's *The Origin of the Political: Hannah Arendt or Simone Weil?* demonstrates that Weil and Arendt serve as something like inverse mirrors to one another, each unwittingly illuminating what is left undeveloped in the other. Arendt's Latin allegiance is contrasted, on the whole unfavorably, to Weil's even more emphatic championing of Greece. For example, Esposito states that "it would be possible to demonstrate the ways in which Weil overturns all of Arendt's affirmations not by negating them, but, rather, by uncovering the double foundation of violence and deceit that underlies the Latin framework upon which Arendt's assertions rest."[27] Without going into the finer points of Esposito's argument, it highlights the self-schism that is still possible for Greece and lauded by Weil, but not for Rome, approaching something like the tension between a strain of Heidegger that insists on nonrelation and worldlessness and Nancy's equally Heideggerian emphasis on "being with" and the plenitude of the world. It might be summed up in the following formulation: "It is precisely because of this ability to split, to be *oneself* and one's contrary simultaneously, that the experience of the Greeks is unrepeatable. This is especially the case in reference to the Romans, who, along with the Jews, constitute their most radical negation precisely for the reasons vindicated by Arendt in the name of their glory" (54). One wonders if this difference also rests on a greater affinity for and non-antinomic relation to the world on the part of the latter grouping. In what will be developed, the purity of Weil's and Heidegger's Greece-over-Rome stance is reflected, at least in Weil's case, in the simultaneous support of a heretical Christianity that can be fully detached (but in reverse chronology) from its Jewish antecedent.

The proximity of Weil and Heidegger is particularly striking in the context of Esposito's opposition between Weil and Arendt, Greece and Rome, not only for their parallel dispositions toward Greece and Rome and similar modes of argumentation but also for their corollary distaste for the perceived strength and despotism of the ancient Hebrews. As Esposito writes, "what is surprisingly familiar in the relation between Weil and Heidegger's writings is not so much the overall framework of an opposition between Greek and Roman worlds that is always developed to the detriment of the latter.... Rather what is familiar is the proximity of their argumentative modalities.... Weil's thesis is precisely as follows: The Roman *numen* is different from that of the Greek gods because, unlike the latter, who can only ever signal a necessity greater than themselves, the former represents the essence of a despotic will akin to the God of the Old Testament. This is in fact the very manner in which Heidegger approaches the spirit of Rome" (56). In effect it is the self-negation, the avowed weakness, of the Greeks that raises them above the less refined brute strength of the Romans, itself following the model of Jewish unvanquishability in the Old Testament.

In "The Great Beast," from *Gravity and Grace*, Weil elaborates on this Roman-Jewish juxtaposition with particular crudeness and heavy-handedness, the heavy itself being the mark of pejorative strength: "Rome is the Great Beast of atheism and materialism, adoring nothing but itself. Israel is the Great Beast of religion. Neither the one nor the other is likeable. The Great Beast is always repulsive. . . . In Rome, perhaps, where was only gravity. With the Hebrews too, perhaps. Their God was heavy" (167). The anti-Semitism in Weil's writing is intertwined with a coherent set of thematics, almost all of which overlap with Heidegger's more subtle expression of the same motifs: the upholding of weakness over strength, detachment over society and relation, and the worldless in its break from the world. Whereas Weil's foundational anti-Judaism may be downplayed because of her heritage and her untimely death before the full extent of what transpired in the Nazi death camps was known (it has been speculated that surely she would have viewed things differently had she known, or had she studied Kabbalah or Jewish mysticism), Heidegger's anti-Judaism is less possible to put aside in the wake of the publication of the *Black Notebooks*.[28] Moreover, whereas Weil's work unifies and consolidates the different threads under discussion here, Heidegger's slightly less crass anti-Judaic pronouncements fail to cohere, and are themselves bifurcated from each other with a differently dissonant form of nonrelationality.

Of note are two threads that appear in the *Black Notebooks*, associated with the much commented upon anti-Judaic reflections that have recently come to light, and underscoring the difficulty of dissociating the anti-Judaic, or even anti-Semitic, refrain from the heart of Heidegger's philosophy. One thread is that of the "gigantic" (*das Riesige*), associated with calculation and machination, and serving as a mark of the West's decline in the modern era with the advent of technology. As Heidegger cautions in "The Age of the World Picture," the gigantic presents itself in "the tendency toward the increasingly small," so that it appears to have vanished or been eliminated, as when an airplane traverses great distance in a short time. Thus he warns that "we think too superficially if we suppose that the gigantic is only the endlessly extended emptiness of the purely quantitative."[29] As Marx reminds us in *Capital*, quality and quantity are easily entangled. In the same fashion, the gigantic's leading trait of calculability slides over into the incalculable: "But as soon as the gigantic in planning and calculating and adjusting and making secure shifts over out of the quantitative and becomes a special quality, then what is gigantic, and what can seemingly always be calculated completely, becomes, precisely through this, incalculable. This becoming incalculable remains the invisible shadow that is cast around all things everywhere when man has been transformed into *subjectum* and the world into picture."[30] In language anticipating Derrida, it is not simply the gigantic but the gigantic in play with the infinitesimal that leads to the species-negating play of the calculable and the incalculable. This same warning that the gigantic is not simply gigantic appears in *The Black Notebooks* (*Überlegungen XIII*) when Heidegger emphasizes that "the gigantic consists not in a sum total of unusual extent but in the already unconditionally secured and constantly operative possibility of measurelessness."[31] Almost like the Kantian sublime but working affectively in the opposite direction, Heidegger's gigantic marks an upending conjunction of the calculable and the incalculable, the managed and the measureless. As with Deleuze's society of control, there is at once more freedom and more control.

This seems relatively benign until we consider the slightly earlier formulation from *Überlegungen VIII* that reframes this refrain introducing different terms: "One of the most concealed forms of the *gigantic*, and perhaps the oldest, is a tenacious facility in calculating, manipulating, and interfering; through this facility the worldlessness of Judaism receives its ground."[32] Now we are confronted with the same nexus of terms from Weil's denunciation of "Israel" (jotted in her notebook at roughly the same moment), a combined cunning and tenacity that amounts to an unseemly show of strength. The gigantic, at least in Heidegger's aggressive deprecation of Judaism, appears equivalent to the strength under attack in Weil, and without the counterbalance of the minute and the incalculable as seen in the previous citation from the *Black Notebooks*. Yet it raises the question of why Jewish worldlessness is "one of the most concealed forms of the *gigantic*."[33] Judaism for Heidegger seems to encompass at once the brute strength that for Weil remains shamefully unconcealed, and a form of calculation that somehow covers this over.

In *The Banality of Heidegger*, Nancy captures this conundrum as it pertains to the gigantic, including Heidegger's concomitant dictum that that which is groundless (epitomized by Judaism) should destroy, or at least exclude, itself. Nancy writes that "the figure of the Jew configures the very type of a devastating necessity: the gigantic, calculation, and a rationality that is busy de-differentiating the world and properly dislodging it: withdrawing it from every kind of ground and soil."[34] While Nancy goes on to question how the call for exclusion or destruction can be possibly carried out by an entity that is already groundless to begin with (21), he nonetheless accepts, in this passage and throughout, Heidegger's general constellation of terms. What fails to cohere at an even more basic level is how the gigantic and the worldless could coincide in one entity. While the anti-Judaic pronouncements of Heidegger and Weil overlap in remarkable fashion—including their recurrent favoring of rootedness[35]—one would not find the gigantic and the worldless elided in Weil as they are in Heidegger's *Black Notebooks*. Weil at least retains monotheistic orthodoxy's suspicion of the world, something also acknowledged in early Heidegger. Inextricably attached as he is to the plenitude of the world and an absolute "deconstruction" of Christianity, Nancy readily questions Heidegger's impulse to devastation (and why the Jew is its emblematic figure) but does not acknowledge that the de-differentiating and dislodging of the world is itself a monotheistic, and especially a Christian, goal: the world ends and passes away, but God's kingdom does not.

Nevertheless, in his supplement to *The Banality of Heidegger* (written after the publication in German of volume 97 of the *Black Notebooks* [*Anmerkungen I–V*]), Nancy adduces a magisterial analysis of Heidegger's confounding relation to Christianity, one which—as the example above also illustrates—does not conform with recognized variants, even heretical ones. At a basic level, as Nancy notes at the outset, Heidegger effectively posits that "Christianity should have been capable of resisting the decline of the West" (64) and that it "failed at something that should have fallen to it" (68). But this is quickly disoriented by the figures of the Judaic and the Greek. Even for Heidegger, Christianity is fundamentally indissociable from the Judaism from which it arose; meanwhile there is a Greek originality that "remained outside of Judaism, that is, of Christianity" (Nancy, 69, cited from *Anmerkungen I*, 20). Nancy thus pinpoints the impasse, that for Heidegger some primordial Christianity, itself practically Greek, retains a univocal exceptionality whereas Western Christianity has long since fallen, it is now wedded to Judaism and has "made a pact with destruction" (69). Since Christianity can't be Greek in the way Heidegger would want, and is instead imprisoned within Judaism, what is otherwise closer to crass anti-Semitism modulates in Heidegger into something like anti-Judeo-Christianity.

Nancy considers Heidegger's predicament in two distinct ways that expose a tension at the heart of Nancy's own vexed relation to Christianity, and which will thereafter return us to Weil, *for it is a tension that does not exist in her heretical Christianity, which ultimately maintains something closer to an apostate relation to Judaism*, and makes her anti-Judaism stronger for it.[36] But first, Nancy summarizes Heidegger's position on Christianity in the *Black Notebooks* as follows: "Because Christianity is Jewish, it has nothing to do with the destining of being. It harbored, however, a univocality that could have raised it to the level of an opposition to the destruction, Jewish in its principle, of this destining. Christianity is therefore Jewish and non-Jewish. But well before Heidegger Christianity contorted itself into this kind of double bind" (70). Nancy then highlights Paul as one traversed by this double bind. This is hardly a contentious observation, though it might be noted that it was the fourth-century debates, resulting in the Councils of Nicea and Chalcedon, that helped establish and codify the parameters of Christianity's relation to Judaism alongside other denominations that came to be labeled heretical, such as Arianism, Nestorianism, Pelagianism, and the like. To separate Christianity too forcefully from its Jewish provenance itself became a heretical position, something for which the Cathars or Albigensians were effectively exterminated in the thirteenth and fourteenth centuries.

While writing the Jewish provenance along with its scriptures into both Eastern and Roman Orthodoxy certainly didn't forestall a millennium of Christian anti-Semitism, it did make it harder to account for it *theologically*. If a scholar cognizant of Christian rite offhandedly equates Christianity as such with anti-Judaism, this stands out to one who has eyes to see. Nancy provides a second summary of Heidegger's position a page later:

> Heidegger sees the disaster of this world. He interprets it simultaneously as a Greek and as a Christian; he wants to be above the fray and to endure a forgetting that being itself could bring to an end by "returning," as he writes in 1946 in "The Anaximander Fragment." But as a Christian—since he is one, despite everything; he even is one in the most banal way, steeped as he is in theology and spirituality—he finds it necessary to disqualify the people who have not recognized Christ. (71)

In this juxtaposition of Greek Heidegger and Christian Heidegger, and almost by sleight of hand since the sentence in question is disrupted by a significant biographical parenthetical, Nancy effectively states that Heidegger feels compelled to "disqualify" the Jews *because* he is a Christian. If that were the case, it would be as a Christian heretic. But Nancy has just shown Heidegger's position to be so confoundingly bifurcated as to not fit clearly into a recognized position, however heretical.[37] Opposing Christianity to Judaism in a fashion Nancy imputes to Heidegger is in fact what Weil does, and does coherently and moreover in a manner that fits almost seamlessly into a long tradition of Jewish apostasy.

It is not the aim here to give an in-depth consideration of what constitutes Jewish apostasy, as any given case is arguably more akin to the exception that proves the rule.[38] The most general hypothesis is that there is a long tradition of Jewish apostasy, and a striking feature of the apostate position is that in at least certain cases it also upholds the heretical Christian position of a dissociation of Christianity from Judaism. Such a tradition might be bookended by the Apostle Paul on one end and Simone Weil on the other.

In *A Radical Jew: Paul and the Politics of Identity,* Daniel Boyarin succinctly presents the stakes and indeed the paradox of this position with respect to Paul. Just as Heidegger notes in passing in his *Phenomenology of Religion* lectures that "Paul's argumentation is here rabbinical-Jewish-theological" (49), Boyarin develops this point much more explicitly, arguing that Paul "writes *as a Jew.* . . . Paul's argument is almost prototypical midrash."[39] While rigorously detailing the Jewish dimension of Paul's thought, Boyarin simultaneously takes seriously the paradox that if Paul's approach could be said to be consummately Jewish, he nonetheless uses it to abrogate Judaism: "Paul is using methods of interpretation that would not surprise any Pharisee (I suspect) or Rabbi, although the results he arrives at would, of course, shock them to their depths."[40] Boyarin gets at the heart of the problem with any too easy Jewish subsumption of Paul. While it is all well and good to note aspects of Paul that remain prototypically Jewish (Jacob Taubes will make the claim, for example, that Paul's Greek is the equivalent of Yiddish[41]), there has to be *some* concession to what Paul is actually saying and doing. Hence the extreme double-bind: Paul is using the resources of Jewish thought to abolish Jewish culture and tradition.

Gersholm Scholem's magisterial work on Sabbatai Zevi, the seventeenth-century Jewish mystic who declared himself the messiah but shortly thereafter converted to Islam, extends this perspective to consider that even Sabbatai Zevi's apostasy has something of a Jewish character. Rather than regarding this saga as an unfortunate chapter of Jewish history, Scholem takes seriously the post-apostasy writings of Sabbatai Zevi's followers, above all Nathan of Gaza, who brilliantly read Sabbatai Zevi's apostasy as part of a Jewish messianic mission that entails a descent into the realm of evil (*qelippoth*)—equated with Sabbatai Zevi's 1666 conversion to Islam—as a means of purification. And in fact this break from Halakhic law, as it is justified by Sabbatai Zevi's followers through recourse to Jewish mystical writings, is for Scholem nothing less than the advent of Jewish modernity.[42] In this sense, there is something fundamentally Jewish even in the idea of the messiah becoming radically other.

That there is a distinctive Jewish element in the denial of Judaism, something apostate at the core of Judaism, and furthermore that this is linked to a certain modernity, is a phenomenon that Isaac Deutscher considers in "The Non-Jewish Jew." Deutscher sums up this problematic with particular acuity when he writes that "the Jewish heretic who transcends Jewry belongs to a Jewish tradition. . . . Spinoza, Heine, Marx, Rosa Luxemburg, Trotsky, and Freud . . . all went beyond the boundaries of Jewry. They all found Jewry too narrow, too archaic, and too constricting. They all looked for ideals and fulfillment beyond it, and they represent the sum and substance of much that is greatest in modern thought, the sum and substance of the most profound upheavals that have taken place in philosophy, sociology, economics, and politics in the last three centuries."[43] Leaving aside the complexities of the case of Spinoza, the examples Deutscher cites pertain predominantly to political and literary frameworks. However, things become even more vexed when a theological dimension is added to the mix, and specifically when Judaism pushed beyond its limits intersects with Christianity. In Weil's case, and arguably in figures like Paul and even Spinoza, it is not just any form of Christianity that is touched on, but a heretical Christianity insofar as it posits a *radical break* between Judaism and Christianity.

If for our limited purposes we accept something of a pattern of apostate relations to Judaism in thinkers such as Paul, Spinoza, Sabbatai Zevi, and arguably Marx and Freud, Weil is then the crowning example of Jewish apostasy's intersection with a heretical form of Christianity, heretical precisely for its severing of Christianity from the Jewish tradition. Although it could be argued that Weil did not know the Jewish tradition well enough to have developed a true apostate relation to it, she was certainly well versed in the history of the Cathars or Albigensians, who among other things emphasized the absolute separation between Judaism and Christianity, and whose erasure at the hands of Latin Christianity she found lamentable.[44]

Weil, then, belongs to a luminous tradition of Jewish thinkers who reject Judaism in spectacular fashion, often using tools of Jewish learning to dismantle major tenets of the faith. It might be posited that Heidegger and Nancy use Christianity in the same fashion, with Heidegger adding, as it were, a painfully banal dose of anti-Judaism. Whereas Nancy develops a relational concept of world fully distinct from a Christian or monotheistic one, Heidegger's sense of *world* is so vertiginous in its movement between worldless, world-forming, and world-destroying that it does not leave us on solid ground. Heidegger's apostasy or heresy is not readable in the fashion of Weil's. Perhaps, as Taubes writes, "at the borderline between Jewish and Christian . . . things get so hot that one can only [get] burn[ed]."[45] Or perhaps the Jew's very worldlessness could be generative, like the rock, of other models of being beyond relation that it is the merit, albeit unintended, of Heidegger's philosophy to have envisioned.

Notes

1. See Michel Sourisse, "Simone Weil et Heidegger," *Cahiers Simone Weil* 12, no. 3 (1989): 226–39; Maria Villela Petit, "Simone Weil, Martin Heidegger, et la Grèce," *Cahiers Simone Weil* 26, no. 2 (2003); Chiara Zimboni, *Interrogando la*

cosa: riflessioni a partire da Martin Heidegger e Simone Weil (Milan: IPL, Istituto Propaganda Libraria, 1993); Ramón Xirau, *Cuatro filósofos y lo sagrado: Teilhard de Chardin, Heidegger, Wittgenstein, Simone Weil* (Tabasco, Mexico: Cuadernos de Joaquín Mortiz, 1986).

2. Martin Heidegger, *The Fundamental Concepts of Metaphysics: World, Finitude, Solitude*, trans. William McNeill and Nicholas Walker (Bloomington: Indiana University Press, 1995), 176–77 (hereafter cited in text). German references are taken from Heidegger, *Die Grundbegriffe der Metaphysik: Welt—Englichkeit—Einsamkeit* (Frankfurt am Main: Klostermann, 1992). For more on the question of Heidegger and world, see Jeff Malpas, *Heidegger's Topology: Being, Place, World* (Cambridge, MA: MIT Press, 2006), and Sean Gaston, *The Concept of World from Kant to Derrida* (London: Rowman and Littlefield, 2013). Focusing exclusively on the work from the late 1920s, Gaston's chapter on Heidegger breaks his treatment of world into three rough categories: the historical world, the world as phenomenon, and the comparative world (79), and highlights what he terms and underscores as "Heidegger's most lasting contribution to the concept of world in the history of philosophy: *world remains a problem*" (85). That world persists as a problem is the possibility Heidegger opens toward a non-anti-Judaic reading of his *Black Notebooks*. See my extended consideration of Nancy's concept of "world" in "Nancy, Agamben, and the Weakness of the World," *diacritics* 43, no. 4 (2015): 28–50.

3. Heidegger's very separation of the philosophical from the theological, and the sense by the early 1920s that theology is comprehended in the more general category of philosophy, is itself a contentious claim that runs squarely against the grain of a Thomist insistence that such a thing as Christian philosophy exists, grounded in the central tenet that God is Being. For more on the latter debate as it played out in France, see Émile Bréhier, "Y a-t-il une philosophie chrétienne," *Revue de métaphysique et de morale* 38, no. 2 (April–June 1931): 133–62. Nearly all of Étienne Gilson's oeuvre could be read as a positive counter to Bréhier's negative response to the titular question. For more on Heidegger's complex and shifting relation to theology, see Hue Woodson, *A Theologian's Guide to Heidegger* (Eugene, OR: Wipf and Stock, 2019); Judith Wolfe, *Heidegger and Theology* (London: Bloomsbury, 2014); Jean Beaufret, "Heidegger et la théologie," in *Dialogue avec Heidegger IV* (Paris: Éditions de Minuit, 1973); and Françoise Dastur, "Heidegger et la théologie," *Revue philosophique de Louvain* 92, nos. 2–3 (1994): 226–45.

4. Giorgio Agamben, *The Open: Man and Animal*, trans. Kevin Attell (Stanford, CA: Stanford University Press, 2004), 55, 65, 68. See Aristotle's *On the Soul* in *The Complete Works of Aristotle*, vol. 1, ed. Jonathan Barnes (Princeton, NJ: Princeton University Press, 1984).

5. Derrida echoes even more pointedly the questions Heidegger poses here, first in *Of Spirit: Heidegger and the Question*, trans. Geoffrey Bennington and Rachel Bowlby (Chicago: University of Chicago Press, 1989); then in *The Animal That Therefore I Am*, trans. David Wills (New York: Fordham Univer-

sity Press, 2008); and in *The Beast and the Sovereign*, vols. 1 and 2, trans. Geoffrey Bennington (Chicago: University of Chicago Press, 2009 and 2011).

6. Jean-Paul Sartre, *Critique of Dialectical Reason*, trans. Alan Sheridan-Smith (London: HLB, 1976), 181–82.

7. For an elaboration on these passages and their import with respect to Heidegger and Nancy, see my "The Mineralogy of Being" in *Architecture in the Anthropocene: Encounters among Design, Deep Time, Science and Philosophy*, ed. Etienne Turpin (Ann Arbor, MI: Open Humanities, 2013).

8. Jean-Luc Nancy, *Being Singular Plural*, trans. Robert D. Richardson and Anne E. O'Byrne (Stanford, CA: Stanford University Press, 2000). See *L'intrus* (Paris: Galilée, 2000) for Nancy's meditation on his heart transplant. This sense of "being with" is taken up notably in José Esteban Muñoz, *Cruising Utopia: The Then and There of Queer Futurity* (New York: NYU Press, 2009). For Nancy's poetic response to Muñoz, see "Ode to José Esteban Muñoz," trans. Damon R. Young, *Social Text* 32, no. 4 (121) (Winter 2014): 9–12.

9. Jean-Luc Nancy, "The Heart of Things" in *The Birth to Presence*, trans. Brian Holmes et al. (Stanford, CA: Stanford University Press, 1994), 171.

10. Jean-Luc Nancy, *The Sense of the World*, trans. Jeffrey S. Librett (Minneapolis: University of Minnesota Press, 1997), 63.

11. Nancy, *Sense of the World*, 8.

12. Jean-Luc Nancy, *A Finite Thinking*, ed. Simon Sparks (Stanford, CA: Stanford University Press, 2003), 181.

13. Nancy, *Finite Thinking*, 181.

14. See Jeffrey Jerome Cohen, *Stone: An Ecology of the Human* (Minneapolis: University of Minnesota Press, 2015), for an illustration of stone being good to think with, albeit one that dismisses Heidegger's model rather swiftly (see 50, 311n61).

15. Martin Heidegger, *The Phenomenology of Religious Life*, trans. Matthias Fritsch and Jennifer Anna Gosetti-Ferencei (Bloomington: Indiana University Press, 2004), 69, 49. Cited hereafter in text.

16. See Noreen Khawaja's extended discussion of authenticity in Heidegger in *The Religion of Existence: Asceticism in Philosophy from Kierkegaard to Sartre* (Chicago: University of Chicago Press, 2016).

17. Nancy, *Finite Thinking*, 178.

18. Alain Badiou in *Saint Paul: The Foundation of Universalism*, trans. Ray Brassier (Stanford, CA: Stanford University Press, 2003) similarly connects the radicality of Paul's militancy to his lack of concern with the life of Jesus.

19. Nancy, *Birth to Presence*, 171.

20. Simone Weil, *Gravity and Grace*, trans. Emma Crawford and Mario von der Ruhr (London: Routledge, 2002), 20, 24. Hereafter cited in text.

21. That said, it should be noted that in *Being and Time*, trans. Joan Stambaugh (Albany: State University of New York Press, 2010), Heidegger writes the following with regard to the facticity of *Dasein*: "Two beings, which are present within the world and are, moreover *worldless* in themselves, can never

'touch' each other, neither can they '*be*' '*together with*' one another" (56). Whatever one may think of Speculative Realism and the Object Orientated Ontology it generated, the idea therein of objects being withdrawn is effectively an exploration of the above formulation, and a bolster for the claim that Heidegger's concept of worldlessness is far from a pejorative framework for subsequent ontological investigations.

22. Simone Weil, *Waiting for God*, trans. Emma Craufurd (New York: Harper Perennial Modern Classics, 2009), 25, 40.

23. Susan Sontag, "Simone Weil," in *Against Interpretation* (New York: Farrar, Strauss and Giroux, 1966); Leslie Fiedler, "Introduction" to Weil, *Waiting for God*. For a detailed analysis of the paradoxes of Weil's American reception which emphasizes Weil's strength, see Deborah Nelson, *Tough Enough: Arbus, Arendt, Didion, McCarthy, Sontag, Weil* (Chicago: University of Chicago Press, 2017).

24. See critical commentaries by Emmanuel Levinas, "Simone Weil and the Bible" in *Difficult Freedom: Essays on Judaism* (Baltimore, MD: Johns Hopkins University Press, 1990); and Martin Buber, "The Silent Question" in *At the Turning: Three Addresses on Judaism* (New York: Farrar, Straus and Young, 1952). For an extended consideration of Weil's ethics alongside those of Levinas, see Yoon Sook Cha, *Decreation and the Ethical Bind: Simone Weil and the Claim of the Other* (New York: Fordham University Press, 2017).

25. Simone Weil, *Attente de Dieu* (Paris: La Colombe, 1950), 240.

26. Weil, *Gravity and Grace*, 161.

27. Roberto Esposito, *The Origin of the Political: Hannah Arendt or Simone Weil?*, trans. Vincenzo Binetti and Gareth Williams (New York: Fordham University Press, 2017), 54. Hereafter cited in text.

28. There is already substantial literature on this topic: Peter Trawny, *Heidegger and the Myth of a World Jewish Conspiracy*, trans. Andrew J. Mitchell (Chicago: University of Chicago Press, 2015); *Reading Heidegger's* Black Notebooks 1931–1941, ed. Ingo Farin and Jeff Malpas (Cambridge, MA: MIT Press, 2016); *Heidegger's* Black Notebooks: *Responses to Anti-Semitism*, ed. Andrew J. Mitchell and Peter Trawny (New York: Columbia University Press, 2017); and Donatella Di Cesare, *Heidegger and the Jews: The Black Notebooks*, trans. Murtha Baca (Cambridge, UK: Polity, 2018).

29. Martin Heidegger, "The Age of the World Picture" in *The Question Concerning Technology and Other Essays*, trans. William Lovitt (New York: Harper and Row, 1977), 135.

30. Heidegger, "Age of the World Picture," 135.

31. Martin Heidegger, *Ponderings XII–XV: Black Notebooks 1939–1941*, trans. Richard Rojcewicz (Bloomington: Indiana University Press, 2017), 112.

32. Martin Heidegger, *Ponderings VII–XI: Black Notebooks 1938–1939*, trans. Richard Rojcewicz (Bloomington: Indiana University Press, 2017), 76. See Peter E. Gordon's discussion of the troubling ramifications of "worldless" Judaism in "Prolegomena to Any Future Destruction of Metaphysics: Hei-

degger and the *Schwarze Hefte*" in Mitchell and Tawny, *Heidegger's* Black Notebooks.

33. Notably, and by contrast, for Vico it is specifically the Jews who always "possessed the proper human proportions" and never passed through the age of the gigantic. See Giambattista Vico, *The New Science*, trans. David Marsh (London: Penguin Books, 1999), 9.

34. Jean-Luc Nancy, *The Banality of Heidegger*, trans. Jeff Fort (New York: Fordham University Press, 2017), 20. Cited hereafter in text.

35. Beyond the scope of this essay, another significant affinity between Weil and Heidegger is their emphasis on the importance of rootedness or groundedness, notoriously in Heidegger's "blood and soil" motif in *The Black Notebooks*, and in more nuanced form in Weil's *The Need for Roots*, trans. Arthur Wills (London: Routledge, 2002). In a perplexing juxtaposition, Weil condemns Jews and National Socialists alike for their "dangerous malady" of uprootedness: "The Hebrews were escaped slaves, and they either exterminated or reduced to servitude all the peoples of Palestine. The Germans, at the time Hitler assumed command over them, were really—as he was never tired of repeating—a nation of proletarians, that is to say, uprooted individuals" (47).

36. For more on the question of Nancy's "deconstruction" of Christianity and its relation to recognized heretical tendencies such as Weil's, see my "Nancy, Agamben, and the Weakness of the World."

37. While attempts to link Heidegger directly to Gnosticism seem somewhat unconvincing (such as Robert Avens, *The New Gnosis: Heidegger, Hillman, and Angels* [Dallas, TX: Spring, 1984]), more significant is the work on Gnostic and dualist traditions that Heidegger may have influenced. See, for example, Hans Jonas, *The Gnostic Religion: The Message of the Alien God and the Beginnings of Christianity* (Boston: Beacon, 2001); and Steven M. Wasserstrom, *Religion after Religion: Gershom Scholem, Mircea Eliade, and Henry Corbin at Eranos* (Princeton, NJ: Princeton University Press, 1999), esp. 135–39. There is work still to be done on the linkages between Heidegger's dualist tendencies and Adolf von Harnack's influential work from 1921, *Marcion: The Gospel of the Alien God* (Eugene, OR: Wipf and Stock, 2007).

38. For a consideration of this topic in the modern period, see *Jewish Apostasy in the Modern World*, ed. Todd M. Endelman (New York: Holmes and Meier, 1987).

39. Daniel Boyarin, *A Radical Jew: Paul and the Politics of Identity* (Berkeley: University of California Press, 1994), 137.

40. Boyarin, *Radical Jew*, 142.

41. Jacob Taubes, *The Political Theology of Paul*, trans. Dana Hollander (Stanford, CA: Stanford University Press, 2004), 3–4.

42. Gershom Scholem initially discusses Sabbatai Zevi in *Major Trends in Jewish Mysticism* (New York: Schocken Books, 1946) and then in more depth and more favorably in the later booklength study devoted to him, *Sabbatai Sevi: The Mystical Messiah* (Princeton, NJ: Princeton University Press, 1973).

43. Isaac Deutscher, *The Non-Jewish Jew and Other Essays* (London: Verso, 2017), 26. He also writes about the "moral and political heritage that the genius of the Jews who have gone beyond Jewry has left us" (41).

44. For more on Weil and theology, see Miklos Vetö, *The Religious Metaphysics of Simone Weil*, trans. Joan Dargan (Albany: State University of New York Press, 1994); and A. Rebecca Rozelle-Stone and Lucian Stone, *Simone Weil and Theology* (New York: Bloomsbury T&T Clark, 2013). See also Weil's *Intimations of Christianity among the Greeks*, trans. Elizabeth Chas Geissbuhler (London: Routledge, 1998).

45. Taubes, *Political Theology of Paul*, 143. See also Daniel Boyarin, *Border Line: The Partition of Judaeo-Christianity* (Philadelphia: University of Pennsylvania Press, 2006). In something of the same spirit, Eduardo Mendieta writes in "Metaphysical Anti-Semitism and Worldlessness" of being "brought to the razor's edge between the abyssal profundity of risky thinking and the depthless banality of philosophical kitsch" (40), in Mitchell and Trawny, *Heidegger's Black Notebooks*.

5

Flesh and *Écart* in Merleau-Ponty and Nancy

MARIE-EVE MORIN

Comparing Merleau-Ponty and Nancy

Those familiar with both Merleau-Ponty's and Nancy's works are bound to notice the affinities between the two. An expression, a thought, or a claim in the work of one author will often strike a resonance in the work of the other. In this chapter, I want to focus on the resonance created between both works by the word "*écart*," a resonance that can be overlooked in the English text—the French word is variably translated in Nancy as separation, displacement, apartness, gap, or swerve,[1] and in Merleau-Ponty as separation, divergence, deviation, and sometimes also spread. Before we delve into this resonance, however, I want to address some difficulties or challenges that the comparison of Merleau-Ponty's work with Nancy's necessarily raises.

The first challenge is one faced by any comparative study. These kinds of studies can be of little use if they merely enumerate the similarities and differences between two bodies of work. Furthermore, by forcing two disparate works to speak to each other, to translate themselves in a foreign vocabulary, such studies run the risk of missing the singularity of each thought. This challenge is exacerbated in the case of Merleau-Ponty and Nancy since there is no direct reverberation from Merleau-Ponty's work in Nancy's thinking. There are of course some indirect lines of influence, but these are too tenuous to guarantee the fruitfulness of any comparative study on their own. Nancy moved to Paris shortly before Merleau-Ponty's death, earning his *licence* in 1962, his *diplôme d'études supérieures* in 1963, and his *agrégation* in 1964, all from the Sorbonne. During his time at the Sorbonne, Nancy worked closely with Georges Canguilhem, who is well known for his criticism both of vitalism and of the reductionist approach to life that tries to understand organisms on the basis of the mechanical model, which criticism he recognizes is indebted to Merleau-Ponty's first book, *La structure du comportement* (1942).[2] Yet, this influence will remain indirect and, as Nancy says, belongs to his "philosophical prehistory."[3] Nancy did read *La structure du comportement* and *Phénoménologie de la perception* (1945), since these books were required readings in the philosophy program, but this meant that his encounter with Merleau-Ponty's thought remained trapped within an "academic horizon": Nancy never encountered the "Merleau-Ponty vivant" we get a hint of in his lecture courses or unpublished notes. Even though he had passed away just a few years earlier, Merleau-Ponty was already an academic reference of the past for Nancy, one who, like Sartre, didn't belong to the contemporary landscapes of the 1960s that marked the development of Nancy's thought.

It is through the encounter with Derrida[4] that "philosophy suddenly found, for [Nancy], the actuality of its movement, of its act and gesture"[5] and that he for the first time heard "the music of the present."[6] In Nancy's words: "Derrida represented living philosophy for us: there was somebody doing philosophy right in front of our eyes, producing concepts that we would have to work with."[7] It is through Derrida that Nancy took the measure of the event or rupture of Western philosophical thinking initiated by Nietzsche, Heidegger, and Freud, and it is Derrida who enabled him to read Husserl. Nancy's reading of Husserl starts with the "Origin of Geometry" and is already mediated by Derrida's concern with writing and the impurity of the origin. Here again, we could find an indirect relation between Nancy and Merleau-Ponty, for whom the manuscript on the origin of geometry was also an important text, one to which he devoted a lecture course in 1959–60. Yet, Derrida never heard Merleau-Ponty's lectures, and his interpretation of the manuscript developed "in total independence" from Merleau-Ponty's.[8]

More generally, these biographical anecdotes point to the fact that Merleau-Ponty's and Nancy's thinking seek to answer different questions, move in a different milieu, and undeniably have a different "feel." As a result, the conclusion of a careful comparison between the two works might be that the similarities we identified on the surface are in fact nothing more than that: superficial similarities. They might serve only to hide radical differences so that we must conclude, after a thorough study, that Merleau-Ponty's and Nancy's works belong to two different universes of thought.

Nancy alludes to that difference when he describes his relation to Merleau-Ponty's thought. He characterizes his own universe as German and metaphysical, and Merleau-Ponty's as French and physical.[9] For Nancy, the question of Being remains the fundamental question, even though it is soon to be inflected by Derrida's notions of writing and différance, whereas when Merleau-Ponty turns seriously toward the work of Heidegger at the end of the 1950s, his own thinking has already reached a certain maturity.[10] Nancy summarizes this difference between the French and the German climates with the following sets of oppositions: on the French side, we find a thinking of existence as "life" and "flesh," a thinking of the "participation in being" as being-in-the-world and "inherence" of the self in the world. On the German side, we find a thinking of existence as *Dasein* and as the "putting into play of the meaning of being in the being of *Dasein*," that is, a thinking of a "distance opened within presence," of the "transcendence of being as *Ereignis*." As Nancy admits, the difference is "as wide as it is narrow."[11]

The other challenge faced by a comparative study of Merleau-Ponty and Nancy is the dearth of textual evidence: there are only a handful of direct references to Merleau-Ponty in Nancy's texts, most of which are critical. Yet these few mentions give us hints as to the concrete issues at stake in the relation, or nonrelation, of Nancy's thought to Merleau-Ponty's. We can group these references around two general topics: art and the body.

Nancy explicitly states that, for him, Merleau-Ponty's thinking of art was determining because he was "the first to have penetrated the gesture of the artist in and vis-à-vis the world rather than vis-à-vis the determinations of the work."[12] Indeed, in *Le plaisir au dessin* (2007), after having used passages from "Indirect Language and the Voices of Silence" and "Eye and Mind" as epigraphs, Nancy engages in a meditation on Matisse's claim that the painter follows the "desire of the line," the same Matisse whose gesture had also fascinated Merleau-Ponty in "Eye and Mind." At the same time, one can hardly say that Nancy directly engages with Merleau-Ponty's texts in his writing on the arts, be it in *Le plaisir au dessin* or in *Les muses* (1994), where Merleau-Ponty seems to be addressed mostly as a precursor of Deleuze.

The second set of references, those around the body, pertain to the questions of self-sensing, hence to the constitution of selfhood. First, we find, in *Corpus* and other related texts, critical references to the phenomenologies of the body proper or of the flesh as well as to the touching-touched relation. There, Nancy takes issue with the way in which my own body as self-sensing body is always thought in terms of propriety and unity.[13] As sensing, my own body is opened to what is other, but as self-sensing, it always ends up "return[ing] to a primary interiority."[14] It is this desire for unity and interiority at the core of the phenomenology of touch that Derrida also takes up in *On Touching*. Of course, Derrida recognizes that even for Merleau-Ponty the touching never coincides or merges with the touched, and it is indeed insofar as we preserve this difference between touching and touched that there can be sensing. Yet, this sensing is also a protoreflection; it folds back upon itself to give rise to the synthesis of one's own body. In Derrida's words: "This detour by way of the foreign outside . . . is . . . what allows us to speak of a 'double' apprehension (otherwise there would be one thing only . . .) and what allows me, after undergoing this singular experience, . . . to say 'this is my body.'"[15] By contrast, what interests Derrida in Nancy's understanding of touch as contact between bodies are the dislocations, syncopes, spacings, partitions, spasms, or caesurae: in other words, everything that interrupts the circle of self-presence, introducing an irrecoverable heterogeneity within it. For Nancy, the self is radically affected by differance so it doesn't and cannot come back to "itself."[16] As a result, there is no self-touching-itself that flips into a primary interiority but a self-touching-you (*se-toucher-toi*) or a self-touching-skin (*se-toucher-peau*).[17]

Of course, we could argue that what is true of Merleau-Ponty's early phenomenology is not true anymore in his later ontology. In a sense, Nancy acknowledges as much when, in a short text titled "Strange Foreign Bodies," he takes up the analysis of the touching-touched again, this time emphasizing—in an obvious though implicit reference to the late Merleau-Ponty—the figure of the chiasm, which points to the radical openness or exposure of the touching-touched body to the world. Here is the passage:

> My hands touch one another; my body recognizes itself coming to itself from an outside that it itself is, taking into itself again the world outside it. The chiasm of the flesh that is described so well by the most insightful phenomenology of the body . . . reminds us that our being entwined with the world has always, from the start, exposed us right down to our most intimate depths. The "inside" is always between outside and outside, and this between—the between of its lair, its cave of myths and phantoms of interiority—is, in the end, nothing but another outside.[18]

Nancy's affinity with Merleau-Ponty's thinking, then, is to be found not in the direction of the lived body or the body proper but in the direction of a chiasm or torsion between inside and outside, one that teaches us that we are exposed "right down to our most intimate depths." Such is also the lesson Nancy finds in Merleau-Ponty's lecture notes on passivity and the notes on the Freudian unconscious, which he admits having read with interest. These notes show a displacement of the metaphysics of presence toward a thinking of the "subject" as non-presence-to-self, as coexistence with the world and with others prior to the division between subject and object, and between ignorance and knowledge. At the same time, Nancy is not convinced. In the same text where he praises the lecture notes on passivity and the notes on the Freudian unconscious, Nancy also quotes the following sentence from Merleau-Ponty's "Eye and Mind": "Vision . . . is the means given me for being absent from myself, for being present at the fission of Being from the inside—the fission at whose termination, and not before, I come back to myself" and confesses that this return to oneself remains incomprehensible for him.[19]

In the remainder of this chapter I follow some of Merleau-Ponty's late discussions of the flesh and the chiasm to see whether they allow us to reconceive the self in a way that is radically opened or exposed. My goal is not to prove that Merleau-Ponty is a precursor of Derrida, and of Nancy. I do not intend to argue that Merleau-Ponty foresaw the need to complicate the thought of the subject as self-presence and the necessity of relinquishing the philosophies of consciousness in order to do so, but remained unable to accomplish a real break with the metaphysics of subjectivity either because of his untimely death or because of some deeper desire for integrity, unity, wholeness, and hence a certain form of presence. Proving such a claim would require that we sift through Merleau-Ponty's work to find the seeds of a deconstructive thinking that took root only later on.[20] As will become clear in what follows, it is indeed possible to find such seeds. But as will also become clear, we find much in Merleau-Ponty's lecture courses, posthumous texts, and unpublished notes that goes against such a view. If I choose to follow Merleau-Ponty's later reflections on the flesh and the chiasm, it is not so much to settle the issue of whether he was or was not a proto-deconstructionist (to use that word). Given the unfinished status of Merleau-Ponty's later work, it is probably impossible to settle this question once and for all. Rather, I do so because I think that reading Merleau-Ponty and Nancy together can allow us to develop a better interpretation of their respective thinking. To anticipate, I think that each can provide a corrective to a certain tendency in the work of the other and in our interpretation of it: Merleau-Ponty to the flattening out of relations between singularities and the forgetting of the dimension of desire, Nancy to the overabundance of proximity and promiscuity that risks erasing all separation into a general confusion. In order to show this, I will focus on the role of *écart* in their understanding of self-sensing self and of being more generally.

Sensing in the *Phenomenology of Perception*

Merleau-Ponty recognizes that the *Phenomenology of Perception* remained caught in bad ambiguity insofar as it is still entangled in a philosophy of consciousness.[21] Thus, it can only cast the living body as both subject and object, oscillating between the two traditional categories, or as a "mediator"[22] between consciousness and the thing, between the for-itself and the in-itself, without developing the specific way of being of the body itself in a positive way.[23] As a result, Merleau-Ponty's descriptions of perception or of sensing, that is, of the contact between body and world, also remain caught in a bad dialectics, oscillating between passivity and activity, receptivity and creativity. Of course, in the *Phenomenology of Perception*, the description of perceptual experience does acquaint us with a being that is passive in its activity and active in its passivity, a being who is never sovereign with regard to the sense of its experience without being fully one with the world, a thing among things. What will become clearer in the later works is that the phenomenology of perception requires a new ontology, the development of a new kind of Being (*genre d'être*) between being and non-being, between the in-itself and the for-itself, and hence between the pure activity of a sovereign subject and the pure passivity of the thing. Without such an ontology, the description of perception (or of sensing) remains caught in a bad ambiguity.

In the *Phenomenology of Perception*, it is already clear to Merleau-Ponty that to perceive is neither to have things produce sense-data that are received through a purely causal (i.e., passive) mechanism, nor to synthesize bits of a meaningless sense-data in the mind by subsuming the sensory given under a given concept. The contact between body and world in perception is neither passive nor active, but one of "dialogue," of solicitation and response. Perceiving for Merleau-Ponty is never merely passive because it necessarily involves an exploration: focusing, bringing to the fore, losing something in the background, moving around, and so on. Yet, it is also not merely active: the perceived responds to my exploration, which is itself but a response to its solicitation. Here is how Merleau-Ponty phrases this relation:

> Without the exploration of my gaze or my hand, and prior to my body synchronizing with it, the sensible is nothing but a vague solicitation. . . . Thus, a sensible that is about to be sensed poses to my body a sort of confused problem. I must find the attitude that will provide it with the means to become determinate and to become blue; I must find the response to a poorly formulated question. And yet, I

only do this in response to its solicitation. My attitude is never sufficient to make me truly see blue or truly touch a hard surface. The sensible gives back to me what I had lent to it, but I received it from the sensible in the first place.[24]

The relation between body and world, between sensing and sensed, is paradoxical because each is dependent on the other for its own existence: there is no sensing without a sense that presents itself, but no sense presents itself without my engagement with it. This is the meaning of the expression *co-naître*, coming to presence together, in a relation of co-determination. This also means that it is not possible to say which comes first, which side acts and which suffers, which gives sense and which receives it.[25] This co-determination Merleau-Ponty will infamously name "communion."

I am indeed "open to the world," but because this openness is thought in terms of communion and communication, there is a sense in which what I open unto, what I "gear into" as Merleau-Ponty often says, is something that is adequate to, or commensurate with, the powers of my body. The breach or gap in the body that makes it sensible and sensing—that is, self-sensing, sensing itself from the inside and from the outside at the same time—is what also opens the self to this outside that is the world. Only a self-sensing self can sense the other—since it already senses "itself" also as other, that is, from the outside. But given the way in which Merleau-Ponty describes sensing, the other that is sensed is not foreign or strange: it is this other with which I communicate and commune.[26]

Whereas in the *Phenomenology of Perception* Merleau-Ponty uses communion to characterize sensing, in the later works sense (and sensing) will explicitly be thought in terms of divergence or *écart*. When Merleau-Ponty first introduces the motif of the *écart* in his 1953 lecture course at the Collège de France, *Le monde sensible et le monde de l'expression*,[27] it is to conceptualize what is sensed in a diacritical way rather than as an essence or a given signification that could be possessed in isolation as an "I know that."[28] The point is not, or not yet, to think of the *écart* at the heart sensing itself. Here, rather, Merleau-Ponty is taking the analyses of the *Gestalt* and of the *bougé* (shifting, haziness) of perception found in the *Phenomenology* and investing them with a normative dimension: the background is a level, dimension, or norm and the figure a certain style of divergence from or modulation of this norm that is at the same time destabilizing and motivating.[29] What interests me here is to follow the way in which the *écart* plays out in Merleau-Ponty's understanding of the flesh in *The Visible and the Invisible* to ask whether it is central to his understanding of the self as self-sensing, and—since carnal being is a prototype of Being—of being itself. If it does indeed turn out to be so, then this will make a rapprochement with Nancy. Before we can assess this claim, however, it is necessary to delve into Merleau-Ponty's later work on the flesh.

Merleau-Ponty, *Écart*, and the Flesh

The ambiguity of the concept of flesh has been outlined by many commentators. Indeed, Merleau-Ponty not only uses the word *flesh* to refer to the Husserlian *Leib*, but also speaks of the flesh of the visible, the flesh of things, or the flesh of the world, so that flesh becomes what he calls "an element of being."[30] Whether these different uses of the word *flesh* are compatible is not my worry here.[31] Rather, I want to look at how the concept of the flesh allows Merleau-Ponty to rethink the openness and passivity of my own sensing body and ask whether this openness would be radical enough for Nancy or whether Nancy would still claim that, in the end, it still "returns to a primary interiority."[32] What interests me here, then, is the role that divergence plays in the flesh and the relation between the flesh and the structure of the chiasm in its imminent reversibility.

Merleau-Ponty uses the word *flesh* (*chair*) to refer to my own body insofar as it is self-sensing, the body that was already the topic of the analysis of *Phenomenology of Perception*. Here again, as in the *Phenomenology*, Merleau-Ponty emphasizes the reversibility of sensing, and the fact that the sensing body is always of the world. But Merleau-Ponty now draws the ontological consequences of that discovery: rather than the synthesis of the body schema, the reversibility of sensing means the descent of my body into the world (VI, 134). My body as touching is necessarily also touchable so that the distinction between subject (touching) and object (touched) is shown to be inadequate to capture the constitution of my own body. The important thing to notice here is that the visible/tangible is first in the order of explanation: rather than explaining visibility starting from vision, we need to explain vision starting from visibility. The reversibility of the flesh also leads Merleau-Ponty to posit the priority of the sensible over the sensing in the order of being. Undoing the dichotomy between noumenon and phenomenon, Merleau-Ponty starts from a visibility without vision, or a sensibility without sensation.[33] The world is sensible in itself: the world is not only sensible *for* a sensing being that would be the ground of its (the world's) sensibility; rather the world is already pregnant with all possible (and incompossible) sensibilities, so that vision or touch happens as a fold in the midst of a world that is already visible/tangible without being constituted as such by a conscious subject:

> Because my eyes which see, my hands which touch, can also be seen and touched, because, therefore, in this sense they see and touch the visible, the tangible, from within, because our flesh lines and even envelops all the visible and tangible things with which nevertheless it is surrounded, the world and I are within one another, and there is no anteriority of the *percipere* to the *percipi,* there is simultaneity or even retardation.... When I find again the actual world such as it is, under my hands, under my eyes, up against my body, I find much more than an object: a Being of which my vision is a part, a visibility older than my operations or my acts. (VI, 123)

Merleau-Ponty's position is somewhat counterintuitive: it seems obvious that something can be said to be visible or tangible only in reference to a seer or toucher. Both visible and tangible can only be what they are by being correlated to a seeing or touching power: a consciousness or a body that would be responsible for its visibility or its tangibility. But this is exactly what Merleau-Ponty is denying. "The flesh of the world," Merleau-Ponty writes, "is of the Being-seen, i.e. is a Being that is *eminently percipi*, and it is by it that we can understand the *percipere* . . . [which] is finally possible and means something only because *there is* Being, not Being in itself, identical to itself, in the night, but the Being that also contains its negation, its *percipi*" (VI, 250–51). The event of vision happens in the midst of the world ("vision happens among, or is caught in, things—in that place where something visible undertakes to see, becomes visible for itself by virtue of the vision of all things"[34]), a world that is already visible insofar as it already contains latencies, incompossibilities, and fissures to which my body—this seer-seen (*voyant-vu*) or this visible seer (*voyant visible*)—responds.

Understanding the event of vision as the folding or coiling over of a visible segment of the world allows us to complicate the relation between interiority and exteriority. The coiling over does not create an inside, a private world (ego), but rather opens the "coiled body" to an intercorporeity. Vision does not happen inside the body (within consciousness) and outside the world, but as a fold within the world. Vision is the outside of the world (and hence inside), but this outside is inside the world (and hence outside itself). Because the folding of the flesh is dehiscence, a separation in the midst of the flesh without being a full distinction, it leads to a contortion of the inside/outside divide: "There is inside and outside turning about one another" (VI, 264). Consciousness envelops the world (the world is for consciousness) but is also enveloped by it (since it is within the world that consciousness takes place). This is what Merleau-Ponty means when he says that the world is inserted between the two leaves of my body because my body is inserted between the two leaves of the world:

> The body unites us directly with the things through its own ontogenesis, by welding to one another the two outlines of which it is made, its two lips: the sensible mass it is and the mass of the sensible wherein it is born by segregation and upon which, as seer, it remains open. It is the body and it alone, because it is a two-dimensional being, that can bring us to the things themselves, which are themselves not flat beings but beings in depth, inaccessible to a subject that would survey them from above, open to him alone that, if it be possible, would coexist with them in the same world. (VI, 136)

At this point, we can see how the ontology of the flesh has in a sense led us to a self that is not fully transparent to itself, but rather is what it is thanks to a visibility that is older than all its intentional acts and that it can never fully recuperate within itself. It is this originary delay that opens the self and makes it sensing or sensible. In a note from May 1960, Merleau-Ponty speaks more specifically of the primordial divergence at the heart of the self:

> The *touching itself, seeing itself* of the body is itself to be understood in terms of what we said of the seeing and the visible, the touching and the touchable. I.e. it is not an act, it is a being at (*être à*). To touch *oneself,* to see *oneself,* accordingly, is not to apprehend oneself as an ob-ject, it is to be open to oneself, destined to oneself (narcissism)— Nor, therefore, is it to reach *oneself,* it is on the contrary to escape *oneself,* to be ignorant of *oneself,* the self in question is by divergence (*d'écart*). (VI, 249)

This note, with its mention of *être à* and of *écart,* could almost have been written by Nancy.[35] Recasting selfhood as differance, Nancy will emphasize the essential *écart* at the heart of any self and understands existence (or sense) as the essential movement of *être à*.

Nancy, Selfhood, and Différance

As we know, Derrida coins the neologism *différance* to underline both the spatial meaning of the French verb *différer* (to differ, to be distinct, discernible, separate) and its temporal meaning (to defer, postpone, relay through a detour). Differance names both spacing and temporization: it names the dynamic division of an interval that allows for meaning, for presence. What is "first," then, is the gap or spacing that divides and relates: a spacing that allows for identity (or "self"-identification) but only as an effect of the spacing that has always split any present into two, leaving each haunted by the trace of another.

Following the Derridean logic of differance, Nancy will emphasize the irreducible (or originary) spacing or gap at the heart of the self thanks to which something like a self can exist, that is, be present (to itself and to other). Since the spacing or diaresis of the self is "originary," there is, properly speaking, no self-presence prior to any differentiating: the self is an effect of the spacing so that the self has always already started by altering itself and can never catch up with what would be a pure origin to coincide with itself.

Self-identification, then, the relation of the self to self, does not take the form of a subject or an ipseity. It is not the Hegelian "self-restoring sameness" or "reflection in otherness within itself,"[36] a detour through an outside at the end of which the subject reappropriates this exteriority and comes back to itself. Rather, selfhood consists in a movement of being-to or being-toward, in which the "*to* of the to-itself [or the toward-itself] . . . is first and foremost the fissure, the gap [*l'écart*], the spacing [*l'espacement*] of an opening."[37] Hence, when Nancy says that the self is "to itself by and in alterity," this should not be understood to mean that the self "possess[es] this 'other' as a correlate or as the term of a relation that would happen to 'relate' to itself. Thought rigorously, it is not a matter of 'other' or of 'relation.'"[38]

We are now in a position to understand what Nancy means by sense: Playing on the double-meaning of the French word *sens* as meaning and direction, as well as on the homophony between *le sens* and *les sens* (the senses), Nancy understands sense as the movement of being-to or being-toward that makes up the self as a result of its originary alterity or alteration. It is because of the originary spacing at the heart of the self, the differance that rends the self and means that it is always already affected with some otherness or exteriority, that the self senses (itself and others), that is it exposed to (itself and others): "Sense depends on relating to itself as an another or to some other. To have sense, or to make sense, to be sensed, is to be to oneself insofar as the other affects this ipseity in such a way that this affection is neither reduced *to* nor retained in the *ipse* itself. On the contrary, if the affection of sense is reabsorbed, sense itself also disappears."[39] As Merleau-Ponty would say: to be destined to oneself is not to reach oneself but to escape oneself. If the self were to reach itself in (self)-sensing, if the otherness that affects the self and makes it sensing were reducible to the self, then there would be no sensing. For both, the self that is reached or touched in the movement of being-to or being-toward is not identical to the point of departure of this movement. In fact, being-to or being-toward, sensing, only happens in the divergence or gap between the two so that no points of departure or arrival can properly be said to be. What is is only by divergence.

Yet, one question remains: Does Merleau-Ponty's appeal to narcissism in the note quoted above not reinforce Nancy's worry that even though the sensing body is an *être-à*, even though it is essentially opened to (itself), it remains in the end thought of on the model of the circle of self-presence closing in upon itself? The sensing body would be like Narcissus, who never experiences anything but his own reflection. If this is how we should understand Merleau-Ponty's use of the term *narcissism*, then it would undermine the role of the *écart* by subordinating it to a prior unity.

Narcissism?

We must start by recalling that earlier in *The Visible and the Invisible*, when Merleau-Ponty used the term *narcissism*, it was to speak of a narcissism of all vision, or a narcissism of the flesh. Since vision doesn't happen in an ego, and the flesh is not only my sensing body, narcissism here doesn't mean that I am stuck within my ego, stuck with my representations. Rather, vision is narcissistic because it happens by dehiscence or folding of the flesh, when a visible begins to see.

At the same time there is, for Merleau-Ponty, a certain narcissism of *my* vision. Insofar as the one who sees is always also seen and the one who touches is always also touched, touching the other ("escaping *oneself*") is also the way in which we come back to ourselves or are destined to ourselves, yet always through an *écart*. Without this *écart*, this shift, there would be no sense. On the one hand, my act of vision always implicates my visibility so that in seeing (the other) I find myself as visible. On the other, the visible already includes my vision so that in seeing it I also catch a glimpse of my own vision of it. Yet it is important to note that this chiasm of the seer and the seen is not specular and that the visibility or the vision that I "see" through the other never coincides with my vision in act.

The best image to think of this chiasm between visible and vision is that of incongruent counterparts.[40] Take a right-hand glove. It is always already lined with an invisible left-hand glove, but it cannot be this left-hand glove without the now visible right-hand glove becoming the invisible lining of a left-hand glove. A glove is always both a right-hand and left-hand glove but in different senses of being (passive/active, actual/virtual). At the same time, we cannot say that both the right-hand and the left-hand gloves are mere appearances of a non-handed "idea" of glove. The idea of "glove" could never be differentiated into right-handed and left-handed without descending into the world (in this case, three-dimensional space). So what we have is ontological complicity between right-handed and left-handed, each being the necessary doubling or lining of the other, without any identity between the two.[41] There is a necessary gap or divergence between the two that makes any congruence or superposition impossible.[42]

The relation of right-handed and left-handed within one glove exemplifies the relation between sensing and sensed within my body, and by complication between my body and the other *visibilia*. Think of the visible, what is seen, as a left-hand glove already lined with a virtual vision. The seer-seen that is my body is a convulsion of the *visibilia*, one that reverses the gloves so that *visibilia* is actual vision lined with visibility, rather than a visible lined with a virtual vision. Sensing is then a kind of handshake between my body (right-handed glove) and a *visibilia* (left-handed glove). As with the glove, the chiasm that exists between vision and visible, touch and touchable, is a not straightforward reversibility. Between the two, there is a gap or blur that prevents coincidence and that I experience when my body passes from touching to being touched, a zone of indeterminacy or undecidability that "I" never occupy, being always either touching or touched, but is experienced as a kind of blur, shift (*bougé*), or overhang (*porte-à-faux*) between the two (VI, 148, 256, 260).

This chiral understanding of reversibility can help us make sense of Merleau-Ponty's uses of the image of the mirror in *The Visible and the Invisible*.[43] Often his language seems to imply that seer and visible bounce off each other in perfect reciprocity. For example, speaking of the narcissism of all vision, Merleau-Ponty writes:

> the vision [the seer] exercises, he also undergoes from the things, such that, as many painters have said, I feel myself looked at by the things, my activity is equally passivity—which is the second and more profound sense of the narcissism: not to see in the outside, as the others see it, the contour of a body one inhabits, but especially to be seen by the outside, to exist within it, to emigrate into it, to be seduced, captivated, alienated by the phantom, so that the seer and the visible *reciprocate one another and we no longer know which sees and which is seen*. It is this Visibility, this generality of the Sensible in itself, this anonymity innate to Myself that we have previously called flesh, and one knows there is no name in traditional philosophy to designate it. (VI, 139; my emphasis)

In this passage, the chiasm seer-seen is presented as a reciprocation and the emphasis is put on the flesh, Visibility itself, as the element in which this reciprocal relation takes place. Since Merleau-Ponty also says that the flesh "*is a mirror phenomenon* [phénomène de miroir]" (VI, 255), it seems only natural to interpret the chiasm as straightforwardly reflexive. The mirror (or your eyes) would give me access to a part of myself as through a ricochet. Here we would have a detour through an exteriority (reflection) that would allow the self to come back to itself with a more complete, but ultimately undisturbed, understanding of itself. While the Hegelian model allows for a reflection-into-self of otherness, that is, for the identification of the mirror image that is not I as myself, there is no such moment of recuperation in Merleau-Ponty, no more than in Nancy. Indeed, taking mirroring literally means taking seriously the fact that the image in the mirror is reversed and cannot be superposed onto my body as it is in the world. The image is not merely me as if I were there, but is my other side (*mon envers*). So understood, mirroring does not allow the seer to catch her visibility and complete herself by integrating her external image into herself. The image does teach her something about herself but something that, rather than leading to a more complete and unified sense of self, opens a gap or split within herself. This might explain why, when describing the relation between seer and visible a couple of lines before the long passage quoted above, Merleau-Ponty uses the strange image of two mirrors facing each other. Rather than a simple ricochet movement that would end where it begins, closing the circle, what this image implies is an open series of reflections where beginning and end indefinitely escape.[44]

Écart as Encroachment or Separation

By emphasizing the chirality of reversibility, we have attempted to provide an interpretation of narcissism and mirroring that accounts for the irreducibility of the gap or divergence between the two sides of the chiasm. Our goal was to underline a common motif in Merleau-Ponty and Nancy. There still remains a crucial difference, however, in the way in which each conceives of the "between" of the touching-touched chiasm. For both, as we have shown, there is always a divergence or an *écart* between touching and touched, or seer and seen, so that no coincidence or superposition is possible. Yet Merleau-Ponty considers this gap to be always already spanned (*enjambé*). It is worth quoting the passage in full:

> But this incessant escaping, this impotency to superpose exactly upon one another the touching of the things by my right hand and the touching of this same right hand by my left hand, or to superpose, in the exploratory movements of the hand, the tactile experience of a point and that of the "same" point a moment later, or the auditory

experience of my own voice and that of other voices—this is not a failure. For if these experiences never exactly overlap, if they slip away at the very moment they are about to rejoin, if there is always a "shift" [*du bougé*], a "spread" [*un écart*], between them, this is precisely *because my two hands are part of the same body, because it moves itself in the world*, because I hear myself both from within and from without. I experience—and as often as I wish—the transition and the metamorphosis of the one experience into the other, and it is only as though the hinge between them, solid, unshakeable, remained irremediably hidden from me. But this hiatus between my right hand touched and my right hand touching, between my voice heard and my voice uttered, between one moment of my tactile life and the following one, *is not an ontological void, a non-being: it is spanned by the total being of my body, and by that of the world*; it is the zero of pressure between two solids that makes them adhere to one another. (VI, 148; my emphases)

What is clear in this passage is that the *écart*, the divergence that renders the coincidence or superposition of the two sides of the chiasm impossible, is not an "ontological void," because the two sides are always already two sides *of* one body, one world, one flesh. Of course, one could retort that the flesh is "one" in the sense that it is an "element" or a "general thing," an "*incarnate* principle" (VI, 139; my emphasis) that exists only transspatially, as spread out differentially across individuals.⁴⁵ To which we would reply that the role of this element, despite its differentiation, is to ensure the adherence of the two sides to one another, their communication and—dare we say—communion. It is as if at the moment that he thinks the *écart* as principle—this would ultimately be what flesh is: the primordiality of *écart*, or of incarnate differance, if one wants— Merleau-Ponty cannot help but posit the flesh as a grounding principle behind the *écart*.

For Nancy, it seems that the limit that exposes bodies to themselves and each other is exactly such an ontological void. The limit, the *extra* between the *partes*, is nothing but the sharing of the parts—their separation or spacing and their mutual exposition: "The limit is nothing, but it has or it parts two distinct edges."⁴⁶ Or again: "The limit is therefore the interval, at once parted [*écarté*] and without depth or thickness, which spaces the plurality of singulars; it is their mutual exteriority and the circulation between them."⁴⁷ If sense circulates between the singulars, it is not because something always already spans the two edges, or because one thing passes into the other, but rather because they remain separated on and exposed on the edge of the limit. Merleau-Ponty's emphasis on promiscuity and encroachment (*empiétement, Überschreiten*) remains foreign to Nancy. For Merleau-Ponty, encroachment is the universal structure of world (VI, 234) and applies to all the chiasms or intertwinings (*entrelacs, Verflechtungen*) described in the fourth section of *The Visible and the Invisible* as well as in the Working Notes; for example, that between perceiving and perceived, body and things, perception and movement, sensation and language. Speaking of what happens between singularities, Nancy also uses the image of the intertwining or the knot, but insists on the absolute separation of the different strands being knotted:

> This "between" . . . does not lead from one to the other [i.e., no passage]; it constitutes no connective tissue, no cement, no bridge. Perhaps it is not even fair to speak of a "connection" [*lien*] about it: it is neither connected nor unconnected, but falls short of both. Or rather, it is what lies at the heart of the connection: the *inter*lacing [*l'entre*croisement] of strands whose extremities remain separate even at the very center of the knot [*nouage*]. The "between" is the stretching out [*distension*] and opened by the singular as such, as its spacing of sense. That which does not remain within the distance of the "between" is only immanence collapsed in on itself and deprived of meaning.[48]

For Nancy, even though everything is always in contact with everything, the "law of touching" always remains "separation" and "heterogeneity."[49] Without this separation and heterogeneity that allow for the "with" of being, there is nothing but the black hole of immanence: nothing comes to presence because nothing distinguishes itself from anything else.[50] As Nancy writes in a different context: "Nothing *gets through*, which is why it touches."[51] This is why when speaking of the entanglement of singularities, Nancy will prefer to speak of mêlée rather than mixture: a mixture is the confusion of two things in a new homogeneous thing, whereas a mêlée is an event.[52]

Merleau-Ponty, for his part, always insists on the fact that there is no coincidence between one side of the chiasm and the other, and hence that each remains heterogeneous to the other. At the same time, the fact that one encroaches on the other also means that there is a minimal zone of transgression or overlapping (VI, 123, 218, 248), where the two are confused or blurred.[53] This is why Merleau-Ponty would never say, as Nancy did in the quotation above, that the zone of contact is "without depth or thickness." On the contrary, depth is for him the dimension of encroachment and latency. As we know, for the Cartesian ontology, there is no enigma of depth, depth being merely height or width seen from a different angle. This means that "the encroachment or latency of things does not enter into their definition. . . . I know that at this very moment another man, situated elsewhere—or better, God, who is everywhere—could penetrate their 'hiding place' and see them openly deployed."[54] Against this Cartesian ontology, Merleau-Ponty asserts depth as the relief and structure of the world. Depth is "this invisible link that 'holds together all things,' and that holds us with them within it."[55] Depth signals the co-belonging of the perceiving and the perceived, the fact that vision (and sensing more generally) happens from within the perceived world. As Emmanuel de Saint Aubert puts it: "Depth is rather a way of being of the world, which solicits in us a way of being to espouse its style. A way for the world to give itself to us and to call us in return to open ourselves to it, a way for it to wait for us and desire us, to invite us to abandon ourselves to its depth in order to perceive it."[56] The dimension of depth then is also that of desire: vision— or sensing more generally—is desire because it responds to the visible world in which everything encroaches upon everything. Depth is not visible, but is also not the opposite or the negation of visibility; rather it is the invisible dimension that makes possible what Merleau-Ponty calls the vertical world, the world that assembles incompossibles (VI, 228). Merleau-Ponty calls this world vertical because it is not spread out (horizontally) in front of me. In this world, *visibilia* (including that *visibilie* that is my body) encroach upon one another.

It would be wrong, here, to think that because of the absence of encroachment this dimension of desire is absent from Nancy's work. The body, insofar as it is ex-posed, is always for Nancy a body of pleasure, a pleasure that is not linked to desire-satisfaction but rather to *jouissance*, to that kind of pleasure which is always *a reaching*.[57] Yet, even in *jouissance*, the limit remains and is never breached. In *jouissance*—and *jouissance* is but the extreme experience of touch, of the body touching-touched, of the chiasm the body—the body "reaches its limit, passes to the limit, makes itself limitless" but even here there is no confusion and no blurring. The passage to the limit does not cross the limit; it approaches indefinitely. This passage, then, "does not cross [*ne franchit pas*] but brushes [*frôle*], touches, and in touching lets itself be touched by the outside."[58]

Conclusion

For both Merleau-Ponty and Nancy, *écart* as divergence, spread, or spacing is essential for sense. It is what opens up the body and makes it self-sensing. It is also what allows anything to make sense: a patch of color, a sound, another body, a thought. Yet as we saw, in the end, Merleau-Ponty and Nancy have different ways of conceiving this *écart*: as encroachment and promiscuity, or as unpassable limit. Where does that leave us? Maybe with a double worry, and a double warning.

On behalf of Merleau-Ponty, one might worry that Nancy's insistence on the uncrossability and unpassability of limits operates a flattening out of the encroachments, overlaps, and envelopments, of the depths and shadows that give the world (and others) their presence in the flesh. This worry is voiced by Christopher Watkin in his *Phenomenology or Deconstruction?* Nancy would transpose Merleau-Ponty's characterization of the intertwining of the visible and the invisible into "a 'flattened' understanding of the relation between world and sense in which sense is patent and exposed in the spacing of the world."[59] From Merleau-Ponty would come a call not to forget the dimension of desire that is present in Nancy.

On behalf of Nancy, however, one might worry that Merleau-Ponty's insistence on encroachment and promiscuity against the Cartesian (and Sartrean) *partes extra partes* leads him to the opposite excess: excess of proximity in a general regime of confusion where separation is lost. Saint Aubert, at the end of his long study *Être et chair*, raises this worry: "Here, as elsewhere," he writes, "the vertigo of the enveloping-enveloped, of a regime of *Ineinander* . . . comes close to blurring all differentiations. . . . The 'logic of promiscuity' . . . has the tendency to evacuate, in the end, the fundamental existential virtue of space that is *separation*."[60] From Nancy would come a call not to forget the separation—the birth to presence—that the dehiscence of the flesh also evokes.

Yet despite the fruitfulness of the dialogue I have tried to create between Merleau-Ponty and Nancy, their ontologies remain ultimately at odds. One will still have to choose between Merleau-Ponty's ontology of the sensible and Nancy's ontology of the singular plural. Yet, by bringing the ideas of one thinker to bear on those of the other, one can do so with a renewed attention paid to what both they, and we as interpreters, might be on the verge of forgetting.

Notes

1. In Nancy's corpus, we also find a series of words related to *écart*. Aside from the verb *écarter* (to displace, to disperse, or to separate) and *s'écarter* (to sway from, to diverge, to move aside), and the noun *écartement* (displacement, disjunction, swerve, separation, and sometimes also spacing), Nancy often uses terms such as *espacement* (spacing), *béance* (gaping), dehiscence, distinction, or distention.

2. See Georges Canguilhem, "Preface to the Second Edition," in *The Normal and the Pathological*, trans. Carolyn R. Fawcett (New York: Zone

Books, 1991), as well as *The Knowledge of Life*, trans. Stefanos Geroulanos and Daniela Ginsburg (New York: Fordham University Press, 2008), and *La formation du concept de réflexe aux XVIIe et XVIIIe siècles* (Paris: PUF, 1955).

3. Jean-Luc Nancy, "Merleau-Ponty: An Attempt at a Response," in *Merleau-Ponty and Contemporary Philosophy*, ed. Emmanuel Alloa, Frank Chouraqui, and Rajiv Kaushik (Albany: State University of New York Press, 2019), 298.

4. Derrida was the assistant of Paul Ricœur, who supervised both Nancy's diplôme and his doctoral theses. It is unclear how much contact Nancy had with Derrida while at the Sorbonne, but they knew each other's works from afar before becoming closer collaborators and friends in the early 1970s. See Derrida's letter to Nancy from April 22, 1969, in Benoît Peeters, *Derrida: A Biography*, trans. Andrew Brown (Cambridge, UK: Polity, 2013), 216.

5. "On Derrida: A Conversation of Sergio Benvenuto with Jean-Luc Nancy," trans. Marcel Lieberman, *Journal of European Psychoanalysis* 19, no. 2 (2004), www.psychomedia.it/jep/number19/benvenuto.htm.

6. Nancy, "Attempt," 298.

7. Nancy in Peeters, *Derrida*, 217.

8. See Peeters, *Derrida*, 128.

9. Nancy, "Attempt," 299.

10. See also Emmanuel de Saint Aubert, *Vers une ontologie indirecte: Sources et enjeux critiques de l'appel à l'ontologie chez Merleau-Ponty* (Paris: Vrin, 2006), chapter 3, especially §1, where Saint Aubert shows that Heidegger's thought had little influence on the development of Merleau-Ponty's ontology since Merleau-Ponty only read Heidegger carefully in the late 1950s when his thought had already reached a certain maturity. See also Jacques Taminiaux, "Was Merleau-Ponty on the Way from Husserl to Heidegger?," *Chiasmi International* 11 (2009): 21–31, where Taminiaux shows the independence of Merleau-Ponty with regard to Heidegger's thought in his late lecture courses.

11. Nancy, "Attempt," 299.

12. Nancy, "Attempt," 301.

13. This is why Ian James's emphasis, in his introduction to Nancy's work, on the continuities between Nancy's and Merleau-Ponty's thinking of space and of the body is problematic. It makes of Nancy more a phenomenologist than he really is. See Ian James, *The Fragmentary Demand: An Introduction to the Philosophy of Jean-Luc Nancy* (Stanford, CA: Stanford University Press, 2006), chapter 3. In *Phenomenology or Deconstruction?*, Christopher Watkin reads Merleau-Ponty and Nancy (as well as Ricœur) in order to assess the relation between phenomenology and deconstruction with a view to developing a phenomenological ontology that does not fall prey to Derrida's critique of the metaphysics of presence. Derrida here is the foil, and each thinker is chosen as a representative of a different kind of "phenomenology." As a result, Watkin is not really concerned with staging an encounter or dialogue between Merleau-Ponty and Nancy on their own terms. Rather, he accepts James's demonstration of the

influence of Merleau-Ponty on Nancy's thought and uses Nancy as representing "deconstructive phenomenology." See Christopher Watkin, *Phenomenology or Deconstruction? The Question of Ontology in Maurice Merleau-Ponty, Paul Ricœur, and Jean-Luc Nancy* (Edinburgh: Edinburgh University Press, 2009), esp. 137.

14. Jean-Luc Nancy, *Corpus*, trans. Richard A. Rand (New York: Fordham University Press, 2008), 128.

15. Jacques Derrida, *On Touching—Jean-Luc Nancy*, trans. Christine Irizarry (Stanford, CA: Stanford University Press, 2005), 175.

16. At the same time, Derrida worries that despite everything that separates Nancy's thinking from the phenomenologies of touch, his "post-deconstructive realism," as he calls it, is still implicated in the metaphysics of presence. Without going into detail, this would be the case because Nancy still makes the limit or the intangible, which is the object of touch, accessible in some way. Reading *On Touching*, one gets the impression that the conclusion is that Merleau-Ponty is not enough like Husserl and Nancy is not enough like Derrida, so that the real, productive encounter is really, and from the beginning, that between Husserl and Derrida.

17. On these expressions see Derrida, *On Touching*, 281–82.

18. Jean-Luc Nancy, *Corpus II: Writings on Sexuality*, trans. Anne O'Byrne (New York: Fordham University Press, 2013), 82.

19. Nancy, "Attempt," 299. The quotation from Merleau-Ponty is from "Eye and Mind," in *The Primacy of Perception*, trans. James M. Eddie (Evanston, IL: Northwestern University Press, 1964), 186. For a more detailed analysis of Nancy's and Merleau-Ponty's theories of embodiment along these lines, see my "*Corps propre* or *corpus corporum*: Unity and Dislocation in the Theories of Embodiment of Merleau-Ponty and Jean-Luc Nancy," *Chiasmi International* 18 (2016): 353–70.

20. Gary Madison does argue that Merleau-Ponty anticipates Derrida's deconstruction of logocentrism and his concept of différance. Furthermore, rather than showing that Merleau-Ponty falls short of Derrida, he goes on to argue that Merleau-Ponty's philosophical humanism is a "decided 'advance' over Derrida's" and other poststructuralists' antihumanism. See Gary Madison, "Did Merleau-Ponty Have a Theory of Perception," in *Merleau-Ponty, Hermeneutics, and Postmodernism*, ed. Thomas W. Busch and Shaun Gallagher (Albany: State University of New York Press, 1992), 98. On the relation between Merleau-Ponty and Derrida, see also Jack Reynolds's excellent study, *Merleau-Ponty and Derrida: Intertwining Embodiment and Alterity* (Athens: Ohio University Press, 2004). Contrary to the essays found in M. C. Dillon's volume, *Écart and Différance: Merleau-Ponty and Derrida on Seeing and Writing* (Atlantic Highlands, NJ: Humanities, 1997), which all seem to assume that both thinkers are "highly different, and even paradigmatically opposed" (Reynolds, xiv), Reynolds seeks to bring the two into dialogue by undermining some of the assumptions of the essays in Dillon's collection (including Dillon's

own work), particularly the one according to which Derrida would be a semantic reductionist.

21. See Merleau-Ponty, "An Unpublished Text," in *Primacy of Perception*, 11. See Bernard Waldenfels, "The Paradox of Expression," in *Chiasms: Merleau-Ponty's Notion of Flesh*, ed. Fred Evans and Len Lawlor (Albany: State University of New York Press, 2000), 93–94.

22. Merleau-Ponty, *Phenomenology of Perception*, trans. Donald A. Landes (New York: Routledge, 2012), 146.

23. See among others: "Consciousness is being toward the thing through the intermediary of the body" (Merleau-Ponty, *Phenomenology*, 140).

24. Merleau-Ponty, *Phenomenology*, 222.

25. The inadequacy of the passive/active dichotomy is not limited to perception. It is also apparent in cases of habitual actions, which are not understandable either in terms of passive, mechanistic reflexes, or in terms of willful intentional actions. Habitual actions rely on bodily knowledge and require a certain abandonment to that bodily knowledge. They are actions, but not those of a conscious, willful I. This is why Merleau-Ponty will say that there is an anonymous life of the body underneath my personal life. I cannot really say that it is I who sees the blue sky or I who dances in the same way as it is I who understands this book or decides to become a mathematician. Rather, one perceives or one dances in me. Yet, this depersonalization does not mean that I am reduced to reacting mechanically to my environment.

26. Of course, it would be possible to provide a more generous reading of the *Phenomenology* that highlights the proximity with the later work. Indeed, Merleau-Ponty also uses the term *coexistence* to speak of the communion or communication that sensing is. Whether this coexistence helps us bring Merleau-Ponty closer to Nancy would depend on the valence we give to the co-, to the sharing of existence: union or parting. On communication and how "co-naissance" does not imply co-incidence, see Donald Landes, "Le sujet de la sensation et le sujet résonant: Communion et renvoi chez Merleau-Ponty et Nancy," *Chiasmi International* 19 (2017): 143–62.

27. See Maurice Merleau-Ponty, *Le monde sensible et le monde de l'expression*, ed. Emmanuel de Saint Aubert and Stefan Kristensen (Geneva: MetisPresses, 2011), 49–50, 56–57. On these passages, see Emmanuel de Saint Aubert, "Conscience et expression: Avant-propos," in Merleau-Ponty, *Le monde sensible*, 17–19. The *écart* is also a recurring theme of the 1954–55 lecture courses on institution and passivity. See Maurice Merleau-Ponty, *Institution and Passivity: Course Notes from the Collège de France (1954–1955)*, foreword by Claude Lefort, trans. Leonard Lawlor and Heath Massey (Evanston, IL: Northwestern University Press, 2010), 7, 11, 131, 133, 136–37, 206.

28. See Merleau-Ponty, *Le monde sensible*, 55.

29. See Saint Aubert, "Avant-propos," 33–36.

30. Merleau-Ponty, *The Visible and the Invisible*, trans. Alfonso Lingis (Evanston, IL: Northwestern University Press, 1969), 139. Henceforth referred to in the text as VI.

31. Barbaras thinks they aren't. See Renaud Barbaras, "The Ambiguity of the Flesh," *Chiasmi International* 4 (2002): 19–26. See also "The Three Senses of Flesh," in Alloa, Chouraqui, and Kaushik, *Merleau-Ponty and Contemporary Philosophy*, 17–34. Finally, see the appendix in Lawrence Hass, *Merleau-Ponty's Philosophy* (Bloomington: Indiana University Press, 2008), 121–23, for a summary of the multiple meanings of the word "flesh" in Merleau-Ponty's later works.

32. Nancy, *Corpus*, 128.

33. To clarify this suspension of the subjective dimension in Merleau-Ponty's description of the being-perceived, it would be necessary to retrace Merleau-Ponty's path through the *Nature* lectures. On the importance of these lectures for Merleau-Ponty's ontology, see Renaud Barbaras, "Merleau-Ponty and Nature," *Research in Phenomenology* 31 (2001): 22–38.

34. Merleau-Ponty, "Eye and Mind," 163, translation modified.

35. In Nancy, *être-à* is most often translated as being-to or being-toward. See for example the section "The End of the World" in *The Sense of the World*, trans. Jeffrey S. Librett (Minneapolis: University of Minnesota Press, 1997).

36. See G. W. F. Hegel, *The Phenomenology of Spirit*, trans. A. V. Miller (Oxford: Oxford University Press, 1979), §18.

37. Jean-Luc Nancy, *A Finite Thinking*, ed. Simon Sparks (Stanford, CA: Stanford University Press, 2003), 7.

38. Nancy, *Finite Thinking*, 7. It should be noted that for Nancy, this understanding of selfhood does not apply exclusively to conscious beings, nor is it limited to sensing or living beings. It applies to every singularity (even, in a way, to the stone) and constitutes the meaning of being: to be is to be toward. On this point see my "*Corps propre* or *corpus corporum*."

39. Nancy, *Finite Thinking*, 6.

40. My explanation of chiral reversibility is highly indebted to two excellent articles by David Morris: "The Chirality of Being: Exploring a Merleau-Pontean Ontology of Sense," *Chiasmi International* 12 (2010): 165–82; and "The Enigma of Reversibility and the Genesis of Sense in Merleau-Ponty," *Continental Philosophy Review* 43 (2010): 141–65.

41. That is: in the space in which they are found. If we move to a higher dimensional space, then we can superpose the two gloves but they also lose their chiral sense as incongruent counterparts. For example, paper cutouts of our two hands can be superposed by turning one over, but three-dimensional sculpted hands can't.

42. For an explanation of this point, see Morris, "Chirality of Being," 166–67, and "The Enigma of Reversibility," 145–47. See also VI, 263 for the passage on which Morris's interpretation is based.

43. The question of how to interpret mirroring or narcissism is already at stake in the old debate between Lefort, Dillon, and Madison in *Ontology and Alterity in Merleau-Ponty*, ed. Galen A. Johnson and Michael B. Smith (Evanston, IL: Northwestern University Press, 1990). The question, which is similar to mine here, is whether the flesh means the reversible and reciprocal relation between two terms, or whether it allows for genuine otherness, that is, whether the *écart* is enough to account for an experience of transcendence and otherness. I am obviously more sympathetic to Dillon's reading than to Lefort's, but I take Madison's reading—for whom flesh is differance: "the trace of the other, the inscription of the other, in the subject's own selfhood" (31)—as going too far.

44. On the relation between the image of the mirror and narcissism in Merleau-Ponty as well as the influence of Wallon and Lacan, see Emmanuel de Saint Aubert, *Être et chair: Du corps au désir: L'habilitation ontologique de la chair* (Paris: Vrin, 2013), chapter 3, §1. See also Maurice Merleau-Ponty, *Child Psychology and Pedagogy: The Sorbonne Lectures 1949–1952* (Evanston, IL: Northwestern University Press, 2010), 87, where Merleau-Ponty discusses Lacan's interpretation of the myth of Narcissus and concludes that "the mirror equally permits the subject to isolate himself and to establish a reciprocal system—to facilitate the other's interference [*intrusion*]."

45. On trans-spatiality, see Barbaras, "Merleau-Ponty and Nature," 35. Aside from the unpublished note mentioned by Barbaras, Merleau-Ponty also mentions the idea of trans-spatiality in his *Nature* lectures, for example in his discussions of Whitehead and von Uexküll. See Maurice Merleau-Ponty, *Nature: Course Notes from the Collège de France*, ed. Dominique Seglard, trans. Robert Vallier (Evanston, IL: Northwestern University Press, 2003), 113–22, 173–78.

46. Jean-Luc Nancy, "Rives, bords, limites (de la singularité) / Banks, Edges, Limits (of Singularity)," *Angelaki: Journal of the Theoretical Humanities* 9, no. 2 (2004): 41–53, here 47.

47. Nancy, "Rives," 46.

48. Nancy, *Being Singular Plural*, trans. Robert D. Richardson and Anne E. O'Byrne (Stanford, CA: Stanford University Press, 2000), 5, translation modified.

49. Nancy, *Being Singular Plural*, 5.

50. On the black hole, see Nancy, *Corpus*, 75.

51. Nancy, *Corpus*, 11.

52. Already in the *Phenomenology*, *être-au-monde* meant *être mélangé aux choses*, "intermingled with things" (466), and Merleau-Ponty could write: "we are mixed up with the world [*mêlés au monde*] and with others in an inextricable confusion" (481). In *The Visible and the Invisible*, Merleau-Ponty also uses the word "confusion" as synonymous with encroachment (see VI, 47) and also the word *mélange* ("compound": VI, 102; "blending": VI, 35). On the difference between mixture and mêlée in Nancy, see "In Praise of the Melee," in *Finite Thinking*, 277–88.

53. In "The Philosopher and His Shadow," speaking of the "ontological rehabilitation of the sensible" effected by Husserl's description of the touching-touched, Merleau-Ponty writes that "the distinction between subject and object is blurred in my body" as well as "in the things." Merleau-Ponty, *Signs*, trans. Richard C. McCleary (Evanston, IL: Northwestern University Press, 1964), 167.

54. Merleau-Ponty, "Eye and Mind," 173, translation modified.

55. Saint Aubert, *Être et chair*, 300. Saint Aubert is quoting a note by Merleau-Ponty from *La nature et le monde du silence*, dating probably from fall 1957.

56. Saint Aubert, *Être et chair*, 392.

57. Jean-Luc Nancy, *Corpus II*, 17. On *jouissance*, see also Jean-Luc Nancy with Adèle van Reeth, *Coming*, trans. Charlotte Mandell (New York: Fordham University Press, 2016).

58. Nancy, *Corpus II*, 98, translation modified.

59. Watkin, *Phenomenology or Deconstruction?*, 147. See also 171, 206.

60. Saint Aubert, *Être et chair*, 380.

Sexistence: Nancy and Lacan

EMILY APTER

Jean-Luc Nancy's notion of *sexistence* may be situated against the political backdrop of "Third Wave" feminism labeled thus by the editors of a recently published volume on French feminisms in the twenty-first century.[1] If First Wave was marked by the suffragette movement and the struggle for equal citizenship, and if Second Wave crystallized around women taking possession of their bodies and legislating reproductive rights, Third Wave is defined by the trans, which, as a category, encompasses everything from "how to call sex" without heteronormative pronouns to queer kinship and transgenerational alliance, to diversified race and class positions, to a transvariability that surpasses historically marked categories of transsexual and transgender identity. Transnational feminism, Black feminism, transfeminism, genderqueer, ecofeminism, intersex: these are among the social movements that, according to the editors, buoyed Third Wave feminism since the mid-nineties, in tandem with the emergence in philosophy of new materialisms attuned to modes of subjective embodiment, body modification, and reimagined ways of living together. Renewing a connection to activist intervention, Third Wave feminism bypasses an earlier feminism built on "woman" as prime subject, and substitutes trans as a space for combatting social exclusion, gender violence, and political inequality across sexual multiplicities and polymorphous desires. Following on this diagrammatic timeline, I would conjecture that we are on the cusp of a Fourth Wave feminism that would retain the term *feminism* to underscore the fact that we have yet to reach an era that has superseded *femen* or historic struggles for parity within binary difference, even if we must acknowledge that *feminism* restricts the conceptual field of sexual ontology.

Fourth Wave feminism, drawing on psychoanalysis, philosophy, and translation theory, would, under these conditions, refer to *philosophizing in sex,* to theorizing states of being in sex that approach sexuality not in terms of what or who is the object of erotic interest or attraction (gay, bi, cis, straight, queer, trans . . .), but in the generic terms of what Luce Irigaray characterizes as *a civil right to exist and to be sexuated* that interrogates open-endedly "Who am I sexually?" or "How do I 'be' in sex?"[2] Jean-Luc Nancy's name for this sexual ontology is *sexistence*, a richly suggestive neologism that lends itself to myriad critical uses. There is of course an argument to be made that the gender indifference of *sexistence*, its fluctuations syncopated with the universal pulsations of Eros, installs a metaphysical aloofness from the roiling decades of LGBTQI identity politics. It would seem to herald an apolitical phase of sexual politics. Certainly, Nancy's sexual philosophy, like that of Joan Copjec, Alenka Zupančič, and Slavoj Žižek (all of them committed to unpacking Lacan's formulation of "impossible" sex), sits at a distinct remove from Third Wave activism or a politics bound to identity etiquettes. Nancy makes this position clear in an interview with Irving Goh, reasoning as follows:

> Fundamentally, it is only a manner of saying that sex is as singular as the person and that it is an accumulation of an enormous quantity of energies, representations, valences, emotive charges, and modes of excitation, which can never be reduced to a type. If I say, "He is heterosexual," I am not saying anything much: How is he "hetero"? Which female does he attract? How does he himself experience his desires? Nothing is more secret than my sexual "being": in fact, it expresses itself only in the sexual act.[3]

Sexistence deals with bodies in pleasure rather than bodies demonstrating for justice in the street. It touches only glancingly on the long history of debate around sexual difference. But this does not mean that *sexistence* has no politics. It contains a politics of recognition—of difference as such. It recognizes diversity in a concept of relation that proclaims (and even revels in) its "insufficient reason" for sex.[4] In taking up the problem of "being in sex" it engages the politics of community and the philosophical foundations of relationality. And it commits to reintroducing Eros to the sexually euthanized subject of philosophy (Heideggerian substance, the *subjectum* of

Dasein), a political feat of disciplinary realignment with larger consequences for the non-quarantine of sexual freedom.[5]

"Je = sexe. Je s'exe, tu s'exes, nous sexistons. Toute une alchimie précède ce montage si complexe."[6] How to render this in English? "I sex," or "you sex yourself, are sexed," "we sexist"? An entirely new grammar issues from this conjugation. Nancy's improvisational transliterations in *Sexistence,* like Lacan's homonymic play, "*ça s'oupire*" in Seminar XX (*Encore*)—which signals climax, sigh (*soupirer*), syncopated respiration, sleeping together, and the idea that the relationship is getting worse (*s'empirer*)—pushes the outer limits of translatability.[7] In English, the clunky construction—"doing something to oneself"—comes across as overkill compared to the spare reflexive pronoun *se* in French. Perhaps the *jeu de mots* that comes closest to the novelty of *je s'exe* is "sexting." But where French *s'exister* (or the variant *sexêtre* coined by Mehdi Belhaj Kacem), signals a subtle confluence of being and sexing, or sexing self and other at one and the same time, English "sexting" is ontologically skewed by its connotation of selfie sex on the social media exchange.[8]

S'exister and *sexistence* are quite possibly Nancy's most original contributions to the phenomenology of sexual expressionism. With these singular denominators of sexual ontology, Nancy not only focuses on the problem of how "to be" in sex and gender (existentially and grammatically), he also asks what it means "to sex" or "have sex" relationally. Taking on Lacan, specifically the famous axiom "Il n'y a pas de rapport sexuel" (There is no sexual relation), Nancy posits a "there is" of sexual relation in his own formula "L''il y a' du rapport sexuel" (which can be rendered: There, is the there is of sexual relation; There *is* sexual relation; or, more awkwardly yet more faithfully, The "there is" of sexual relationship, which takes stock of the quotation marks around "il y a" and the strange sound of the definite article *le* before it). In insisting on the "there is" of sexual relation in the ontology of relation, Nancy underscores the happening of being that occurs in the act of sex—this is the event of *rapport* as relation.[9] Nancy taps into the oldest sense of rapport as report, which opens up the question of how sex is accounted for and named in juridical reports of intimate relations. At the same time, "the sexual" of relation cannot be predicated because it is neither discrete substance nor thing. "The sexual [writes Nancy] is its own difference, or its own distinction. Being distinguished as sex or as sexed is what makes sex or sexed-ness." He will further expatiate on this idea, moving into the territory of *Geschlecht,* with its vocabulary of species, sexes, and kind:

> For every living sexual being and in all regards, sex is the being's differing from itself, differing understood as differentiating itself according to multiple measures and according to all those tangled processes that go by the names *masculine/feminine, homo/hetero, active/passive,* and so on, and differing understood as the species multiplying indefinitely the singularities of its "representatives." That is to say, there is no difference of the sexes, but there is, first and always, sex differing and deferring itself. (C II, 9, 10, 11)

Nancy's concept of the "sexual" as "its own difference" may be difficult to grasp, but as a formula it reworks the Lacanian proposition that there exists "only one sexuality," albeit, for Lacan, one that is dominated by the masculine, phallic function and that comprises two different "modes of entry."[10]

In *L'"il y a" du rapport sexuel* (an approximate version of which appears in English in *Corpus II*), sex is cast as an act of differing and deferring, of "relating [in the sense of supporting, retailing] oneself" (C II, 11). Reading this text alongside two others—*Coming* and *Sexistence*—we might approach *sexistence* to an ontology of sex that, in Alenka Zupančič's terms, locates the "being" of sex in a compound sexual drive, composed of different partial drives, such as looking, touching, sucking" (or, as Nancy will assert, "kissing/fucking," both of which signify in the French verb *baiser*). According to Zupančič, these expressions of compound drive serve to denaturalize the "artificial naturalization of the originally denatured drives."[11]

How does Nancy access denatured drives? By tracking in language a desire "obscure to itself," manifest in "the perpetuation [*poussée*] of the species," and the "drive [*pulsion*] that exceeds that thrust."[12] In the mounting fury of *poussée* and *pulsion*, drive works its way, like a *demiurge* through repertories of corporeal postures and verbal conjugations. In this scheme, verbs like *faire* (to do someone/something), *coucher* (sleep with), *baiser* (kiss/screw/fuck), *prendre* (take, possess), *pénétrer* (penetrate), *branler* (stimulate, masturbate), *toucher* (touch, pleasure)—all of which fluctuate between auto- and alloeroticism—are designated delegates of the drive.

In the lexicon of *sexistence*, *jouir* and *jouissance* stand out as notable untranslatables.[13] Nancy's gloss on what takes place in "coming" furnishes the predicate of "the there is" of sexual relation. Additionally, as Charlotte Mandell notes, *jouissance* "designates the entire, limitless usage of a possession, with the twofold connotation of appropriation (or *consummation*, consumption) and pleasure carried to its height. (It stems from the Latin *gaudium*, joy, delight.)"[14] From this legal sense of "limitless usage of a possession" (comprising accumulation and absorption), we pass to "the sexual meaning of delectation or of voluptuousness," to "sex and/or the mystical." Such a state of ecstatic being merges with an *ethic of the pathic* associated by Lacan with the analytic of knowledge. Pathos unleashes yet another series of theatrical associations, especially if we consider its usage by the Greek sophist Gorgias. Gorgias identified pathos with a fusion of affect and effect resembling autoaffective transport; being overcome by something (as by a powerful drug) or subject to a violence that, according to Gorgias commentator William Fortenbaugh, is analogous to rape. I will not go into how the unsettling transition from pleasuring to sexual violence contained in Nancy's notion of transport overwhelms conventional notions of property in the person essential to legislations of sexual safety. Here, I will only trace how, in his reworking of Lacan's axiom of sexual nonrelation, Nancy gestures toward a "to be" and a "there is" of *sexistence*.

L'"il y a" du rapport sexuel (2001)—the prequel and theoretical nub of *Sexistence*—puts two foundational Lacanian axioms in apposition: "There is no sexual relationship" (*Il n'y a pas de rapport sexuel*) and *"Jouissance* is impossible" (*La jouissance est impossible*). Like St. Paul's good news, what is announced here is nothing short of spectacular. "What is, is not?" (*il n'y donc pas ce qu'il y a!*) Nancy incredulously exclaims (C II, 2; I, 11). He notes that since Hegel and Heidegger we have been familiar with the idea *that being is not*. But the scandal in this case lies not with affirming the nonexistence of what exists, but rather in understanding that "the 'there is' itself, is no kind of being at all" (C II, 2). Delving further, he continues:

> Does the same hold for sexual relation, which is not? In a certain way this may be the whole question. It is not impossible that in the end we will discover that "the sexual relation" behaves like the "to be" [*l'être*] (understood as verb and act) in relation to what will therefore be "being" [*l'étant*] for it (that is, the entwined couple). (C II, 2; translation modified)

Lacan's formula does not just involve trying to wrap one's head around the counterintuitive notion that there is no relationship in sex, or that a sexual relation is no relation at all, but that the "*is*"—the copula of the existent (*l'étant*)—is what Lacan most radically put into doubt as to its functions and significations (I, 12). Kenneth Reinhard, commenting on Badiou's response to the Lacanian axiom in his 1993–94 seminar on Lacan, reminds us that the *is,* for both Lacan and Badiou, performs the work of contesting the reign of "oneness." Lacan's variation "*y a de l'Un*"—"there's some oneness"—foregrounds the multiplicity of sexual being while inoculating metaphysics against the temptations of the One or singular subject.

Nancy takes this contestation of the One not as pretext for militating in favor of plural sexualities or singularities in multiples, but as impetus for dissolving the subjective boundaries between partners and distributing difference among man, woman, hetero, homo, and trans (none of which belongs to a binaristic entelechy). Sometimes his mode of interrogation seems tongue in cheek, as when he applies a kind of scholastic probity to the conundrum of what it means to fuck. "When I fuck, I'm fucked, but how are we to understand this? Who fucks whom, and what does it mean to fuck or to be fucked?" Fucking, the act of reciprocal pleasuring, abolishes divisions between subject and subject, doing and being done to, agent and transitive object. It baffles the "is" of existence or Being writ large (*l'être*), replacing it with a delocalized "is," concretized through positive acts of *indifferentiating* being (C II, 3). The problem of the "there is," viewed thus, becomes a problem of placement. Where is the "is" of sex? Where is its there? For Nancy, the *there* (pronoun *y*), is intervallic; a "spacing of taking place and the play of between-place" (C II, 9). This spacing, essential to the scoring of sexual performance, belongs to "the performative pragmatics of coitus," including coitus interruptus (C II, 3).

Nancy's sexual "pragmatics," privileging perlocutionary act over causative result, have the added benefit of displacing castration fear as the master trope of desire. When active spacing is patched in over fearful lack, a quest for another mode of articulating interdiction in acts of sex is initiated. Drawing on the resources of the French word *jouissance* (and Lacan's play on the term as *jouis-sens*, "coming sense," "to come with sense," "to enjoy sense-making"), Nancy displaces castration anxiety, effecting a shift toward a contraceptive theory of "impossible" pleasure within sex that doubles as a mode of philosophizing. His strategic use of the word for birth control, *contra-conception*, which can also be taken to mean concept philosophy without concepts, yields nothing short of a major achievement of antiphilosophy: "And what if *jouir* meant *to conceive without a concept* (to enjoy or to suffer [*pâtir*] in general)? Knowledge of jouissance, or knowledge of relation, is a matter of knowing exactly what is not an object of knowledge" (C II, 13). "Knowing what is not an object" implies another mode of knowing, one that proceeds from "some mode other than renunciation" (i.e., castration, lack, sexual difference) toward articulation of the impasse in the sexual relation, even as it serves as the general indicative of the "not thing" of relation. In Nancy's theoretical practice, knowing becomes a different way of conceiving that releases knowledge's hold by giving full force to the power of the *contra* against its own *cept* (a Latin root word meaning "seized, taken"; "to cept" something is to appropriate it). Moreover, his notion of conception without concepts lines up with the idea of a sexual politics without categories (a politics, that is, minus its delegates for screening and sorting sexual subjects). In place of categorial sexes we have differentials of "sexed-ness." "Being distinguished as sex or as sexed is what makes sex or sexed-ness," Nancy asserts, and later: "there is no difference of the sexes, but there is, first and always, sex differing and deferring itself" (C II, 9 and 11). To conceive or write "sex differing" is to risk neutering sexual difference by denying the capacity of the "negative instance" in Lacanian *jouissance* to forge, in Joan Copjec's words, "a new understanding of the common, one that in preserving the asymmetry of the different ways sexual life is approached . . . preserves the common itself" (neutering is just what Copjec accuses gender theory of doing to the sex of sexual difference).[15] Nancy never confronts this issue directly, and his own contraceptual transcription of "sex differing" arguably tries to dodge it through recourse to deconstructive strategies of dissemination—homonymic plays, scolia—that steer clear of the Lacanian schemata of sexuation, based on the formalization found in number, set theory, and topology.

Let us resume some of the major interventions of *L'"il y a" du rapport sexuel*, all crucial to theorizing sexual ontology. First, Nancy has gestured toward an alternative logic of interdiction in the activity of sex, in the process momentously defenestrating the Oedipal paradigm and the preeminence of castration. Second, he has transvaluated (albeit in a Derridean vein) the conditions of "difference" in "sexual difference" by setting the problem backward, which is to say, by presuming that ontological difference (like relation) is itself de jure sexual.[16] This ontological difference is postdual, transindividual, essentially trans. Though Nancy's ontological subject of sex, at this juncture, runs the risk of etherealizing the gendered bodies and lived experiences of individual subjects (opening itself to relapse into the frigid ideal of what Marion calls *amour sans l'être* [love without being]), it makes up for this loss of personal identity—for this dehiscence—by personifying sexual materialism; its sensorium and choral work of pulse, sob, and throb.[17] Third, through the marvelous trope of contraception, he enjoins us to think in sex as one thinks in a language, or across languages; affording, as it were, a translative mode of conceiving sexual ontology. Fourth, he has rezoned sites of pleasure, writing his way into what I would call *sexy being* drawing on Nancy's phrase *Le sexe s'y zone, si je peux dire* (a phrase that the English "sex zones itself" utterly fails to convey).

Sexy being returns us to the ethic, or rather the *ethos* of pathos in acts of sex, from tremulous communion to melancholia. Tapping into the dangers of emotion warned against by the guardians of rhetoric and associated in music with the sublime Grave, the voiced C minor chord, the heroic affect of fiery Allegro (found in Beethoven's Sonata no. 8, Opus 13, called by the composer *grande sonate pathétique*), pathos transmits states of trance, transport, and entropic repletion (the self-exceeding experience of dizziness, giddiness, or *étourdissement*).

In one particularly lyrical passage of *L'"il y a" du rapport sexuel* on the zone, this pathos comes across as the co-creative unison of sex and thought. Silhouettes of bodies in acts of making love index the abstraction of sense-making from the movements of corporeal anatomies and vice versa:

> Le sexe s'y zone, si je peux dire: il s'y divise (*zoné*, en grec, c'est 'ceinture' en tant que séparation, delimitation). La différence d'une zone à l'autre (du sein au ventre ou à l'oreille, des lèvres aux aisselles—mais peut-on même nommer les zones de noms déjà anatomisées?
>
> ... Les zones valent comme vaut l'*eros* qu'elles ne produisent ni ne contiennent, mais qu'elles *sont* en tant qu'elles s'excitent. (I, 41)

> Sex zones itself, if I can put it that way. It divides itself (*zoné* in Greek means 'belt' in the sense of enclosure, separation, delimitation). The difference between one zone and another (from breast to belly to ear, from lips to armpits—but can we even name the zones using names that are already anatomized?
>
> ... Zones are valuable as the *eros* that they do not produce or contain but that they *are* insofar as they are excited. (C II, 16)

Contraception redraws the cartographic boundaries of erogenous zones by mobilizing pathos and the excitable agency of auto-affective verbs. *Le sexe s'y zone* allows us to hear sex speak up for itself. The phrase demonstrates how—by means of forcing—language marks out certain terms or syntactic structures for greater things or higher office. The simple line—*Je vais et je viens*—from the Serge Gainsbourg song "Je t'aime . . . moi non plus" suddenly becomes a milestone in the history of sexy being. *Zonage* becomes the bodybuilder of an expanse of erogeneity that knows no limits, embarking us on "*l'iliade du rapport*" (the "illiad" of relation)—an adventure of resectorization, resexuation, and inter*sex*ionality. Elsewhere, *consommation* (consummation, climax) becomes the designated carrier of "an ethic of sense-burning" (drafted from Paul Celan's *brûlure de sens*; "The kiss, at night, / burns sense into a language"), posed against the logic of lack. In *Sexistence, joy* (the English word), comprehends and overflows its prosaic usages ("joy of cooking," "joy of sex," Shakespeare's "Joy delights in joy"), emerging as the magic token that allows "nature to exceed itself and come towards existence" (S, 127, 128, 134). In ways that recall Luce Irigaray's forays into giving voice to parts of bodies and mobile pleasure centers, Nancy perfects a phenomenological eloquence that, while mimetic of sexual positions and the expirations of heaving bodies, stops short of body essentialism.[18] This is precisely how he models sex without concepts, as a mode of conceiving that proceeds by hearing; that is, by listening to what sex is talking about: "*car le sexe désire se dire. Il se désire dit, nommé, désigné.* [because sex wants to speak itself. It wants itself said, named, designated]" (S, 56). In *Sexistence* Nancy will enlist the full complement of erotic fiction and poetry on behalf of untying sex's tongue.[19] The book reads as a compendium of arousal culled from authors known and lesser known, including Proust, Rimbaud, Whitman, Edith Wharton, Henry Miller, Georges Bataille, Léopold Sédar Senghor, Ingeborg Bachmann, Pierre Jean Jouve, Paul Celan, Michel Deguy, Hélène Cixous, Joë Bousquet, and Philippe Beck. This turn to literature forms part of a mission to change philosophy, which as a field has historically retreated from love and sex in metaphysics, ontology, and phenomenology. This is the central thesis of Jean-Luc Marion's *Le phénomène érotique*, which claims that philosophy has gone silent on the subject of love, while he himself, as a philosopher, has fallen prey to "erotic aphasia."[20] Now even if it may be objected that many philosophers (notably Plato, Descartes, Hegel, Heidegger, de Beauvoir, Derrida, Irigaray, Butler, Badiou, Malabou) have in fact expatiated on love, sex, *Geschlecht,* the germ of sexual difference, and the gender of *Dasein* (and that Marion would have done well to cite them rather than presuppose his own unique corrective), it seems clear that Nancy, with the idea of *sexistence* and the example of his own philosophizing in sex, has effected a major shift in how to think sexual ontology.

In addition to "thinking sex" through the auspices of a sensuous materialism of sex acts (or a phenomenology of supra-sensible feeling), Nancy produces, in a novel way, the "inverted echo" of "what is given by the structure" of Lacanian thought (C II, 1). I would argue that in taking on Lacan's controversial constative *il n'y a pas de rapport sexuel* in a register at once "performative and pragmatic," Nancy offers a strong translation of Lacan, and more specifically, sublates the central problem of impasse which appears in various guises as resistance in transference, *jouissance,* the Real (of sexual difference), blocked relation, impossible knowledge, the Borromean knot, the quilting point (*point de capiton*), the closed instituted space (in topology) covered with open sets that exclude their own limits, and "the Pass."

Normally, when we think of impasse we think of blocks on the road, byways of obstruction and stuckness, including infrastructural metaphors, blocked transportation systems. *Impasse* in French literally means dead end, with the expression *faire l'impasse* referring to disregard, overlook, bluffing (as in a card game), or skipping part of an examination. It designates something disregarded, in the sense of neglected, ignored, wasted, passed over, used up. Impasse is often used interchangeably with obstruction (French *engouement*), referring to a word that gets stuck in the throat or a route full of hurdles. A prime example is the road nicknamed "La Route de la Chicane" (playing off the multiple associations of *chicaner*, to haggle with or cheat someone) that leads to the ZAD (*Zone à défendre*), squatted by the airport protesters in Notre-Dame-des-Landes. Transformed into a makeshift obstacle course forcing vehicles to zigzag and swerve on a serpentine path, strewn with car carcasses, refuse heaps, mounds of old clothing, and remnants of shelters, it recalls the smoking cars and human debris captured in the long tracking shot of Godard's film *Weekend* and complements contemporary works of hactivism aimed at disabling government operations. If here, obstruction and impasse are deployed as tactics of resistance (notionally exemplified by civil disobedient stances like Bartleby's "I would prefer not to" or Heather Love's politic of "queer refusal"), elsewhere they function as defeat mechanisms, as when Herbert Marcuse, in *One-Dimensional Man*, associates stymied subjective emancipation with "administered individuals" who have transformed "their mutilation into their own liberties and satisfactions."[21]

Jacques-Alain Miller identifies impasse in Freud as that which succeeds the termination of an analysis, a point of "insuperable resistance" coinciding not, as one might think, with the successful conclusion of an analytic experience, but with its failure:

> What is it that blocks the experience? What, according to Freud, does not come to pass? It is the clause which prescribes to a man how to be a man for a woman, and to a woman, how to be a woman for a man. Freud finds that this clause, which anticipates, fails to appear, and there he posits the castration complex as irreducible. But what did Freud expect of the experience if not a formula for the sexual relation? He hoped to find it inscribed in the unconscious; hence his despair at not finding it.[22]

What was for Freud an irreducible residue becomes for Lacan an opportunity for the Pass, with specific reference to the rite of passage to becoming an analyst of the Freudian School. The Pass was introduced by Lacan in 1967 and evolved into a delicately timed, stringent protocol involving first, a petition from the "passand" to two "passers"; next, an act of testifying before a cartel of witnesses; and finally, a call by the jury on whether the nomination to the position of Analyst had or had not occurred. Given this formal process, one assumes that the Pass consecrates accession to secret knowledge in addition to conferring a promotion in professional status. But the term is misleading when it comes to defining the kind of knowledge acquired, because it is knowledge at an impasse, knowledge that reports on the impossibility of *rapport*. In this sense, as Adrian Johnston emphasizes in his historical account of the Pass, the "passand" travels toward an unfordable chasm between the sexes, otherwise known as sexual difference.

> In one of his most famous seminars, the twentieth (*Encore*, 1972–1973), he [Lacan] theorized sexual difference as "sexuation," depicting the non-biological, denaturalized subject-positions of masculinity and femininity in terms of formal logic. Therein, he purported to uncover an inherent, ineliminable structural discrepancy/gap separating the sexes, an inescapable condemnation of sexed subjects to being essentially, necessarily out-of-sync with each other (and even with themselves as split subjects). Lacan summarized this with an infamous one-liner: "*Il n'y a pas de rapport sexuel*" (There is no sexual relationship). This declaration scandalized many at the time.[23]

It is easy to interpret "There is no sexual relation" to mean simply that desiring subjects can never directly relate to each other because desire is diverted through language. Language, the medium of the symbolic order and the name of the father, is the effective thwart of *rapport*. Relationality may try to happen in sex, but language denies its access code to the Real. And then we are left with absolute non-relation, to which we attribute the dualist divide between masculine libido and feminine jouissance and their formalization in mathemes of sexuation, the impasse of impossible knowledge, and the Pass which is no pass, but rather a transit to an aporia.

Nancy seems to accept this impassive stance of relation between the two. But he comes at the problem differently. What if sex, as a phenomenon, *is* relation *tout court*? What if *is* is sex? Nancy, one could say, retrieves the positive contents of the "there is" of relation by transvaluating relation as a term of *sexistence*. Where the impasse of absolute knowledge in Lacan authorizes a patriarchal ontology of sexual difference, Nancy will turn relation into a thinking organ of being that has sex, speaks desire, makes love, and envelopes philosophy in an erotic embrace.

Notes

1. Karine Bergès, Florence Binard, and Alexandrine Guyard-Nedelec, eds., *Féminismes du XXIe siècle: Une troisième vague?* (Paris: PUR, 2018).

2. Luce Irigaray, *J'aime à toi* (Paris: Grasset, 1992). See the chapter "Revêtus d'une identité civile," loc. 946 in Kindle.

3. Jean-Luc Nancy and Irving Goh, *The Deconstruction of Sex* (Durham, NC: Duke University Press, 2021), 34.

4. Nancy's short text, also titled "Sexistence," frames the problem of "diversity" in terms of why sex matters. His own very particular reading of diversity and relation are thus situated within the vast problematic of the rationality of sex (its principle of sufficient reason), habitually accounted for by theories of reproductive destiny and the perpetuation of the species. "As we are learning, the diversification of genomic characteristics is not necessarily the surest benefit of sexuality even if it is a compelling force. . . . Biology struggles to give a "sufficient reason" for sex. Perhaps it is necessary to consider that sex matters just as much in terms of relation (*rapport*): diversifying or not, sexual relation (*le rapport sexuel*) introduces a supplementary dimension—diversifying in its own way—within the species, or even, in some cases, at the limits with other species. Yet how might this relation as such offer a sufficient reason (*ratio sufficiens*)?" Jean-Luc Nancy, "Sexistence," trans. Irving Goh, *diacritics* 43, no. 4 (2015): 111–12.

5. The section of the book *Sexistence* (Paris: Galilée, 2017) titled "Philosophie?" is where Nancy takes up philosophy's desertion of the erotic. His reference point is Jean-Luc Marion's *Le phénomène érotique*.

6. Nancy, *Sexistence*, 119. Further references to this work will appear in the text abbreviated S.

7. Kenneth Reinhard translates Lacan's *s'. . . oupire* as "yearsening." See Kenneth Reinhard, "Introduction to the Seminar on Lacan," in Alain Badiou, *Lacan: Anti-philosophy 3*, trans. Kenneth Reinhard and Susan Spitzer (New York: Columbia University Press, 2018), 30.

8. Mehdi Belhaj Kacem, *Être et sexuation* (Paris: Stock, 2013). Nancy invokes Kacem's term in a footnote (Jean-Luc Nancy, *L'"il y a" du rapport sexuel* [Paris: Galilée, 2001], 57). Further references to this work will appear in the text abbreviated I.

9. Jean-Luc Nancy, *Corpus II: Writings on Sexuality*, trans. Anne O'Byrne (New York: Fordham University Press, 2013), 6–8. Unless otherwise noted, references to this work will be to this edition, abbreviated C II.

10. The phrasing here is adapted from Balibar's summary of Lacanian sex in *Citizen Subject: Foundations for Philosophical Anthropology*, trans. Steven Miller (New York: Fordham University Press, 2017), 295.

11. Alenka Zupančič, *What Is Sex?* (Cambridge, MA: MIT Press, 2017), 9.

12. Nancy and Goh, *Deconstruction of Sex*, 22. The full paragraph by Nancy is as follows: "The body inclined toward sex [*le sexe dans le corps*], the sexual body [*le corps sexué*], or corporeal sex constitute the reality—simultaneously the most immediate and the most obscure—of our existence as it presents itself simultaneously as individuated and as shared with an entire (human) species, which, itself, communicates with all the living (and the nonliving, throughout life). A body is sexual [*un corps est un sexe*], and we can understand this in terms of the body relating itself simultaneously to the species and to (at least) another body that it desires. Obscure to itself, this desire

responds simultaneously to the perpetuation [*poussée*] of the species and to a drive [*pulsion*] that exceeds that thrust [*poussée*]."

13. *Jouissance* thoroughly resists translation. It is variously rendered in English as orgasm, pleasure, to pleasure someone, oneself, or something, having enjoyment, possessing sex, having the other. Joan Copjec reminds us that "the word is derived from an old legal term, *usufruct*, which grants one the use of one's means, permits one to enjoy them, but not to acquire legal title to them or use them up." See her "The Sexual Compact" in *Sex and Nothing: Bridges from Psychoanalysis to Philosophy,* ed. Alejandro Cerda-Rueda (London: Routledge, 2016), 110.

14. Charlotte Mandell, translator's preface to the English-language edition, in Jean-Luc Nancy with Adèle van Reeth, *Coming*, trans. Charlotte Mandell (New York: Fordham University Press, 2017), Kindle edition (np).

15. Copjec, "Sexual Compact," 136. Will Greenshields notes: "Copjec effectively argues why we should avoid attempting to replace sex and nothing with sex and an infinite series of somethings in the name of a well-meaning pluralism." I would agree, but remain less convinced by her argument for retaining a heteronormative Lacanian model of sexual difference based on the "split" between masculinist libidinal desire and a feminine *jouissance* whose time of articulation is yet to come. Greenshields, review of *Sex and Nothing,* ed. Alejandro Cerda-Rueda, *Reframing Psychoanalysis*, http://reframe.sussex.ac.uk/repsychoanalysis/2017/01/10/sex-and-nothing-review-by-will-greenshields/?pdf=417.

16. This move would be unacceptable to Lacanians like Ellie Ragland-Sullivan, who dedicates a chapter of *The Logic of Sexuation: From Aristotle to Lacan* (Albany: State University of New York Press, 2004) to the topic "Why the Sexual Difference Makes All the Difference."

17. See Nancy's short text "Sexistence," in which the act of love is depicted as "an élan, a surge, a rush without reserve and without horizon." *Diacritics* 43, no. 4 (2015): 111. See, too, Jean-Luc Marion, *Le phénomène érotique* (Paris: Grasset, 2003), 17.

18. Nancy, like Sarah Ahmed, takes a phenomenological approach to describing sexual orientation, but unlike Ahmed, Nancy abstains from bringing the lived experience of gender politics to bear on his rendering of sexual feeling and experience. See Sarah Ahmed, *Queer Phenomenology: Orientations, Objects, Others* (Durham, NC: Duke University Press, 2006).

19. Catherine Malabou unties the tongue of the clitoris in *Le plaisir effacé: Clitoris et pensée* (Paris: Rivages, 2020).

20. Marion, *Le phénomène érotique*, 9.

21. As Douglas Kellner notes: "A central dilemma in Marcuse's theory—sharply formulated in *One-Dimensional Man*—that continued to haunt him: 'How can the administered individuals—who have made their mutilation into their own liberties and satisfactions . . . liberate themselves from themselves as well as from their masters? How is it even thinkable that the vicious circle be broken?'" "Marcuse and the Quest for Radical Subjectivity," *Dogma*

(February 2000), accessed August 10, 2018, http://www.dogma.lu/txt/Kellner-Marcuse01.htm.

22. Jacques-Alain Miller, "Another Lacan," originally delivered as a talk in Caracas in 1980, trans. Ralph Chipman, *The Symptom* 10 (Spring 2009), http://www.lacan.com/symptom10a/another-lacan.html.

23. Adrian Johnston, entry "Jacques Lacan," in *Stanford Encyclopedia of Philosophy*, accessed August 10, 2018, https://plato.stanford.edu/entries/lacan/.

7

Sublime Seizures in Lyotard and Nancy
The Political Blooming of Art and Technology

TIMOTHY MURRAY

Technology and the sublime may seem like strange bedfellows. While technology could suggest various manifestations of mechanics, order, control, rationality, and finitude, the sublime might lead us in far different directions. Gesturing to its Kantian articulation, the sublime evokes not only emotion but also judgment and perception, at least the conceptual variability of aesthetic judgment related to taste and beauty, on the one hand, if not also the perceptive excess of the mathematical sublime, on the other. Such early modernist notions of the sublime also bear the stamp of the affective poetics of the seventeenth-century French poet and aesthetician, Boileau, and his classical source, Longinus. Longinus established the early link between art and the sublime in his essay "On the Sublime," which Boileau translated in 1674 as one of the frameworks of his endorsement of rhetorical affect, in contrast to philosophical reason. For both writers, the sublime signifies the colorful rhetoric of passion as well as the shimmering marvel of style. Characteristic of the sublime is the enigmatic verve of its "je ne sais quoi," in Boileau's words, "that seizes, strikes, and makes one feel,"[1] as if a mirrorical Medusa shield were shining back at the beholder. Paradoxically, this grounding of affect in the stylistic marvel of artistic form itself is also an essential feature of what continues to align the sublime with philosophies of technology.

The sublime seizure of artistic form figures centrally in contemporary French philosophy where the subtleties of *techne* inform the thinking of the broadest range of writers, from Jacques Derrida, Bernard Stiegler, and Gilles

Deleuze to Paul Virilio, Louis Marin, and Christine Buci-Glucksmann. The dynamic "touch" of art is particularly pronounced in the work of Jean-François Lyotard and Jean-Luc Nancy, two of the most prolific late twentieth-century French philosophers of art. For Lyotard, the force of artistic touch ranges from the open gestures of drawing to the formlessness of painting. His frequent comments on artistic affect are replete with references to the *je ne sais quoi* of the early modern sublime. It is via the "non-place" and "non-object" of painting's foundational clinamen, suggests Lyotard, that art touches its interlocutors as "ce non-cela."[2] The *non-cela* enigmatically carries the envelope of sentiment and seizure of its *je ne sais quoi* as it figures in the abstract sites of "non-place" and "non-object" that would confound today's proponents of object-oriented ontology. As if echoing the sublime seizures of Boileau, Lyotard celebrates artistic line as an act of sharing [*partage*] that "touches and shares with the other."[3]

Speaking of painting and performance in reference to Daniel Buren, Lyotard elaborates on how viewers must first be touched, "affected," as the addressee of the work. "By *affected*, I mean that the viewers find themselves thus transformed by their perception (their sensorial organization) and in their sentiment (in their affective disposition)."[4] "You will touch me," he adds in relation to the interlocution of paintings by Valerio Adami, "only by being touched in the process."[5] Touch is as reciprocal for Lyotard as it is unfigurable. Indeed, touch itself carries something of the evanescence of the sublime as Lyotard expresses it. The artwork is a *"retouche,"* in the sense of "something that tries to secure and represent touch and never succeeds because touch happens in the place and moment of a space-time other than that of preserving and rendering."[6] The philosopher even describes his own commentary as something of a *retouche* itself as it fails to account adequately for the *je ne sais quoi*, the *non-cela*, that so enframes, compels, and drives it. The philosopher thus finds himself touched by his encounter with the subliminality of his own thinking and writing on art.

Similarly, Jean-Luc Nancy frames his book *The Muses* around a central subliminal question: "What does art do if not finally touch upon (*toucher à*)?"[7] Throughout his oeuvre, Nancy positions art as "the privilege of an index, which shows and touches, which shows by touching."[8] Instead of operating as the representational platform for a conception of "world" understood as mere exteriority—*comme milieu ou comme nature*[9]—the artistic operator, *toucher à*, must be understood in the most vulnerable sense of ex-posure, "in the sense of shaking up, disturbing, destabilizing, or deconstructing."[10] Representationality cedes to indexicality. The world-as-picture is shaken to its core by the indexical destabilizations of reciprocal impact in which the representing subject of art is concomitantly subjugated to the affective procedures of subjugation itself. In so describing the privilege of art as its indexicality, "which shows and touches, which shows by touching,"[11] Nancy also situates the intensity of art as that which lies at the affirmational core of technology itself: "the in-finite affirmation of what incessantly *touches* on its end: another *sense* of existence, by the same token, another sense of 'technique.'"[12]

Sublime Offerings

It is within this context of the touch of technique that Nancy reflects elegantly on what he terms "the offering of the sublime." "The judgment or the sentiment of the sublime," he suggests, "offers us a 'seizure,' a possession from within this unboundedness that comes to apprehend a figure."[13] But for Nancy, it is not really the figure itself that matters. Rather, he emphasizes the gesture of the arresting event of figuration, *toucher à*. This enactment or impact of touch is what characterizes Nancy's notion of the sublime as "an aesthetic of movement," which he contrasts with a more stable, rational, bounded, and perhaps formally technological, if not ideological, "aesthetic of the state."[14] Being "an aesthetic of movement," the act of drawing, for instance, is described by Nancy as "a disposition to follow": "the passivity implicated in this 'following' is that of opening up to the distinctive and singular event of an impetus, motion, line, or emotion."[15] What's happening in the sublime, as Nancy reads Kant, is very much the unlimited features not merely of number (as in the mathematical sublime) but more importantly of "the *gesture* of the infinite ... the gesture of *form*ation, of figuration itself, but in the sense of the informe,"[16] or, we might add, in the sense conjoined by both Nancy and Lyotard of the gestural clinamen or *toucher à*. A burst, a trace, an emotion, perhaps also a *non-cela* or a *je ne sais quoi*.

In *The Pleasure in Drawing*, Nancy emphasizes the equivocal nature of the sublime as evoking pleasure and non-pleasure while tainting form with the *informe*.[17] Thus infected are both form and meaning in the wake of the gestures of touch. Nancy elaborates in "The Forgetting of Philosophy,"

> The fact that meaning in this sense infinitely exceeds signification, and that it neither has nor gives signification, makes it neither non-meaning nor fate nor some dull necessity. . . . It is *us* as exposed, to [*à*] a space and to [*à*] ourselves as a space, to [*à*] a time and to [*à*] ourselves as a time, to [*à*] language, to [*à*] ourselves, that is, to [*à*] us others.[18]

À ... à ... à thus evolves through the moving fabric of its repetition into the rhetorical performance of the figure of imprinted, informe(d) exposure.

Thus staged in the indeterminate whirl and swirl of *à, à, à* is the intimacy of movement-in-proximity rather than the safety of fixity-in-distance, the activity of exposure instead of the passivity of contemplation. Nancy thus scripts the sublime as something of the shifting poetics of movement, just as his prepositionally laden prose evokes something in itself of the *informe* of indexical gesture and rhythmical repetition. *À . . . à . . . à*.[19]

Nancy does not hesitate to enfold the *informe* within the framework of technology and the sublime's historical inscription in rhetorical affect. He thus frequently references Heidegger's musings on poetics, especially the prescient warnings raised in "The Question concerning Technology." Particularly compelling and complementary to Nancy's essays on the arts is the stress Heidegger places on the *informe* of techne and the technicity of poiesis in contrast to the replicable dependability of technology's closed economy of innovation for profit. Central to Heidegger's essay is its caution against the enclosure of technological production, regulation, and distribution. Referencing the "revealings" of the technologies of mining, for instance, Heidegger reflects on the invidiousness of the closed circularity of technology.

> The revealing that rules throughout modern technology has the character of a setting-upon, in the sense of a challenging-forth. That challenging happens in that the energy concealed in nature is unlocked, what is unlocked is transformed, what is transformed is stored up, what is stored up is, in turn, distributed, and what is distributed is switched about ever anew. Unlocking, transforming, storing, distributing, and switching about are ways of revealing. But the revealing never simply comes to an end. Neither does it run off into the indeterminate. The revealing reveals to itself its own manifoldly interlocking paths, through regulating their course. This regulating itself is, for its part, everywhere secured. Regulating and securing even become the chief characteristics of the challenging revealing.[20]

The threat of such regulation, on which he also elaborates in his essay "The Age of the World Picture," is not only the transfer of touch into the hegemonic machineries of production but also, and more cruelly, the related deadening of thought and erudition by the repetitive practice of research and experimentation for the mere sake of innovation, especially as practiced within the postwar research university. Lost is the enigma of the movement of thought for the predictable return of state-sponsored results of research, from engineering to history. The German philosopher passionately urges his readers to respond to this state of emergency threatening the cultural potential of creativity and thought. His antidote is that we attend actively to the marvel of form, technicity, and poetics otherwise enveloping and constituting us: "this destining, the coming to presence of technology gives man entry into That which, of himself, he can neither invent nor in any way make."[21] At stake is the preservation and nurturance of the openness of techne's subliminal "That," "the bursting open belonging to bringing-forth, e.g., the bursting of a blossom into bloom, in itself."[22] Nancy even implicitly mimes this theme when he celebrates "art taken absolutely in its modern sense (i.e., upon techne as a mode of execution of being, as its mode of finishing in the explosive brilliance of the beautiful and the sublime, double and rival in sovereignty of the blossoming of *phusis*)."[23] Any competing regulatory research or "aesthetics of the state" is to Nancy a far cry from the effervescent pulsations of art, which he marvelously describes along the formless lines of Heidegger's blossomings and burstings: "it is the impulse and pulse of being-in-the-world and all the senses, sensations, sensitivities, and sensualities are delineations of this impulse and pulse."[24]

Such an aesthetics of pulsing movement, enhanced by the pull of the sublime and the in-formative summons of pronomial this's and that's, also calls forth the vast corpus on art written by Lyotard. Even in the early days of his *Des dispositifs pulsionnels* (1973), prior to his prolific output of catalogue essays and art monographs, Lyotard situates the intensive force of art in the participants' openness to hearing, to being touched by its event. What's at stake is not some grand technological unity or comprehensive form or genre but rather art's simultaneous metamorphosis in affect's "*non-cela*": "in [*en*] tears, in [*en*] gestures, in [*en*] laughs, in [*en*] dances, in [*en*] words, in [*en*] sounds."[25] Similar to Nancy's prepositional summonings, "*à, à, à,*" the artistic participant succumbs within Lyotard's aesthetic inscription of the "*en, en, en*" to the gestural pulsations of art in all their corporeal and affective resonance in the "*non-cela*," from the flow of tears to the resonance of sound.

It is Lyotard who would become most readily identifiable within international theoretical circles as the most vocal proponent of the arts of the sublime. In his frequently cited essay "The Sublime and the Avant-Garde," Lyotard positions the sublime as the mode of sensibility most characteristic of modernity. Through the sublime, he suggests, "the indeterminate destabilizes the didactic project" of the realistic mimesis state. Lyotard embraces the sublime, in a way not incompatible with Nancy, for stepping aside from any dependable artistic imitation of nature to create a world apart [*un monde à côté*] "in which the monstrous and the formless have their rights because they can be sublime."[26] It is particularly "the avant-gardes," from Delauney and Mondrian to Monory and Buren, who pursue the experimenting vocation of "the evocation of the unpresentable. Their sublime is scarcely a nostalgic one, being turned towards the infinity of plastic essays to be made rather than towards the representation of a supposedly lost absolute."[27] Rather than look back to the absolutes of the past, Lyotard positions the sublime in relation to the blossoming techne of the moment. Paramount is the artistic staging of the enigma of the sublime, "*Is it happening?*, the *now*."[28]

In insisting on the enigmatic swerve of such a sublime happening, Lyotard cautions his readers, however, not to become too complacent in aligning the sublime with "*techne*" without continually rehearsing its lineage in relation to the aesthetics of the state.

> By meditating on the theme of sublimity and of indeterminacy, meditation about works of art imposes a major change on *techne* and the institutions linked to it—Academies, Schools, masters and disciples, taste, the enlightened public made up of princes and courtiers. It is the very destination or destiny of works which is being questioned. The predominance of the idea of *techne* placed works under a multiple regulation, that of the model taught by the studios, Schools and Academies, that of the taste shared by the aristocratic public, that of a purposiveness of art, which was to illustrate the glory of a name, divine or human, to which was linked the perfection of some cardinal virtue or other. The idea of the sublime disrupts this harmony.[29]

Lyotard alludes, of course, to the hegemonic tradition of the seventeenth-century French Academies, from Painting and Sculpture to Dance, Music, and Architecture, which were founded in the age of absolutism to propagate a technology and ideology of uniform cultural production. Perhaps the penultimate act of such cultural regulation was the exclusion by the Académie Française from its formative French dictionary of "any loose or licentious term, open to equivocal or evil interpretation."[30] Might not this provide some minor contextualization of the counter-technics of equivocal speaking that so frames the theory of the sublime, commenced by Boileau's poetics of *je ne sais quoi* in the age of the Academies and later developing into the licentious choreography of contemporary prepositions marshalled by the likes of Nancy and Lyotard? Lyotard's caution to keep in check the cardinal harmony of the academies certainly lends ample color to the contemporary philosophical impetus of the sublime. And doesn't Lyotard's assertion of the sublime disruption of this harmony evoke in so many ideological ways what Nancy terms the subliminal "aesthetics of movement" in contrast to any "aesthetics of the state"?

What distinguishes both philosophers' prolific writing on art from that of so many of their philosophical peers is their common emphasis on this imperative of thinking the complexities of the sublime within this contradictory context of the form and heritage of technology. Lyotard joins with Nancy on building a discourse on art whose foundations contrast the state/corporate investments in technology with the *informe* of technicity as ghosted by the sublime and by what Nancy terms its affiliated "(é)motions." But not blindly celebrating the promise of the sublime, both philosophers consistently pause to clarify the technological context in which it can best activate. Nancy elegantly muses on how the technology of perspective bears the absolutist state lineage of techne, as summarized above by Lyotard. Within the conventional mise-en-scène of exhibition, for instance, the subject is said by Nancy to be held pre-positionally as *présent-à-distance* and thus encased in the structural foundation of the Occidental perception of the world. In *The Ground of the Image*, Nancy traces how the evolution of modernist ocular technologies positions the confident framework of perspective, *à-distance*, as the structural foundation of the Occidental perception of the world:

> Between the Renaissance and the nineteenth century, European thought (the world that was in the process of westernizing itself, of imagining itself "as world") shifted from the painting to the projection screen, from representation to presentation, and from the idea to the image, or, more precisely, from the fantasy or the fantasm to the imagination.[31]

Optically grounded precepts that pivot between being and fantasy frame Nancy's notion of the world imagining itself (Occidentally) as "world." In the context of the conventional architectonics of artistic exhibition, furthermore, the viewing subject is thus always situated pre-positionally as *présent-à-distance* and thus held back as "immobile" before both the artwork and the hegemonic cultural condition sustaining it. Nancy elsewhere critiques this positioning as falling within the restrictive, absolutist paradigm of what he caustically calls *"techno-logie."* It is no coincidence that this same ontological character of immobile positioning, *à-distance*, is comparable to Heidegger's regulating economy of closed perspective and capitalist technology developed for accreditation, distribution, and profit rather than for the sublime offerings of erudition and (é)motion.

This is a point pursued even more vigorously throughout Lyotard's oeuvre. As early as *The Postmodern Condition* (1979), Lyotard warns ominously of subjection to procedures of social and cultural performativity, which have come to dominate cultural and intellectual production over the past quarter century. "It was more the desire for wealth than the desire for knowledge that initially forced upon technology the imperative of performance improvement and product realization.... Technology became important to contemporary knowledge only through the mediation of a generalized spirit of performativity. Even today, progress in knowledge is not totally subordinated to technological investment."[32] Particularly in the age of the digital, warns Lyotard later, in *The Inhuman*, the quivering touch of the present is negated in the face of the pre-determined future of technological fulfillment and the disturbing infelicities of the emergent digital-industrial complex.

> The growth of techno-scientific systems appears to be drawn by this ideal of *Mathesis Universalis* or, to use Borges's metaphor, the library of Babel. Complete information means neutralizing more events. What is already known cannot, in principle, be experienced as an event. Consequently, if one wants to control a process, the best way of so doing is to subordinate the present to what is (still) called the "future," since in these conditions the "future" will be completely pre-determined and the present itself will cease opening onto an uncertain and contingent "afterwards."
>
> Better: what comes "after" the "now" will have to come "before" it. In as much as a monad in thus saturating its memory is stocking the future, the present loses its privilege of being an ungraspable point from which, however, time should always distribute itself between the "not yet" of the future and the "no longer" of the past.[33]

Effaced by such a techno-scientific ideal is the enclosure of the empowering question of the sublime, "What is happening?, now," by the certainties of the hollow repetition of innovation. It is no exaggeration to suggest, now, that the inscription of thought and creativity in the shackles of performativity has become sadly evident across the specters of the cultural sphere, from the museum to the academy. In receiving our artistic response to queries about productivity and performativity, is it still possible for the neoliberal administrators of culture and education to hear the slightest empowerment, if not wonder and glee, in the parodic retort, "What is happening?, now."

Technological Stains, from Differend to Écotechnie

Let's not forget, however, that both Lyotard and Nancy continue to have faith in the performance of their craft. The promise of art and technology, not to mention philosophy, continues to depend on the thought of technique, techne, and poiesis, as fulfilling the threatened enigma of technology. Nancy enthusiastically embraces the singular plurality of the arts and technology as the ground of thinking the world "with," "*avec*," in its plurality. He even celebrates the effervescence of the exposition of technicity *à côté*, as the fundamental soul of philosophy. "To philosophize," he says in *The Forgetting of Philosophy*, "is to think exposition itself."[34] Writing on Buren, Lyotard similarly calls for the philosophical imperative of thinking "the problem of exposition of exposition." This means considering the techne of exposition, as Nancy would say, *à côté*. "These asides [*ces à côtés*] are not invisible, but are seen from an other vision, de-centered [*désaxée*]. Not exposed but proposed. Visual exposition, like the symphony, composes the asides, makes them contribute to positioning the facial axis, fashioning them, regulating their allure, but without exposing them. They are on the horizon, not in the foyer. Confined more than domesticated. Lateral, curved expanse, circumspect sidelong glance. They are still strategically positioned as generators of ellipsoid volume."[35] Curious perspectives, curved operators, sidelong circumspections. The exposition of exposition in terms that curve, glance, scrape, and caress. The touching event of *à côté*.

In his 1988 book on the import of digital technology, *The Inhuman*, Lyotard similarly recommends enlivening the contours of technology with the similarly enigmatic "complexification of the transformers." With the verve of visual anamorphosis or the sway of choreographic pivot, these transformers are, *à côté*, what he terms an "immaterialist materialism" through which a technological stain will leave the vibrant trace of what has not been inscribed.[36] Regarding exposition of the avant-gardes in painting, Lyotard insists in a similarly elliptical fashion that "they do not try to find the unpresentable at a great distance, as a lost origin or end, to be represented in the subject of the picture, but in what is closest, in the very matter of artistic work."[37] Put otherwise, he adds, "the inexpressible does not reside in an over there, in another word, or another time, but in this: in that (something) happens. In the determination of pictorial art, the indeterminate, the 'it happens' is the paint, the picture."[38]

While Nancy cautions against Lyotard's well-known association of the sublime with the artistic presentation of that which otherwise has been unpresentable or uninscribed—since Nancy stubbornly insists on Lyotard's alignment of the unpresentable with the notion of a primordial state awaiting the genius of sudden presentation[39]—their dazzling essays on art continue to share the uncanny emphases on the *à côté*, not to mention the resistance of touch to technological hegemony. For both artistically sensitive philosophers, the fluid field of art's vital surgings enhances a horizon of entwining technicity that envelops the social within the plural, whether Nancy's affirmational "being-in-plural" or Lyotard's more agonistic concept of the *differend*. "In the *differend*," writes Lyotard, "human beings who thought they could use language as an instrument of communication learn through the feeling of pain that accompanies silence (and of pleasure which accompanies the invention of a new idiom), that they are summoned by language, not to augment to their profit the quantity of information communicable through existing idioms, but to recognize that what remains to be phrased exceeds what they can presently phrase, and that they must be allowed to institute idioms which do not yet exist."[40] To Lyotard, the structural failure of technology lies in its indifference, if not its hostility, to what he calls the empowering *differend* inherent in it.[41] Recall his earlier caution to activate against the early modernist predominance of the idea of techne as subjection to overlapping systems of regulation.

Permit me now to repeat a prior mantra. It is not the spirit of techne that poses a threat. Rather it is the threatened negation of techne's *differend* by the imperatives of technological performativity. And this is where the sublime figures so prominently in Lyotard's approach to art. The sublime charge of contemporary experimental art "is thus in accord with the contemporary world of industrial techno-sciences at the same time it disavows it."[42] Again, the promise of techne, of technique, is its summoning of the *informe*, the *differend*, its offering of plurality's allowance itself. And let's not lose sight of the effervescence of the in-common plurality of Nancy's sublime bursts and emotions. As he no doubt would remind us, *techne* can be understood as "a mode of execution of being, as its mode of finishing in the explosive brilliance of the beautiful and the sublime, double and rival in sovereignty of the blossoming of *phusis*."[43]

Yet it behooves us to continue to acknowledge the incessant seizure of the offerings of the sublime by the very economies it might otherwise resist. Lyotard does so by tracing the evolution of the sublime in the contemporary economy of art. Playing off Edmund Burke's eighteenth-century analysis of the sublime, Lyotard reflects on the sublime intensity associated with the ontological dislocations of modern and contemporary art. He finds particularly compelling Burke's dismissal of painting for its allegiance to the classical rule of mimesis. Burke embraces poetry for its ability to more freely combine words in a way that would have the power to move readers aside from, *à côté*, the conventions of verisimilitude, beauty, and painting. The procedures of radical combination and deviation from the norm are what Lyotard also values in the modernist painters whom he reads as following the lead of the Burkean sublime.

The artist attempts combinations allowing the event. The art-lover does not experience a simple pleasure, or derive some ethical benefit from his contact with art, but expects an intensification of his conceptual and emotional capacity, an ambivalent enjoyment. Intensity is associated with an ontological dislocation. The art object no longer bends itself to models, but tries to present the fact that there is an unpresentable.[44]

Yet this same formula becomes exceedingly complicated with contemporary art's activation of the sublime event itself as a means of breaking away from the broader coda of representation and reception.

As Lyotard sees it, "the avant-garde is not concerned with what happens to the [viewing] 'subject,' but with: 'Does it happen?,' with privation. This is the sense," he adds, "in which it still belongs to the aesthetics of the sublime."[45] Paradoxically, the artistic seizure here can be said to lie within the sublime itself. Not within the viewing subject, creating artist, or contemplating philosopher, but, rather, within what Lyotard calls the expanding collusion between the avant-garde and capital. "There is something of the sublime in capitalist economy," cautions Lyotard already in 1983, on the eve of the explosion of the unlimited global networks of digital capital.[46] First comes the Idea or economic aim of infinite resources, prosperity, and power. Any notion of artistic aura becomes subsumed in the calculation of profitability and performativity, reminding us of the prescient warnings of Heidegger about the potential perversions of contemporary cultural institutions, not only the academy but also the museum, gallery, and art markets. This is when the reorganization or intensification of techne from an aesthetics of state to one of movement comes full circle to be coopted by the fluid e-motions of global capital. Through the manipulation of information and the resubordination of technologies, the reality of both art and capital becomes unsteady. Lyotard sees global capital as mimicking the artist's mistrust of rules and experimentation with ever-new materials. "In this way," Lyotard suggests, "one thinks that one is expressing the spirit of the times, whereas one is merely reflecting the spirit of the market. Sublimity is no longer in art, but in speculation on art."[47]

In fascinating ways, Lyotard foresees the politics of Eugene Thacker and Alexander Galloway's groundbreaking book, *The Exploit*, which critiques the new digital sovereignty of looping and evolving biopolitical networks, from science to art. Here speculation itself mutates from thinking vis à vis the individual into the combines of the global market, always continually morphing with an eye on future innovation as one network intersects with another. Here the empowering linguo-biomorphic expressions of Lyotardian touch, affect's *"non-cela,"* "in tears, in gestures, in laughs, in dances, in words, in sounds," become peeled off from aesthetic empowerment as merely transformable bio/data bits to be combined ad nauseum into exchangeable combinations. Turning explicitly to Lyotard's *The Inhuman*, Thacker and Galloway dwell on their skepticism of his continually resistant hope for a "transformative transformation" of "an inhumanity . . . in which all politics is reduced to voting, all culture to fashion, all subjectivity to the stratifications of class. . . . By definition, this potential site of resistance cannot be named unless it is discovered. For Lyotard, this is the domain of our contemporary 'sublime' in the arts, the very site of discovering what is beyond representation."[48] As they read Lyotard, the resistance to the performative speculation of art, when the sublime becomes speculation itself, still remains paradoxically situated within the philosopher's hope in the differential political intensification of the sublime within the arts.

Returning to Nancy, he promises in his 1988 essay, "L'offrande sublime," that he will respond to what he references as Lyotard's politicization of the sublime. He could be referring to Lyotard's numerous inscriptions of the political apparatus into his musings on art. As noted by Thacker and Galloway, this is certainly paramount in the case of Lyotard's essays on art and the sublime. In "Painting as Libidinal Apparatus," for instance, Lyotard links politics to the aesthetics of movement as the dislocation of conventional approaches to painting. At first glance, Lyotard's emphasis on transformation seems to be strictly aesthetic. "It means to transform the energetics at play in what one calls painting, not in a theoretical device but more in a kind of liquefication, in a kind of aleatory production, in the sense introduced by John Cage."[49] Here again the philosopher foregrounds the sense of that repetitive action of the *"non-cela" (en, en, en)*. But, as if interpolating the political inference of Nancy's sublime alternative to an aesthetics of state, Lyotard adds insistently, in regard to aleatory art, that "we must demonstrate how this apparatus that regulates the energetic transformations of pictorial inscription, how it communicates with another apparatus which is the political one."[50] While I am uncertain whether Nancy ever elaborated on Lyotard's politicization of the sublime, we can certainly appreciate the depth of Lyotard's gesture in here situating aleatory energetics, perhaps an aesthetics of movement, as a political apparatus of the sublime, regardless of the obscurity of this notion.

It is conversely possible to locate indirect affirmative traces of this very same gesture in scanning Nancy's own oeuvre where he adopts rather than counters Lyotard's aleatory gesture of the *differend*. Perhaps most suggestive is Nancy's application of something akin to the *differend* in his 1991 essay, "War, Law, Sovereignty—*Techné.*" This is where Nancy institutes a new idiom to refashion techne in the shadow of globalization and the onset of the first Gulf War. To contrast his term for the economics and aesthetics of the state—"*logo-logie*"—he puts into play, *à côté*, the more paralogical notion of "*écotechnie.*" As if echoing Lyotard's musings on the artistic seizure of speculation, where global storage units accumulate the endlessness of artistic wealth collected from the auction houses, Nancy laments

> the "world (dis)order," if it is without reason, end, or figure [as *informe*], nonetheless has all the effectivity of what one calls "planetary technology" and "world economy": the double sign of a single complex of the reciprocity of causes and effects, the circularity of ends and means. The without-end, indeed, but the without-end in millions of dollars and yen, in millions of thermies, kilowatts, optical fibers, kilooctets. If the world is a world today, it is a world first of all under this double sign. Let us call it here *écotechnie*.[51]

Nancy goes on to suggest in the same essay that, while operating within the sublime endlessness of world economy and planetary technology, *écotechnie* parodoxically opens the space of thinking *techne* to something other than the very parameters of war and capital that constitute the double signs of state aesthetics today.

> What one calls "technology," or again what I am calling here *écotechnie* (henceforth to be liberated in itself from capital) is the techné of "finitude" or of spacing. No longer the technical means to an End, but techné itself as in-finite end, techné as the existence of the finite existent, its brilliance, and its violence. We are talking about "technology" itself, but about a technology that of itself raises the necessity of appropriating its sense *against* the appropriative logic of capital, and *against* the sovereign logic of war.[52]

Coming full circle, in much the same way that Heidegger raises up poiesis as the hopeful practice of techne and foresees Lyotard's "What's happening?" as the aleatory *differend* of the political apparatus—as they both position the questioning of technology on the precipice of a state of emergency from which techne could conceivably fall prey to the universal end or force of technology, Nancy stages the exposition of éco*technie* to activate the aleatory spacings of touch and proximity that constitute the potential energetic horizons of technology. The parameters of éco*technie* shake and disturb predetermined assumptions about the culture, capital, and violence of technology, its aesthetics of state, and its relation to art and philosophy.

What I had not fully anticipated in planning this essay's pairing of the writings on art by Nancy and Lyotard is the extent to which their various texts and contrasting approaches would be conjoined by their mutual fascination with technology and the artistic sublime. Even those characteristics most separating them—say, Lyotard's unapologetic commitment to politics and the *differend* of technology or Nancy's more formal affection for the singular pluralities of art and technique—seem to morph into each other when these philosophers consider the sublime platform of art, from economy to exposition. Whether through the marvel of touch, the philosophical thought of exposition, or the complexifications of technology, the fraught discourse of the sublime traverses their many reflections on the expansive and empowering touch of art. Most telling is how their aleatory meanderings through the seizures of the sublime seem to echo each other on the very platform of politics that should most distinguish them, indeed what Nancy obliquely hints as dividing their offerings of the sublime. Even in the face of Nancy's resistance to Lyotard's positioning the sublime as activating the *differend* of what is yet to be articulated, which is an implicit political position for Lyotard, Nancy is most forceful on this very same register when he distinguishes the energetic *differend* of écot*echnie* from the blinding hegemony of *logo-logie*. "It is a matter of *worldliness*," argues Nancy, "as a proliferation of 'identity' without end and without model—and perhaps it is even a matter of *'technology' as techné of a new horizon of unheard of identities*."[53] On the horizon of art, the seizure of the artistic sublime renders inefficacious for both philosophers the tired technology of the new digital state by lending touch to what remains to be articulated in our politically energetic world. The blossoming of the unheard rises again. But here it is far from the matter of any release of presymbolic potential or mere artistic experimentation. Much more consequential is the political imperative of thinking anew on the other side of the technological divide where the universalism of the Idea explodes in the innumerable particles of écotechnical ideas, lines, motions, migrations, and ecologies.[54]

So What's Happening, Now? These creative philosophers of Paris mobilize techne as exposition, not as the echo of the unconscious, of taste, or even of blind intensity, but rather as the artistic mobilization of a new emergent ecology of worldliness, one now under even greater pressure from the natural and cultural weight of the Anthropocene. In the threatening face of ecological implosion and fascist resurgence, the texts of Nancy join the writings of Lyotard in conjoining art, technology, and philosophy to reshape the unifying sovereignties of absolutism and the deadening commodities of globalization into the transformers of plural worldliness. The emergent horizons of art bloom and blossom for both thinkers as the sublime seizures of predetermined ends and, most forcefully, as the sublime offerings of the effervescent touch of emergent horizons in a world of political and ecological ex-posure.

Notes

1. Nicolas Boileau, *Oeuvres complètes*, ed. Antoine Adam and Françoise Escale (Paris: Gallimard, 1966), passage translated by Louis Marin in "On the Sublime, Infinity, *Je Ne Sais Quoi*," in *A New History of French Literature*, ed. Denis Hollier (Cambridge, MA: Harvard University Press, 1989), 341.

2. Jean-François Lyotard, *Que Peindre? Adami, Arakawa, Buren* (Paris: Hermann, 2008 [first published by Éditions de la différence, 1987]), 32.

3. Lyotard, *Que Peindre?*, 66. My translation of *Que Peindre?* throughout.

4. Lyotard, *Que Peindre?*, 177.

5. Lyotard, *Que Peindre?*, 84.

6. Lyotard, *Que Peindre?*, 28.

7. Jean-Luc Nancy, *The Muses*, trans. Peggy Kamuf (Stanford, CA: Stanford University Press, 1996), 18.

8. Nancy, *The Muses*, 36.

9. Nancy, *The Muses*, 18.

10. Nancy, *The Muses*, 18.

11. Nancy, *The Muses*, 36.

12. Nancy, *The Muses*, 37.

13. Nancy, "L'offrande sublime," in Jean-François Courtine, Michel Deguy, et al., *Du sublime* (Paris: Belin, 1988), 51. My translation throughout.

14. Nancy, "L'offrande sublime," 52.

15. Nancy, *The Pleasure in Drawing*, trans. Philip Armstrong (New York: Fordham University Press, 2013), 40.

16. Nancy, "L'offrande sublime," 52.

17. Nancy, "L'offrande sublime," 101–2. Nancy here develops the term introduced by Georges Bataille and later mobilized by Yve-Alain Bois and Rosalind Krauss for their 1996 exhibition at the Centre Pompidou, *L'informe*.

18. Nancy, *The Gravity of Thought*, trans. François Raffoul and Gregory Recco (Atlantic Highlands, NJ: Humanities, 1997), 63.

19. In Timothy Murray, "Philosophical Prepositions: Ecotechnics *là où* Digital Exhibition," *diacritics* 42, no. 2 (2014): 10–34, I first attend to the force of Nancy's repetitive *à, à, à,* in elaborating on the stylistic importance of prepositionality in Nancy's writings on technology.

20. Martin Heidegger, *The Question concerning Technology and Other Essays*, trans. William Lovitt (New York: Harper and Row, 1977), 16.

21. Heidegger, *Question*, 31.

22. Heidegger, *Question*, 10.

23. Nancy, "War, Law, Sovereignty—*Techné*," trans. Jeffrey S. Librett, in *Rethinking Technologies*, ed. Verena Andermatt Conley (Minneapolis: University of Minnesota Press, 1993), 43.

24. Nancy, *Pleasure in Drawing*, 41.

25. Lyotard, *Des dispositifs pulsionnels* (Paris: Union Général d'Éditions, 1973), 284. My translation.

26. Lyotard, "The Sublime and the Avant-Garde," in *The Inhuman: Reflections on Time*, trans. Geoffrey Bennington and Rachel Bowlby (Stanford, CA: Stanford University Press, 1991), 97.

27. Lyotard, "Representation, Presentation, Unrepresentable," in *The Inhuman*, 127.

28. Lyotard, *The Inhuman*, 106.

29. Lyotard, *The Inhuman*, 96.

30. Duncan Maclaren Robertson, *A History of the French Academy, 1635–1910* (New York: G. W. Dillingham, 1910), 12. For a broader discussion of the creation of the French academies in line with the regulation of the monstrosities challenging absolutism, see Timothy Murray, "1634, 13 March: The Académie Française, Created by Cardinal Richelieu," in Hollier, *New History of French Literature*, 267–73.

31. Nancy, *The Ground of the Image*, trans. Jeff Fort (New York: Fordham University Press, 2005), 80.

32. Lyotard, *The Postmodern Condition: A Report on Knowledge*, trans. Geoffrey Bennington and Brian Massumi (Minneapolis: University of Minnesota Press, 1984), 45.

33. Lyotard, *The Inhuman*, 65.

34. Nancy, *The Forgetting of Philosophy*, 52. In "Philosophical Prepositions," 18–19, I justify my insistence on translating *"exposition"* as "exposition": "I will capitalize below on the translation of *exposition* as exposition in order to reference the double guise of exposition and exhibition. In *The Forgetting of Philosophy*, for instance, Nancy contrasts exposition with the exhibition of conventional systems of ocular perspective, which have been understood historically to capture the subject in presence. At the heart of conventional exhibition lies the imperative of an aesthetic of indefinite or infinite proportion through which the various machineries of perspective cast exhibition metaphysically."

35. Lyotard, *Que Peindre?* (Paris: Hermann, 2008), 169. My translation.

36. Lyotard, *The Inhuman*, 44, 45.

37. Lyotard, *The Inhuman*, 126.

38. Lyotard, *The Inhuman*, 93.

39. Nancy, "L'offrande sublime," 53.

40. Lyotard, *The Differend: Phrases in Dispute*, trans. Georges Van Den Abbeele (Minneapolis: University of Minnesota Press, 1988), 13.

41. Lyotard, *The Inhuman*, 21.

42. Lyotard, *The Inhuman*, 127.

43. Nancy, "War, Law, Sovereignty—*Techné*," 43.
44. Lyotard, *The Inhuman*, 101.
45. Lyotard, *The Inhuman*, 103.
46. Lyotard, *The Inhuman*, 105.
47. Lyotard, *The Inhuman*, 106. In 1988, the same year that Lyotard published *The Inhuman*, Antonio Negri argued for the evacuation of the artistic sublime from "the machine of the market." Antonio Negri, *Art et multitude: Neuf lettres sur l'art suivies de Métamorphoses*, trans. Judith Ravel, Nicolas Guilhot, Xavier Leconte, and Nicole Sels (Paris: Mille et une nuits, Librarie Arthème Fayard, 2009), 49.
48. Alexander Galloway and Eugene Thacker, *The Exploit: A Theory of Networks* (Minneapolis: University of Minnesota Press, 2007), 141.
49. Lyotard, *Des dispositifs pulsionnels*, 245. My translation.
50. Lyotard, *Des dispositifs pulsionnels*, 260. My translation.
51. Nancy, "War, Law, Sovereignty—*Techné*," 51.
52. Nancy, "War, Law, Sovereignty—*Techné*," 56.
53. Nancy, "War, Law, Sovereignty—*Techné*," 58.
54. Nancy's text ends up dialoguing in fascinating ways with Negri's appeal in *Art et multitude* for a "third model of the sublime" (apart from the mathematical and affective) as "the common as ethical sublime, the common as aesthetic sublime" which happens in opposition to "the interlacing of anthropogenesis and technogenesis which is the mark at the same time of the constitution and unveiling of the common" (155).

8

D'avec
Mutations and Mutisms in Jean-Luc Nancy

WERNER HAMACHER

The stance of philosophy toward what it encounters must—so one should think—be the stance of not only *one* philosophy among others; it must be the stance *of* philosophy in general, thus of every philosophy, no matter its provenance; thus, according to the logic of the double genitive, it must be the stance determined by philosophy and the stance that determines it. It must, namely, clarify the matter that it encounters—not *one* matter among others, but rather in each case the matter of the matter itself, its essential matter (*Sachheit*)—and it can—so one should think—clarify it only insofar as it experiences it as *its* matter and insofar as it grasps this, *its* matter, as a philosophical matter, as a matter that is determined *by* philosophy and *for* philosophy. The matter of philosophy would accordingly be the implicit philosophy of the matter; philosophy the explication of every inexplicit philosophy, even before it reaches the state of its reflection. Philosophy could not specifically make itself its own theme if, pre-thematically, it had not in each case already taken up a relation to itself. That is to say, its relation to the course of the stars or to the architecture of language would be its relation to itself, would be a stance to the stance itself, a relation to the relation *kat' exochēn*, and hence not merely a relation *to* the relation of all relations, but rather this relation of all relations *itself.* Philosophy—so one should therefore think—would have to be, since its first self-determinations, *autarkeia* in an eminent sense, self-grounding, self-mastery, self-sufficiency, not only in its theoretical, but also in its political praxis, a praxis whose actor was characterized by Plato in the *Republic* (3.387d) as *malista autos autōi autarkēs*, himself most of all furnishing himself with his own ground, mastery, and sufficiency, in need of none other. For this reason the stance that it takes to its themes, theses, and tempi would not be just any stance, interchangeable with another; its stance would not be some erratic leaf turning with the winds of time that it uses to cover up its nakedness; it would rather have to be the wind itself, leaf and nakedness, philosophy *of* philosophy, immediately and through all mediations: and hence itself the all that encompasses its own ambit—the *eukyklos sphaira*, the well-rounded sphere of Parmenides (Fr. 8, 43)—and in all of whose parts, even its inebriated ones, it is. Even before it marks off an outer and an inner, it—this encyclical, esotericism pure and simple—would be the process of *internalizing* (*Er-Innerung*) even what is most external, which Hegel speaks about at the end of the *Phenomenology of Spirit* under the title of absolute knowing, a knowing that is absolute because it holds itself together in its externalizations by *being* them. If, however, philosophy not only *has* a stance that it can also change and even give up or lose, but *is* the stance of all stances, then it cannot be what it nevertheless claims to be; it must—so one should think—be *sophia*, not, however, mere *philosophia*.

Heraclitus does not speak of *philosophia*; he speaks of an *anēr philosophos*, a man who loves the *sophon*, what is wise. Even for Plato it is not yet certain that this *philein* is enough for the beloved, although in this regard Heidegger writes, without further clarification or justification, in his 1955 lecture "What Is That—Philosophy?" (which was initially intended for a French audience): "*philein*, to love, signifies here, in Heraclitus's sense, *homologein*, to speak as the *Logos* speaks, that is, to speak in accordance [*entsprechen*, 'to correspond'] with the *Logos*." And he continues: "This speaking in accordance is in accord with the *sophon*. Accord is *harmonia*. This fact, that one nature fits itself to the other reciprocally, that both from their origin submissively fit each other because they are ordered and fitted to each other—this *harmonia* is the distinctive feature of *philein*, of 'loving,' thought in the Heraclitean sense."[1] Accordingly, whoever loves the logos loves wisdom, and he loves the logos insofar as he speaks in accordance with it—thus in accordance with language—and insofar as he holds (*hält*) himself to it—to *logos*, to the relation (*Verhältnis*). Heidegger's interpretation of this love-relation, thought in the Heraclitean sense, takes as its point of departure a *homologein* that is accomplished solely within the horizon of the logos, and defines this logos as a relation of reciprocity, of "each other" and "to each other," of "fitting" and "accord." Loving what is wise, the *sophon*, amounts therefore to saying all that which says already of its own accord, and saying it in such a way that it is said *as* such saying. Saying everything amounts however to saying all beings, and saying them in their totality and unity, thus in their communality. Heidegger can therefore continue: "The *sophon* says: All beings are in Being. More pointedly: Being *is* beings. Here 'is' speaks transitively and says something like 'gathers.' Being gathers beings in so far as it is them. Being is the gathering—*Logos*."[2] Now if, as Heidegger here means, Being gathers, then its gathering is a *legein*—indeed a *homologein*—and since this *homologein* is at the same time a *philein* in the sense of reciprocity, of "each other" and "to each other," the *anēr philosophos* must be the one who speaks in accordance with the *logos*. He does not merely speak, but rather speaks speaking, does not merely speak one among several languages, does not talk in one idiom among other equally valid idioms, but rather speaks the *one* language 'language,' gathers the gathering, and carries out that transition—and transcendence means nothing other than this—from one to the other, a transition that Heidegger characterizes as transitive Being. "*Being is the transcendens pure and simple*"—one reads in the form of a definition already in *Being and Time*.[3] What is also being said with this explanation is that Being is to be understood as *legein*, *homologein*, and *philein*. Whoever loves, and *a fortiori* whoever loves what is wise, transcends, he goes over, is a transition to another and is this transition in the mode of "one another," of "to one another," and of reciprocity. He corresponds (*korrespondiert*)—Heidegger uses the French *correspondre* as a word that corresponds to the German *Ent-sprechung*, which is emphatically written in two parts[4]—he gathers in his *homologein*, he collects (*kollektiviert*). He is, himself, the collecting of the collective. He, himself, is the corresponding of the correspondence.

That, however, he is capable of such a correspondence means, first of all, that he is himself already addressed from the beginning by language and thus by Being as the gathering of beings. If he is able to come into an "accord" with these beings then it is only because he is already determined (*bestimmt*) by the "spoken appeal [*Zuspruch*] of the Being of beings," as Heidegger asserts: "What speaks itself appealingly [*zuspricht*] to us as the voice [*Stimme*] of Being determinatively at-tunes [*be-stimmt*] our speaking in accordance." Heidegger translates this being attuned or determined (*Bestimmtsein*) into French as *être disposé*, and comments: "Dis-posé [—written in two parts—] here means literally: set apart, cleared, and thus transposed into relations to that which is."[5] Only as one disposed, exposed, set apart in this way, only as one opened up in this way, is one who comports oneself to the Being of beings and in that respect to another—and to that other that one oneself *is*—in each case *in* the transition, and only as set apart is one oneself *the* transition to another. As such a transition, however, one is both, *sit venia verbis*, enothering (*Eranderung*) and enselfing (*Erselbstung*): the happening of the other as of the self as it proceeds homologically, "reciprocally," mutatis mutandis.

Such is over and done with as soon as the *philein* of the *anēr philosophos* is superseded by *orexis*, by the striving after the *sophon*, which happens with Aristotle and even already with Plato. The original accord *with* the logos becomes, according to Heidegger, a striving *after* it, and this transformation of the *with* into an *after* remains decisive for the history of what is henceforth to be called philosophy. Ever since then philosophy has been a derivative occurrence of the ever-failing approximation to an "each other" and "to each other," whose "gathering," whose "*Logos*," and whose constitutive transitivity are denied. It can be left open as to whether this transformation results from earlier thought as a "free consequence" or with the necessity of a dialectical process. Both assumptions, Heidegger's and Hegel's, coincide in the axiom that, at the basis of these transformations, philosophy "remains the same,"[6] and that it therefore "remains" a philosophy of the transformations of the relation to the "with" as well, to the "each other" and to the "to each other," in short that it "remains" a philosophy of the stance to the modalities of the continually common. Even striving *after* the logos, after gathering, after Being, is a mode of the With, and Heidegger's so-called "free consequence," which characterizes Aristotelian philosophy in relation to Heraclitus's thought, is also such a mode, insofar as it is at all a "consequence." The singular of the universality of philosophy is thus justified only by the fact that the plurality of philosophies gathered under its title is initially a plurality of its and of every other commonality, and by the fact that, however deeply those philosophies may differ, indeed differing *before* that which is different, philosophy is nevertheless able to think this differing as transition, transcendence, reference, correspondence, and relation. From the beginning on, the relation of the "one another," of the "to one another," of the With, is retained, whether it be unquestioned and merely implied in what is said or thought, or whether it be made thematic explicitly, as one finds ever since Heraclitus's *diapheron* all the way up to Derrida's *différance*. For philosophy, Being is in each case Being-with, Being-with-another, Being-with-oneself-as-another. Whether it is in the mode of *philia* or of *orexis*, of *erōs* or of *eris*, of *logos* or of *vox*, of the *concept*, the *will*, or *intention*, it remains a relation and the concealed or revealed articulation of the fundamental relation of all relations.

After Heidegger, after Sartre, who reduces him by Hegelianizing him, and after Levinas, who radicalizes him in an ultra-Heideggerian volte-face, Jean-Luc Nancy has advanced this thought in a rapid series of large-scale works. On a number of occasions, he himself characterizes his stance to the whole complex of questions that are connected with this thought as a *remettre au chantier* (starting from scratch). Two pertinent statements provide a sketch of his program in a less artisanal and less poietological way. In *Listening*, from 2002, we read—and the middle of the sentence is given particular emphasis through italics—that "it should be very clear that the whole analysis I am suggesting . . . *at every instance risks not being distinguished from this typically metaphysical circle,* which produces nothing less than the resolution of presence to self at the same time as that of the sensibility of the intelligible and of the intelligibility of the perceptible."[7] What is being said here is that the risk of such indistinguishability between Nancy's reflections and the "typically metaphysical" ones not only isn't dreaded but is precisely and necessarily intended, indeed because, as may be added, these reflections within the "metaphysical" typology touch on a non-metaphysical difference between self-presence and an other that can be reduced neither to a self nor to its presence. In *Being Singular Plural*, from 1994, eight years before, we read: "It is necessary to rewrite *Being and Time*: this is not a ridiculous pretension, and it is not 'mine'; it is the necessity of all the major works, insofar as they are *ours*."[8] What on the one hand is being said here is that the major works are major through us and for us, for a universality of the content of their questions, of their insistence and their incisiveness, a universality that is indubitable because it is itself attested to by the severest doubts; on the other hand it is thereby said that their belonging to *us* cannot allow them to exist as what they are or may have been intended to be; rather, they are always exposed, ever anew, to a We that can be experienced only as a forum of their transformation, their mutation, and their *re*writing. Whoever writes about Being and about time—and no one ever writes about anything else—rewrites *Being and Time* and writes it anew, like Pierre Menard; and even if he writes every word and every comma of *Don Quixote* exactly like Cervantes, he still writes a book that is different to the point of incomparability. Thus, thirdly, it is thereby said that the We, which here reclaims all—and evidently not only the *major*—works for itself, itself preserves (*bewahrt*) and retains something in them and in it, in the We, becomes aware of (*gewahrt*) and exposes something that cannot be reduced to a persisting, and in its persisting continually present moment; that it thus becomes aware of and preserves what cannot remain a *nunc stans* or a *nos stans*, nor, however, a *nous* understood in the Greek sense, a *noēsis noēseōs* (*Met.*, 1074b).

Nancy, whenever he writes *nous* in French, is presumably playing with the Greek *nous* and—who knows—also with the mystical *Nu* of the German negative or ultra-positive theologians, who saw in it the moment of a community with God. But whether he is playing with such homophonies and even homologies or letting them play with him, his *nous* is, *nolens vo-*

lens and with the "necessity" that he himself admits, a "rewriting" of every other *nous, nous, Nu* and even *nu* that was ever heard, said, written, or rewritten and entered into the nexus of correspondences that gather the plurality of beings into the harmony of their Being. This "rewriting" must, accordingly, with the "necessity" of that which does not cease to cease, be the medium of transformations that lets an always new *nous* emerge, in which the "same" *nous*, although it is distinguished from every other, is preserved; it must remain the place of constancy and consistency for the various beings and their Being and thus be a topology of Being, a homotopology and tauto-topology which presents itself as differing from itself. It must, then, whether it knows it and wants to or not, lay bare the medium of its own immediality and its own immediation; it must lay bare in every *nous* and every *Nu* an incomparably other *nous* and *Nu*, and cannot therefore be anything other than its own becoming other (*Veranderung*), thus the othering (*Anderung*) of its own, its *Über-eignung*, its *ex-* and *trans-propriation*. This "rewriting" is, instantaneously, the *author*ization of an always other *nous*; it is, from the beginning on, a *re-nou-er* and *re-nou-veller*.

Just how little the homophony between the French *nous*, the Greek *nous*, and the German *Nu* can be reduced to a mere "wordplay," and just how little a casual "joke" it is to draw attention to it, can be recognized in a famous passage of the *Phenomenology of Spirit* in which the structure of self-consciousness is analyzed by taking Fichte's formal definition of the I as I=I as its point of departure. In this formula, the I appears as a consciousness related to itself as its immediate object and thus related to itself as *other*, namely objective consciousness, yet thus at the same time related to that consciousness that this *other* consciousness has of that whose object it is. The I therefore can always only be a doubled, and in this doubling a reciprocal, consciousness of itself as another consciousness; it can, whether explicitly or implicitly, in each case only be self-consciousness and must as such be a *plurale tantum*. For Hegel the I is thus never "alone"; it is, already in the apparently isolated act of its original self-positing, a co-positing together with another I, which even in its objectification preserves itself as independent of this objectification and by virtue of its independence asserts itself not solely as the other of the I but as another I: it is not "alone," it is all-one. It is not merely consciousness, but self-consciousness as the unity with the same consciousness which is separate from it. Hegel encapsulates this differential unity—this unity of an essentially homogenizing difference—with the expanded formula: "The *I* that is *we* and the *we* that is *I*." The identity with itself, which the I experiences in the We and the We in the I, is characterized by Hegel as "universal, inerasable substance, the fluid self-equal essence," and, in the same train, as "*spirit.*" "We" is accordingly for Hegel both what in Aristotle is called *hypokeimenon* and what is called *ousia*, and it is above all their noetic substratum: *nous*. In the course of his thoughts, he does not fail to make reference to the *present* either, indeed to a *Nu* that is just as point-like as it is vitally moved, not a "mystical" *Nu*, but rather a speculative-dialectical one. The final sentence of the introduction to the self-consciousness portion of the *Phenomenology* reads: "Consciousness has its turning point in self-consciousness, as the concept of spirit, where, leaving behind the colorful semblance of the this-worldly sensuous, and leaving behind the empty night of the supersensible other-worldly beyond, it steps into the spiritual daylight of the present."[9]

The immediate pluralizing of the first-person singular into the first-person plural, of I-consciousness into We-self-consciousness and thus into "*spirit*," as Hegel thinks of it, must, together with its "turning point" to "the spiritual daylight of the present," nevertheless in Nancy butt against the barrier of the incommensurability of every I with others and every We with other We's. When one speaks of an "incommensurable 'with,'" one is not talking about a straightforward "with," a substantial Being-with and Being-with-one-another of separate consciousnesses, since the "fluid self-equal essence" of the We, of spirit, of the present does not hold the I together with itself and with other I's. The incommensurable "'with'" of the stipulated "rewriting" is rather *um*geschrieben—rewritten in such a way that it is *umgeben*, surrounded by quotation marks—and has its self-identity in this *Um*schreibung, yet an identity with which the reciprocity of its elements, and with this in turn its "essence," has nevertheless ceded to a difference with itself that must remain unsublateable, because it first opens up access to an I and to its community with others. The "incommensurable 'with'" that Nancy speaks of[10] must, however paradoxical and inconceivable it may be, be a With that cannot coexist even with itself if, as it must, it is to be able to ground the coexistence of the I with itself. Through Nancy's *Um*schreibung, through the citation of the "'with'" and the "rewriting" of the entire classical We-ontology that is condensed in it, both formulas of existence, consistency, and reciprocity, that is, I=I and I=We, crumble into an unidentifying that makes each of their elements incommensurable with each of their elements. Only because and so long as they are incommensurable do they provide the chance—the possibility that is not founded in any "essence" and is therefore not categorically assured—nevertheless to encounter one another.

"It is necessary to rewrite" thus means: Being-we otherwise, Being-we otherwise than every other We, and thus: otherwise than being. Levinas has not thereby become the author of Nancy's appeal to "rewriting"; rather a definition of Being-with is given that is circumscribed (*umschrieben*) by Heidegger, but that is first explicitly *fort*geschrieben by Nancy in *Being Singular Plural*, in both senses of the word: written further and written away from. This definition runs as follows: Being, since it is in each case absolutely singular and incommensurable with another Being, must "be" otherwise than every other Being, must "be" otherwise than the Being that is graspable under a universal concept, yet must also "be" otherwise than every other "concrete" Being of beings and of *Dasein*, must therefore "be" otherwise than Being. Having, of necessity, to "be" in this way, it "is"—this side of all merely moral imperatives and this side of all categorial possibilities—historical. For it is not what *is* subsistent or what presents a mere modification, transformation, or metamorphosis of substantial Being that can stand under the necessity of being otherwise and otherwise *than* being, but rather only a sort of essence—a sort of *nous*—that is not and is never capable of being consistent in itself and with itself. Thus, it must be admitted that Being-with is—logically, topologically, and ontologically—inconsistent Being and that its distinguishing feature consists in "being" precisely its inconsistency. To "be" its inconsistency means, however: in every moment, every instance, and every *stance* already no longer to tarry in this moment, this instance, and *stance*; it thus means: in every moment and every instance to remain open to other ones and open to indefinitely other ones, thus to other than other ones and thereby open to the Open itself. The definition of Being-with lies in its indefinition; its determination (*Bestimmung*) lies in not having a voice (*Stimme*) of its *own* that would be kept up and determined by it itself; its horizon is the beginning of something ahorizonal.

Being is historical as the aporetic consistency of the illimitably inconsistent: it is historical from a sort of *dis-position* that can never solely be its *dis-position*—and therefore can never persistently be ours—it is historical from its ek-sistence—therefore from the outstanding and standing out of every *nous*—and it is thus historical from its insistent out-of-itself, in which it *remains* otherwise than it may ever have been or may yet become. Otherwise, namely Being-with-another and Being-with-another-than-other, and therefore in an alteration that, as alter-alteration, and in a mutation that, as muta-mutation, precedes every substantial, subsisting, and essential Being of the With, precedes every status, every instance, every *Nu*, and every *nous*, and, in preceding them, exceeds them as well.

There is Being only as Being-with with others; there is Being-with only as historical mutation; there is mutation only as mutation of Being-with. This short series of propositions can serve as preparation for a sequel, which would have to say: historical Being-with is structured as Being-with

with another sort of With, which for its part cannot sustain any community with the With. This proposition would have to risk an assertion that would clearly distinguish itself from the *"typically metaphysical circle"* by saying that Being-with-with-others is Being-with-with-another-than-Being-with, that it is therewith Being-with-with-the-Without-of-Being-with and, put more succinctly, is With-without-With. Accordingly, it can be constituted neither as a substantial community nor as a contingent With in the manner of a metonymic contiguity, but rather must open up an infra-contingent relation to a relation, without being able already to contain this relation in itself and consequently to compel it.

The text of *Being Singular Plural* does justice to the historicality of Being-with in a manifold way. Already in the first few pages it is maintained, in the form of a definition—this time in a "rewriting" of a sentence or a syntagm by Nietzsche—that, "From now on, *we, we others* are." And: "'We' says (and 'we say') the unique event whose uniqueness and unity consist in multiplicity."[11] Now, this existing and consisting of the unique event in its multiplicity—or in its multiple multiplicities—is not a constitution into which it would be brought by way of a mediation between these manifolds. Plurality is primary; its structural and historical pluralizations—and there is no difference between its structure and its history, since the one just as the other exclusively carries out its differentiation—, its pluralizations and thus its alterations and alter-alterations are coprimary; a preexistent medium or a subsequently accessory mediation between them cannot therefore bring them into a relation that would function, in the language of antiquity, as a mixture and *methexis* or, in that of modernity, as a *convenience* and mediation. Plural Being can thus only be thought of as immediately mediated, as self-*en*-mediation (*Selbst*-Er-*mittlung*) rather than as mediation between an already given multiplicity. Being does not move about in what is given, it moves (itself) as giving. It bears no date; it dates. We thus read in *Being Singular Plural*: "Therefore, Being is directly and immediately mediated *by itself*; it is itself mediation; it is mediation without any instrument, and it is nondialectic: dia-lectic without dialectic. It is negativity without use . . . the plural fold of the origin."[12] With the phrase "negativity without use," which presents a "rewriting" of the same phrase used by Bataille and by Blanchot in their confrontation with Hegel, a negativity is presumably being circumscribed here which cannot be deployed as a means or instrument, because it immediately, thus non-instrumentally, characterizes Being in its Being-with-another as distancing, spatialization, and temporalization, not therefore as a negativity of *opposition* or placing-against, but rather as a negativity solely of *dis-position* or placing-apart to the other and with the other. It is not the middle between two or several, but rather their middle-less, radically non-centric, thus endless and beginningless, unrooted apart. Now, this negativity "without use," which, of course, implies a mediation "without use," an immediate sui- and alter-mediation, nevertheless disempowers every secondary or reflexive mediation, every mediation of mediation. In other words, there can never be a mediation through a mediator that would do justice to the structural co-originality of beings-with-one-another in their Being-with.

If the immediate mediation is not a mediation *between*, but rather only a mediation *in* things already mediating one another, then every mediation *with* Being-with is not merely an additional and superfluous mediation; it is a structurally unfounded mediation, one that evades, covers up, and forces away the logic of the With. Through it, the immediate mediation becomes something already mediated, thus becomes an other that is isolated from the primary context of mediation and hypostatized into an independent exponent of this context. For *Being Singular Plural*, it follows from this circumstance that

> the "with" is the permutation of what remains in its place, each one and each time. The "with" is the permutation without an Other. An Other is always the Mediator; its prototype is Christ. Here, on the contrary, it is a matter of mediation without a mediator. . . . Mediation without a mediator mediates nothing: it is the mid-point [*milieu*], the place of sharing and crossing through [*passage*]; *that is, it is place* tout court *and absolutely*. Not Christ, but only such a midpoint; and this itself would no longer even be the cross, but only the coming across [*l'croisement*] and the passing through, the intersection and the dispersal [*l'écartement*], radiating out [*étoilement*] from within the very di-mension of the world.[13]

This first sketch—and by the way one that in its entirety is placed within parentheses—of the major project that stands under the title "Deconstruction of Christianity" may be surprising in at least two regards. It defines the "with" as "permutation"—in the context of Christ, one can also understand this *permutation*, without an excessive tendency to segmentational hearing, as *père-mutation*—and indeed as "permutation of what remains in its place," therefore of that which already has *its* place, remains in this, its place, and is itself this place as "mid-point," thus is absolutely identical with it and in this way is the world. The "with" does, to be sure, remain "the place of sharing and crossing through"; it remains—in proximity to the cross—a crossing, remains—in proximity to the *étoiles*—a "radiating out" (*étoilement*), and remains—in proximity to a *dissection* that would let it be torn apart and let its gathering in the center of its "mid-point" be dispersed—an "intersection," but it, the "with," the "permutation," "remains in its place."

Being-with—as the axiom of *Being Singular Plural* accordingly goes—remains Being-with. It remains Being-with with another Being, yet, as this Being-with, it cannot be a Being-with with *the* Other, with the capitalized one, the one that would redeem, release, or liberate it from its place, its abode. Since the argument of *Being Singular Plural* invokes Christ as the prototype of the mediator, the suspicion looms that the reduction carried out here is directed against a restricted Christianity in order to clear the path for a generalized Christianity: since a mediation without a mediator still always remains a mediation, and precisely for that reason also remains bound to the prototypology of Christianity and can therefore be only more Christian than Christianity—more Christian, as one says, than the Pope—and it must, in order to let this ontological reduction reach its foundation and goal, turn it into the reduction to the archetype, to the *permutation* and *père-mutation* of the mediation remaining in its place and being this place.

The suspicion that the "Deconstruction of Christianity," as it is sketched here, would be carrying out an archi-Christianization is strengthened by the second distinctive feature in the argumentation of the cited passage. It requires, namely, that the "permutation" remain, that it remain in its place and therein remain itself, without taking up another in its movement: it is "permutation without an Other." And yet it also says, in an unmistakably ambiguous way: "Mediation without a mediator mediates nothing." "Permutation" is thus thought of as *mutation*, and this *mutation-mediation* is that of a "nothing," but it is therefore, as Nancy understands this "nothing," a mutation-mediation of a *res*, a matter that, as excluded, marks the empty center of the place in which Being-with moves and transforms itself. Thus, the authoritative instance of the Other, of the capitalized Other, is expanded into an other tout court. This generalized—and, more exactly, ultrageneralized—other, in turn, is characterized as a sort of other that takes the position of a nonbeing, a position that is exorbitant in the structure of Being-with. Being-with is therefore Being with the Not of precisely this Being.

Being-with is Being with its Not. This formulation, which does not appear in *Being Singular Plural*—and cannot appear in it—yet to which everything in it is directed and of which it may be said that it structures the topography, the heterauto-topography of its "center-point," is ambiguous. On the one hand, it says that there is only and exclusively something other within the horizon, because *on* the horizon of Being-with, whether this other be the supposedly big other of the Christian or proto-Christian mediator or the other of any random otherness encountered in sounds, colors, smells, stones, plants, and animals, no matter whether this other is an other of a self or an other of an other: in everything, namely, that is called the other—stone or cadaver, dust or light—experience touches on a nothing and on the Not of experience. With this we have said what *Being Singular Plural* and also later writings in the same vein decisively do not say: namely, that it makes no structural difference whether there is a mediator or merely immediate mediation. Even immediate mediation must, according to the argument not merely of Hegel's *Logic* but also of *Being Singular Plural*, be a mediation that is mediated infinitely in its immediacy, one whose stations, instances, and institutions all together function as a mediator and at the same time as something immediate, so that Being-with is *a limine* in each case Being-with with God and with the impossibility of God. It may be an extravagant understanding of Christianity still to discover, even in this impossibility and thus factical inexistence of God, a trace of divinity, but both the fundamental structure of the Christian legend and its treatment in Christian philosophy up to Hegel and even Kierkegaard and Nietzsche and Heidegger suggest such an understanding as of the fullest-bodied currency. Yet therewith it is said that Being-with must be Being with an other, the capitalized and lowercase one, through and through, and that it, whether explicitly or implicitly, is not only "sharing" and "crossing through," but precisely therefore Being-other even beyond the possibilities of transition and communication, is othering even beyond Being. If the sense of Being-with—thus of Being—is communication (*Mitteilung*), then it is the sharing (*Teilung*) and dispensation (*Austeilung*) of the With to others, then it is the giving-out of the With to others, then it is alteration—to the point of psychosis and debility—then it is Being-other. Being-with is Being-other: thus is the universe of Christianity circumscribed as the play-space of Being-with.

The ontology of Being-with, indeed every ontology, is a heterontology of Being-other. Since, however, this Being-other—which transitions to another and, transitioning in this way, is the other, *transitively*—involves the fusion with it and in this fusion the destruction of the With and its elements, this Being-with as Being-other is necessarily Being-with with its Not. The individual treatises that are brought together in *Being Singular Plural* warn not only of the collapse of the With; they attempt to protect the With from this fusionistic collapse and thereby precisely testify to the fact that this collapse belongs inextricably to the structure of the With. The *co* and the *cum* of *ego sum = ego cum* and of *être = co-n-être* conflicts, as "communication," "commerce," "competition," "concurrence," "conscience," "confusion," and "conformism,"[14] with coexistence not only occasionally and episodically; rather this *co-* is, constitutively, in itself, the ever-acute collapse of coexistence.[15] "Permutation" is effectively mutation "in its place," without a way out of the "crossing over," without any other sound than *unison* (*Einklang*), and thus, *nolens volens*, mono-onto-theo-logy of the world as a whole. No god, but also no demigod, no human being and no humanity, however they are defined, can, as long as they are defined, save "themselves," and thus "us," from being a We in the sense of a "conscience," thus at the same time in the sense of "concurrence" and "competition," a We in the sense of both capital and its bankruptcy. And no philosophy, no *anēr philosophos*, can save "us" from it, for their profession consists precisely in effecting that *accord* (*Einklang*), invoked by Heidegger, with the gathering of beings in their Being—yet further with the disparity of this Being. Philosophy, which corresponds to this self-understanding of its praxis, always *also* acts as the agent of this collapse. No warning, no reserve, no revolt helps against it, for every revolt, every reserve, and every warning is, a priori, conformable and commercializable.

We are, that is to say: *We others*, yet that is to say, precisely for that reason: We were (*waren*), and that is thus to say, moreover: We wares (*Waren*). The With is, *transitively*, Without-With: this formulation designates the endogenous ending of Being-with, of philosophy, of history, of the world.

This formulation, which does not appear in *Being Singular Plural* and yet sketches its ground plan, is, once again, ambiguous. It characterizes not only the absolute immanence of the transcendence of *Dasein* as Being-with; it no less characterizes the latter's absolute *e*manence. "*E*manence" will designate the non-tarrying in the space or at the place of "permutation . . . in its place," its *out*standing character, the ex-position, the placing-out from the sphere—from the *eukyklos sphaira*—of a transcendence to an other; thus an ex-position that is not a transition to another, but a transition to what is impassable; not transcendence, but transcending without transcendence; thus ex-cendence—in a sense that perhaps comes close to what Levinas associates with it, yet which presumably remains different from it. With the sentence "Mediation . . . mediates nothing," what is indeed being said initially is that nothing precedes the mediation (*Vermittlung*), communication (*Mitteilung*), and sharing (*Teilung*) of the With, that there is no preexistent substance or preposited subject of mediation, but only an immediate and instantaneous mediation, and that this mediation is a mediation of what for its part is always already mediated and in this sense is everything. Since, however, this sentence, like countless others in *Being Singular Plural*, asserts the rigorous exclusion of a "nothing" from the happening of mediation, what is also being said with it, *nolens volens*, is that this mediation mediates precisely what is insubstantial and insubjective, and thus, however, mediates what is incapable of mediation and consequently what can be called co-inexistence as much as it can be called incoexistence. The sentence, *La médiation ne médiatise rien* ("Mediation . . . mediates nothing"), thus says: *La médiation médiatise rien*.

Already in the first few pages, *Being Singular Plural* faces the question concerning the origin or creation of the world, and since this question does not permit recourse to a preexisting world, to a substance from which creation issues or to a subject that creates, *Being Singular Plural* faces it as the question concerning the origin or creation from nothing. The answer that follows appears unambiguous: "The *nihil* of creation is the *truth* of sense, but sense is the originary sharing of this truth."[16] What is apportioned, shared, and With is accordingly a *nihil* that would not be a *quantité* or *étantité négligeable*, would not be a being that *also* appears among other beings in the negative modification of a nonbeing, but rather the immemorial Not of a Being that 'is' not the Not of one being among and with others, but rather the Not of *every* being and thus the Not of *every* Being and every Being-with. This *nihil* is marked out—and *un*marked—by the fact that it finds no complement, no correspondence, and no consistency with itself or with another, nor therefore with any unity or totality, whatever their nature may be. It is for this reason that the *mē on* has, at least since Parmenides, been the absolute scandal of thought, and thus the question concerning it has never been able to find a satisfying answer. Of Nothing, it cannot be said *what* it is, because, of it, it cannot be said *that* it is, and because even the negation that could be opposed to it is but a derivative and dissimulation of not-Being. The *nihil* of *creatio ex nihilo* can thus only, in an excessively aporetic fashion, be a *nihil* of this *creatio* itself, a *nihilum ex creatione*; it cannot precede creation like a fallow land of possible Being, as the Greeks thought of material and space—and the *chōra* more than the *topos*. This nothing must be a nothing *with* creation and this creation must be a creation *with* the nothing, thus a creation *with* the *Without-With* and further an *Ent*schöpfung, a de- and excreation. *Being Singular Plural* approximates this thought in the just-cited sentence and the one preceding it: "It is the explosion of *nothing* [rien], in fact, it is the spacing of sense, spacing *as* sense and circulation. The *nihil* of creation is the *truth* of sense, but sense is the originary sharing of this truth."[17] The world is not a creation *ex nihilo*, but rather an *explosio nihili*: The nothing 'is' the sheer apart through which something is at all. Thus, what Plato called *chōra*, Thomas *diffusio* and *distributio*, and Heidegger *Räumung* and *Ent-fernung*, is characterized as "spacing," indeed as an *espacement du rien* which then advances to a "spacing of meaning, spacing *as* meaning." With this transmutation of the *rien* into sense—in every sense of the word—the *rien* is indeed brought to silence, yet it remains preserved within sense as silenced, and lets this sense appear as a spatiotemporal occurrence of the *nihil*: not as a compact *nihil negativum, imaginarium* or *rationis*, but as an extended-extending *nihil originarium* in the sense of Being-with structured as "sharing." Being-with is thus initially and in every respect Being-with with not-Being, With-without-With, thus *is* not, but occurs without Being.

If, therefore, there can be talk of a primary sociation, then it is in each case only of a sort of sociation that proceeds *from* and *with* a no less primary dissociation and opens up a world whose initial and lasting sense must be to preserve and increase the *rien*. *The desert grows*, but the fact that it grows, extends itself in space, time, and language, this is what first lets it be a desert. We would be brought nearer to the truth—and perhaps to the *vérité* of which the above-cited sentences from *Being Singular Plural* speak—by the converse of Nietzsche's sentence: The growing desertifies. The extension naughts. The apart-*from*-one-another first yields the possibility of a part-*of*-one-another, yet it does so only in such a way that, in this, the disparate others relate *to* one another as modes of the *from*-one-another. The from-one-another individuates, but it individuates the *nihil*.

Otherwise than as the ontological and meontological doxa would have it, there is from the very beginning never only one and one single nothing, but rather always a plurality of singular nothings—whether *néants* or *riens*—which do not in themselves and do not simply co-here, but rather, as extensions of extending, open up the dimensions of Being-with: not merely all, but always more and other than all, for the propagation of these naughtings can only be infra-singular and ultra-universal. The *mē* and the *ouk* are also said, which Aristotle does *not* say, in many ways, *legetai pollachōs*. So much Being—so much not-Being. So much *Being*-with—so much *naughting*-with. So much Being-*more*—so much Being-*less* and less-*than*-Being. The phrases "whole of beings" and "beings as a whole," which are used frequently in *Being Singular Plural* as well, may indeed belong, ever since antiquity, to the fixed traditional stock of ontology; they do not for all that do justice either to the excreative movement of the genesis, the exogenesis, of those beings, or to the excreative movement of the structure of the tradition, of the transmutations of non-subsisting *nihila*. They, the beings and "their" *nihila*, are in each case more and less than themselves, know therefore no measure, are thus always too little, but are also always too much for one to say they are or are not. The pseudo-equation: "so much the one—so much the other," swings on the hinges of a "so" and an "as"; yet since in the movement of immediate alteration one can never arrive at a "so" and a Being-so that would not already be outstripped and thus missed, this equation must crumble. And with it the non-equation that insists on a too-much and a too-little, and thus supposes the categorial possibility of a proper measure, must crumble as well. What remains is only the *not*-remaining of the measureless movement of Being-with as With-not-Being. Since this With-not belongs, not unambiguously, to the sphere of logos and its ability to speak in terms of correspondences (*Entsprechungsfähigkeit*), it can only be given as a *mutum*: not as a vowel, but rather solely as a *con*sonant, as an occlusive or plosive, and beyond this as a zone of muteness. What remains must be "the explosion of *nothing*, in fact," the mutations of the With with the *muta*.

To think of creation as "the explosion of *nothing*" is not some provisional insight jotted down in passing in *Being Singular Plural*. Six years after this publication, one reads in "Ex Nihilo Summum" (2002), which deals with a politics without a subject and with Bataille's pertinent formulation, "Sovereignty is NOTHING": "The sovereign cannot be a father—or else the father must be the very person of the nothing (nothing or 'no one' ['*personne*'] is the same 'thing')."[18] One would have to study in all detail the (mute) dash and the "or" or "or else" of this sentence and of countless similarly structured gestures of thought in order to grasp more precisely how an alternative veers into a fundamental alteration and makes the latter become a "rewriting" and mutation of what was initially said. "Not a father—or else the father must be the very person of the nothing." The father, thought by Aristotle up through Hobbes and Hegel to be the prototype of the transition from the *oikos* to the *polis*, from the *domus* to the *civitas*, from the private to the public sphere, becomes, with this sentence, the person of the nothing, and this person, as the French allows, is explained as a no one, a no one of sovereignty and a no one of what is gathered under this sovereignty. This is its *père-*, its *per-mutation*, and it is its elevation or debasement into muteness. The political consequences of this mutation of the father are as manifold as they are contradictory; yet they are only this because "the very person of the nothing," and with it the sovereign, cannot be a simple nothing, but rather only an in principle infinitely articulating and therefore infinitely articulated, segmented, and multiplied nothing. In the continued expansion of its internal and external plurality, each *is* its Not and cannot but show itself, and withdraw, in this Not-Being. Each points into its withdrawal; each speaks its falling silent. Therefore, the sovereignty of each and thus the sovereignty of Being-with can occur only as extension, and therefore this occurrence can never be concentrated in a single fixed point at one with itself.

Being-with is constitutively ex-centric; it is, as *Being Singular Plural* puts it, "bizarre." "Bizarre," because historical; historical (*geschichtlich*), because its occurrence (*Geschehen*) can never be arrested in one place, shape, or position. The politics of the *historical* sovereignty of Being-with—thus of the With-*not*-Being—must accordingly be a politics of the mutation of every position and every person that has ever been touched into positions and persons of the nothing; it must be a politics of the revolt of the nothing—"Ex Nihilo Summum" calls it, less abstractly, but no less mistakably, "the revolt of the people"[19]—and must, in short, be the mutation of the no one into that someone who "is" his Being-no-one. If the metontological axiom requires that, for everything of which it can be said that it is or is not, there be an *ex nihilo*, then it also holds for each that this *ex nihilo* is its *nihilum*. Since the occurrence of With-not-Being takes place only as its emergence and passing by, it must bear witness to itself as the emergence of its passing by. The nothing, in other words, must show itself, the falling silent must mark itself, even if it be through the withdrawal of every marking. What is acted out in monarchies' statist operations of decapitation, in Freud's legend of patricide and Bataille's *Acéphale*-myth, are entitativist phantasies that presuppose what they are attempting to rectify or even merely to explain. A father must already be dead, a king headless, a sovereign already nothing if the band of brothers is to be in a position to set about killing him. These myths, legends, and operations are not the paradigm for the appearing of a nothing; they are its concealment, yet precisely herein they are its attestation as well.

In "Ex Nihilo Summum" it is clearly and distinctly said how this attestation is constituted: "That which is nothing is what subsists this side of or beyond subsistence, of substance and of subject. It is what realizes or reifies existence right where it is detached from its own position: right where it exceeds the stance, the station, and the stability of beings. This point is its contact with the being that permeates it: it is the point of cancellation of the *ontological* difference. Thus"—and here this reflection reaches its culmination—"this difference is cancelled only through being infinitely sharpened. It is thus the point where existence exists as the engaging of its very being."[20] *Punctum saliens*: the point with which Being—a nonbeing, a not-being-with—realizes itself and congeals into a thing (*Sache*) that is a being, a being-with, is exactly that point at which it ceases to be a thing and begins to open itself to Being, Being-with. The difference between Being and beings, the so-called ontological, more precisely metontological difference, cancels itself in what Heidegger in his *Introduction to Metaphysics* calls a *seiendes Sein*, a "Being that *is*,"[21] but it cancels itself only insofar as the Being which is thereby retained bursts open, as naughting, its seat in beings. Heidegger gave the following highly dramatic characterization of this process in his commentary on the first stasimon of *Antigone* in precisely this *Introduction*: "Historical humanity's Being-here [*Da-sein*] means: Being-posited as the breach into which the excessive violence of Being breaks in its appearing, so that this breach itself shatters against Being."[22] What Heidegger is calling a breach, Nancy calls a point. If in the former the appearing of Being (*Sein*)—which is "not *a* being" ("*Unseienden*")—"shatters" Da-sein and with it its Being, what is "at stake" in the latter with regard to that appearing is the Being of *Dasein*. The "ontological difference" is cancelled in both interpretations because both *Dasein* and its Being are cancelled; in both interpretations this "ontological difference" comes infinitely to a head, because the shattering and its threat are preserved as the thoroughgoing structure of historical *Dasein*. Only, in this shattering, beings are no longer experienced, but rather Being is, for, in each case, the first and only time. Being-with is not exempt from this structural rupture: Insofar as it is experienced *as* Being-with, what is also "at stake" with the beings of any community whatsoever is the latter's Being-with, and this Being-with must, whether point or breach, inevitably burst. If, therefore, there can be any talk of a Being-with-one-another, of Being-with-another, of Being-together and Being-with, then it can only be, and can be nowhere else than, where there can *not* be talk of this Being-with.

The "Being that *is*" is neither a tauto- or homology nor an episodic paradox, neither the corroboration nor the provisional interruption of a given context that could be restored. It is rather the fundamental, the affundamental aporia pure and simple, an aporia which structures and destructures every Being of the With, the *an-archē* in every *archē*, the *atē* in every *aitia*. Being-with may be defined as the Being of beings that are with one another, yet this with-one-another is not Being with Being, but rather Being with its Not—and thus Being-with with the Without-Being: With-without-With. If there is talk of a "contact with the being [*l'être*] that permeates it" and of "concretion,"[23] then their *co-* is indeed a With, yet one which touches nothing and which coalesces or coheres with nothing that could correspond to this With and be homologous with it. Nothing is more problematic than the correspondence in Being-with that is suggested by a *co-*, nothing more questionable than the community and universality that it asserts, nothing more dubious than the concession that it is still or after all "its being"—thus always its *own* Being and Being-with—that is "at stake." Being-with is free from correspondence, incapable of consensus, and without concretion, otherwise it could neither be threatened nor burst. *Avec* ("with") is to be thought of as deriving from a *d'avec* ("from"), from a difference *d'avec* . . . , even if this be . . . *rien*. If, as *Being Singular Plural* emphasizes more than once, it is incommensurable, then it is first of all incommensurable with "itself."

Every *co-* is inchoative, the beginning of an end without compare. If in the aporia of a "Being that *is*" the ontological difference is cancelled, then it is cancelled in a circle not only whose center is empty, but whose every point stands as the double point before a breaking off of the circumference. The With, in short, marks the relation to no relation. No *correlation*: but rather a—*sit venia verbis*—*chora-relation* or *hors-relation*. A difference, but none which could ever be reduced to a *differentia specifica* between individual entitative classes of various potency, but rather that infra-singular and ultra-universal difference which, since it remains incommensurable with itself, can be characterized as a *differentia differentiae*—thus as a sort of difference that does not correspond to itself, but rather breaks with itself and breaks its With. One may attempt to think of this nothingness in the With as "the smallest amount of beingness [*étantité*],"[24] but one does not convert it into a being by adding that, even for infinitesimal calculus, there is a minimum only in the infinite and that, even in the infinite, it is still too much for the closure of difference, of the metontological difference.

From the kink in the With, consequences follow which are not readily compatible with several of the reflections in *Being Singular Plural*. Here only two will be named, the one concerning the figure of the symbol and its symbolicity, the other the category of Being-so.

In the critique of Situationism and the critique of the "society of the spectacle" launched by it, *Being Singular Plural* makes the criticism that, in it, "symbolic appropriation" is shrunk down to a mere "productive appropriation" and that the concept of the symbol is stripped of its ontological power that is constitutive for every Being-with; "taking *symbol*," it is noted, "in the strong sense of being a bond of recognition, an ontological instance of the 'in-common.'"[25] After a "Copernican"—and perhaps *co-père-nicienne*—"revolution" has been invoked in the chapter "Co-appearing," namely, that "of 'social Being' revolving [*tournant*] around itself or turning on itself, and no longer revolving around something else (Subject, Other, or Same)," one reads, again in the form of a definition: "The proper value of symbolism is in making a *symbol*, that is, in making a connection or joining, and in giving a face [*figure*] to this liaison by making an *image*. Insofar as the relation is imagined [*se représente*], and because the relation as such is nothing other than its own representation, the symbolic is what is real in such a relation."[26] Thus the following series of assertions is set up: that (1) Being-with is a figure, that it (2) is a representing figure, that it (3) is not only one among other figures, but rather the figure of figuration pure and simple, since it (4) is that sole figure in which the real of Being-with, together with the imaginary and the symbolic, finds its identical representation and at one with it its originary presentation.

With this, it is asserted that (5) Being-with is structured as a symbol. This assumption contradicts not only all classical distinctions between figure and figured (and not just the Lacanian ones) but also initially and above all the insight into the structure of rupture and breach belonging to *Dasein* and Being-with, the insight that both are pervaded not by a merely ontic, but by the "ontological" difference. *Being Singular Plural* continues in this direction and asserts that "'society'" (which is put in scare quotes) is alone the symbolic, "making a symbol of itself, society making its appearance by facing [*face à*] itself in order to be all that it is and all that it has to be. . . . Its unity is wholly symbolic; it is wholly of the with. Being-social is Being that is by appearing in the face of itself, faced with itself: it is *co-appearing* [com-parution]."²⁷ After extensive amplifications of this thought, six years later one reads, in "*Urbi et Orbi*": "Our task today is nothing less than the task of creating a form or a symbolization of the world."²⁸ What is thus required, however, is to create a sort of world and With-world whose every element would be the pure complement of every other of its elements, so that its totality and unity, as it essentially *is* and *has to be*, has the form, and exclusively the form, of a symbol. The circular self-correspondence of Being-with in the ambit of the symbol by which, as *Being Singular Plural* recalls, friends can recognize one another after their separation is however nothing less than a recapitulation of the Parmenidean *eukyklos sphaira*, of Hegelian recognition, and of the homology, harmony, and correspondence of beings in their Being claimed by Heidegger. It contradicts the metontological insight that Being—thus also Being-with—is not a being and brooks no reduction of the breach and the cracked point to a mere agent of continuity between coexisting beings. That there is talk in this context of a *tâche*, of a task or requirement, can be read as a symptom of the ambiguity of the symbol; for, if the symbolization of the world is required, then its fundamental structure is already presupposed as given, as known, and as recognized, while, as merely required and envisaged for the future, it at the same time can be neither given nor recognized. The symbol and with it the self-complementing of Being-with is thus never sufficiently a symbol, recognition never the structure of Being-with. The *syn-* does not suffice to characterize the structure of the *syn-*. If nevertheless it is attempted, then it is at the price of ontologizing, substantializing, and "entitizing" ("*Etantisierung*") precisely what cannot be a being or object or subject of an ontology. *Mit-sein* ("Being-with") cannot be thought otherwise than as *Mit-*Da*-sein*: as commonality in regard to a *Da* that is neither *ibi* nor *ubi*, neither *archē* nor *telos*, but a thither into a placeless, and an out into an unoccupiable other. Only in this way is it co-*ek*-sistence: as in-coexistence and co-inexistence.²⁹

Being-with cannot be constituted *sym*bolically. Even when it is thought of as *hyper*bolically or as *para*bolically constituted, it is subjected to the measure of a rhetorical figure or a form, a measure which must fall short when it comes to Being-with as a *non*being. Walter Benjamin's most important work, *The Origin of German Tragic Drama*, in which the breakdown of the classical and classicistic symbol and the rise of allegory in the art, theology, and politics of the modern age are analyzed, culminates, with the final chapter titled "Ponderación misteriosa," in the vision of absolute singularity, which knows no community with others, but only a sort of community that is inaccessible to others. The "open place"[30]—especially when it is thought of as openness *to* places—the Open, as Heidegger sketches it in his artwork-essay, for instance, does not find its correspondence (*Entsprechung*) in any figuration, but only its *un*speaking (Ent*sprechung*) as adfiguration and affiguration: in the opening *to* figuration, in the resistance *against* it (the *ad* of adversity) and the departure *from* it. Heidegger's occasionally hyphenated *ent-sprechen* provides at least an indication that the sense of "corresponding" can be attributed to it only when there speaks along with it something which does *not* speak, but rather withdraws from all speaking. Thus, in order for *Entsprechen* to be *Entsprechen*, it must leave open within itself a not-speaking (*Nicht-Sprechen*). Being-with is not the with-one-another of beings; it "is" their *not*-with, a with-nothing. Yet just as little as the *rien* of *res* belongs to the order of objective things, so little does the *reor* of saying belong to the system of the said and of the sayable. An "as"—and therefore an "as/so" of which the *symbolon* is supposed to consist—is given only from out of a zero: from out of what does (is) not give(n) (*was [es] nicht gibt*).

With this, the aforementioned second consequence of the destructure of Being-with is touched upon, from afar, namely the category of Being-so. Its discoverer, Aristotle, calls this category *to ti ēn einai hekastō*—the "What was the particular thing such that it is (as this thing)?" (*Met.* 7.4.1029b1, 12 sqq.). This Aristotelian formulation, which was translated by its scholastic commentators as *quod quid erat esse*,[31] was rendered by Ross into English as "what was it to be so-and-so," and by Seidl into German, perhaps not without Ross's influence, and perhaps not without Meinong's, as *Sosein* ("Being-so").[32] Even in its abbreviated version as *to ti ēn einai*, the characterization chosen by Aristotle is, not accidentally, an open question and not a purely affirmative determination. It relates to what he calls *prōtē ousia*, first substance, which, with the *einai*, he designates as an occurrence that continues from its past, from the *ēn*, into the particular thing that is presently being inquired about. First substance, however, is an occurrence: *hē ousia . . . energeia estin* (9.8.1050b2). Thomas thus defines it as *actus essendi*.[33] What is meant by this is the active and, more precisely, occurring Being of an always individual being, insofar as the latter is taken *as such* and thus as that which is "said of itself": *legetai kath' hauto*. With this "of itself," however, what is being asked is to address this being itself, as it is in itself, without subordination to the universality of a genus, without properties and without additional determinations, thus to address it in such a way that, in this address, it is not for its part named and, as named in this way, loses its singularity.

The Being-so of a surface evidently does not lie in its being a white surface, since there are still other surfaces than white ones. Nor, however, can its Being-so be addressed as a surface-being, since its Being (which is to be understood verbally) would thus be addressed as a being and this being as an existing being (*ein Seiend-sein*), thus as separated from its own occurring and no longer grasped as the occurring of the Being of the surface. In order to rebut this transgression of Being-so, Aristotle avails himself of the taboo against tautological double-predication, a taboo he deploys again and again: "That statement . . . is for every individual a statement of Being-so, a statement in which this is stated, though not itself contained therein" (7.4.1029b20–21). Were the Being of surface—or of the good, of the one, of Being—contained in the statement about it, then it would not be the Being of precisely that surface—or of the good, of the one, of Being—but rather, separated from this, would be another Being than that which is to be stated; and this other Being would in turn be the theme of further possible statements, in none of which could the *Being*-so of the thing that is meant be stated. The consequence of this infinite ontological regress into what Aristotle characterizes as an *apeiron* (1032a3) would be the split between Being and beings, and yet it would thus be the loss of both Being and beings to an always indeterminate other. The detachment of that *which* is from its *is*: the separation between a being and its Being—*to onti kai to on [einai]* (1031b1)—would have to make the Being-so and the *ousia* of the individual ungraspable. This ontological disparity cannot be remedied by onomatic harmonizations, for the assignment of a specific name to the specific Being that is meant would have to double precisely this Being by the Being of its name and would thereby leave the specific Being-*so*, even in its specific denomination, unnamed. Moreover, names as Aristotle understands them only name what is common to all things of the same sort (1040a10sqq.), and yet they must therefore miss the specifically intended Being-so of a specific thing. If the interrogative formulation of Being-so—"What *was* the *Being* that occurs for a particular thing"—is to hold together and sustain a continuity of, in a temporal bracket, that which it *was* with that which it *is*, then precisely this coherence through names, through concepts that consist of names, and through definitions that operate with names will indeed be brought about, insofar as the commonality of preterit and present Being is stated. Since, however, this commonality through names must at the same time encompass a broader universality than that of the individual thing in its specific duration, the Being-so of the individual can be stated neither in names, nor in concepts, nor in definitions. The consequence of the requirement that the particular individual must be stated in its coherence with itself, without however this statement doubling this individual, is summarized by Aristotle in the sentence that there can be neither a definition nor a proof of an individual thing, and leads him to the conclusion that nothing stated universally is substance: *tōn katholou legomenōn ouden ousia* (1041a4).

Since neither universal nor particular can correspond to Being-so, Being-so can only appear to be determined as that differential middle between both, which Aristotle characterizes as *eidos*, thus as shape, form, outward look. "Eidos," as he defines it, "I call the Being-so and first substance of a particular thing (in its individuality and unity)"—*eidos de legō to ti ēn einai hekastos kai tēn prōtēn ousian* (1032b1–2). After Cicero's translation of the Greek term as *species*, in the sense of outward look and form, this *eidos* entered into the philosophical terminology of the Middle Ages and modernity. The individual in its Being-so thus comes into consideration solely as species, as a type of genus, and is distinguished from universality solely by the *specific* difference. From this there arises the difficulty that, in spite of the Aristotelian definition, the *ousia* of the individual itself is not stated in its Being-so, but rather the *ousia* is stated merely more closely and better in its *eidos* than in its *genos*. The *Categories* expresses this more clearly than the *Metaphysics*: the species is more substance (*Wesen*) than the genus—*to eidos tou genous mallon ousia* (*Kat.* 5.2b22). *More* substance, thus *more* formal determination and actuality (cf. *Met.* 9.8.1050b2), yet not simply this actuality itself and not the individual in its uniqueness. For Aristotle, in short, Being-so in the sense of *eidos* does not characterize the singular being in its Being. The latter is not—as would have to follow from the inversion—what it was, sustains no relation of continuity to its having-been, but rather always gives itself anew and never according to a pregiven paradigm. The question *ti ēn einai*—what was the particular thing such that it is (as this thing)—remains without an answer capable of universality and remains without an answer capable of singularity.

It is evident which fundamental-ontological problems, that of the "ontological" difference between Being and beings above all else, Aristotle recognized in his investigation of first substance, but it is just as evident that these problems have been solved only by a dogmatic compromise, and thus have remained unsolved by the assimilation of the individual and the *eidos*. The arguments presented by Aristotle make clear that precisely what must of necessity be addressed as a singular, and indeed must be addressed at the beginning of every ontology, in order for it to count *as* ontology—and thus *as* philosophy—can simply never be addressed *so*, i.e., in the manner in which it must be addressed in order to find its correspondence in this speaking as the Being-so of the singular. Of the singular only what is not singular is ever said: in the mode of a "rewriting" without an original, a rewriting which for its part can never serve as an original for a second "rewriting." The ambiguous expedient to which the philosopher therefore has recourse leads from the *legetai kath' hauto* to ana-logy, thus however to a mode of speaking that only remains 'near,' 'in the vicinity of,' thus at an irreducible distance to the address of the Being-so of the singular. It is thereby acknowledged that Being-so cannot be addressed *as* this Being-so, but rather in each case only in such a way that it is displaced from its Being-so and is attested to only from its displacement. Already for its discoverer, this Being-so is therefore accessible solely in its other-than-Being-so. Since it is addressable only as with-an-other-than-Being-so, it can announce itself only as an immediate Being-other-in-itself. Being-with in turn cannot be expressed as Being-with *in itself* or as what could be called 'Being-with-so,' because, as a plural singular, it falls for its part under the condition of unaddressability and can only be spoken of *per analogiam*, thus as disguised, overnamed, mutated, and addressed in silence.

Being Singular Plural chooses a different explanation for this Being-so and finds support for it in an impressively apodictic interpretation that Giorgio Agamben gives of it in *The Coming Community*. There he writes, "The thinking that tries to grasp being *as* being retreats toward the entity without adding to it any further determination . . . : comprehending it in its being-so, in the midst of its *as*, it grasps its pure non-latency, its pure exteriority. It no longer says *some thing as 'some thing'* but brings to speech this *as* itself."[34] *Being Singular Plural* follows this interpretation, although it is hardly compatible with the aporias in Aristotle's idea of Being-so and with reflections in other parts of *Being Singular Plural*, and speaks, recalling Mallarmé yet without taking any distance from him, of the "presence *as such* of every flower in every bouquet," in order to draw from it the consequence that "every spoken word brings to speech this 'as itself,' that is, the mutual exposition and disposition of the singularities of the world. . . . Language is the element of the with *as such*: it is the space of its declaration. In turn, this declaration as such refers to everyone and to no one, refers to the world and to its coexistence."[35] If, however, there is a "mutual . . . disposition of . . . singularities ['as such']," then there are no "singularities" without their being, through their "mutuality," not only specified and formalized in an *eidos* in the Aristotelian sense, but even generalized and thus disguised, desingularized, and silenced. "Mutuality" immediately makes mutation become mutism. The muteness of the singular, of Being-so in its particular plurality, is, however, for its part not one that could *as such* be brought to language, since it belongs to language only in *such* a way that it does not—not yet, no longer, or never—belong *to* it. Language cannot be the element of the With *as such*, since it must deliver every With to another With, to a cited or so-called, to a circumscribed or rescribed "With," and to something other *than* a With. The With is communicable *kat' exochēn* only as immediately refused. So singular as it may be in its Being-so, it belongs to no species, no genus, and no universal. Always only that which is still other than *so* would accordingly be *so*: the simply non-conceptual, which remains immune to statements and definitions.

"Mutuality," if this, in a strictly ontological sense, *is as such* at all, and *so* is namable, introduces a mutation that prohibits even speaking of "language" without at the same time saying nothing *of* it and being silent *about* it. The phrase "bringing to language," which Agamben and Nancy use in the wake of Heidegger's *On the Way to Language*, does not purport that something, and first of all the singular, is already given *in* language or enters into it as such, but only that it is brought *to* it. Such *bringing to* language cannot itself be completely linguistic; still less can it be an integral process or a rotating circulation of linguistic or meaningful communication; least of all can it bring itself, this bringing, to language, without already being *in* it and thus, sunk into its *element*, without being mute and in this way *not* being. Language never speaks in any other way than *with* its structural silence and therefore *with* its becoming mute: as language that is first *en*spoken (er*sprochen*), as a path that is first blazed, as a mutation that moves against and with its *muta* and mutisms. Even the *kata* of the Aristotelian *legetai kath' hauto* designates a "toward" of the matter of language and a "thither" of the language of the matter, one which never results in a simple "so" and "as such." The range of movement both of language and of the matter is opened up in the becoming mute. For this reason, Benjamin is able to write in "The Metaphysics of Youth," "Conversation gravitates toward silence, and the one who hears is above all one who is silent. The speaker receives meaning from him; the silent one is the unappropriated source of meaning."[36] More dryly, Heidegger notes, in a somewhat different sense, in the *Contributions to Philosophy (of the Event)*, "The essence of 'logic' is therefore sigetics." And: "The laws of bearing silence are higher than those of any logic."[37]

Not in *Being Singular Plural*, but in *Listening*, at the latest, is that "bearing silence [*Erschweigung*]" of which Heidegger speaks encountered, how it cannot be otherwise than as the self-encountering of language with itself as what it is not, what it does not strive for, and what it does not signify. As "Vox Clamans in Deserto" already did, *Listening* analyzes the preconditions of every possible language that can be understood as an intentionally and phenomenologically graspable occurrence. The attention in both texts is directed to the mere sounding—of the tone, of the sonority, of the voice—and thus to the experience of the initially only sensible sense, of *aisthēsis*, insofar as it is affected by the *phasis* and the *kleos*, not however by the ensuing *noēsis*. The question that both investigations pursue does not concern the semantic, and not even the semiotic level of language, in which its meanings, the structure of statements, and the content of its communications are generated, but rather the genesis of what precedes this generation: the genesis of *aisthēsis* as the pre-sense before every noetic-noematic sense; the genesis, therefore, of the auto-genesis of *logos*. The argument, which is prepared for in *Listening* by a schematic summary of Gérard Granel's analysis of Husserl's *Phenomenology of Internal Time Consciousness*, runs, for its part, roughly as follows: that in the *living present*, which Husserl becomes aware of in listening to a melody, a unity, with its differential moments of "past" and "future," is indeed brought about through retentional and protentional accomplishments of consciousness, although this unity itself, the *living present* of intention, must for its part be initially constituted by its internal difference from itself, if it is at all to be capable of retentions and protentions. The sui-difference of intention is "forgotten" by Husserl, and, with it, it is also "forgotten" that the *living present* must already be the result of a presentification; that, in Heidegger's terminology, what is present must be the gift of a presencing; that, in the terminology of *Listening*, "the present" must be the gift of a "presence" that for its part can never display the character of something present. If, accordingly, the experience of time in listening is not, initially, the experience of the unity of various dimensions of time, but rather the experience of the difference between them, from which the different *and* their unity first of all emerge, then the relation between difference and the different must become the center of attention. Attention must turn toward what phenomenological intentionality turns away from: "the original 'retreat' of each trait, unity and diversity, which does not offer itself *as such* but, on the contrary, plunges into what Granel calls 'the Tacit' or 'the silent difference that bears fruit in anything perceived.'"[38]

This revocation of the "as such"—thus also of the Being-so of first substance—in "'the Tacit,'" in the stillness and silence of difference, testifies not only to a fundamental weakness of classical *prima philosophia*, but also to a weakness of the more recent one, namely phenomenology and its concepts of intention, retention, and protention. This weakness demands nothing less, as one reads in Nancy, than "the beyond-phenomenological ascent—that is to say ontological, still in the sense that in this case being continuously differs from all being-here-and-now [and] does not stop differing this difference itself."[39] What was earlier called *differentia differentiae* does indeed lead, according to the particulars of this sentence, into the stillness of an ultra- and extra-phenomenology, yet it is nevertheless to remain an *ontological* regression. If, however, the deafness of phenomenology betrays "a philosophical *anesthesia* or *apathy*"[40] and a "philosophizing anesthesia,"[41] then it is only because sense itself, *aisthēsis*, is, as sense differing from itself, a "beyond-sense or sense that goes beyond signification."[42] What is accordingly required is not only a "beyond-phenomenological and beyond-philosophical ascent," but furthermore a *beyond-ontological* ascent, which goes back even before the *to on* and its *logos*, and perhaps even before the *einai* that remains subordinate to that *to on*. We must go back to a listening to silence or muteness, thus to a listening to what never lets itself be heard *as such* but without which something would never be able to be heard.

Although *Listening* remains concentrated on "resonance" as "archsonority" and as "a nonperceptible transcendental of signifying sonority," and although the analysis of resonance, "when all is said and done," pivots on its interpretation as "a return of sound to self in self" and thus on the "*typically metaphysical circle*," as whose geometricians Schelling and Hegel are cited, every "return of sound to self in self" is nevertheless also interpreted in the same text as a reference that does not reach its end in the intentional "to self in self," but rather remains open, in the exposition and "opening up of a body," to another body and to something other than a body, thus to something other than sensible resonances and furthermore to no resonances.[43] Openings, and still more the Open, are not possible objects of merely bodily sensations. There is indeed still talk of "mutual resonances" in this context as well, but there is also talk of something "beyond agreement or harmony," thus of a beyond of that which defines the basic structure of the genuinely philosophical relation—of *philein*, of *legein*, and of *homologein*—for Schelling, Hegel, and Heidegger. When, however, this beyond of "resonances," "correspondences," "agreement," and "harmony" is confined to a beyond of merely the "signifying sense,"[44] when even Derrida's "*archi-écriture*" is interpreted as "a voice that resounds,"[45] the suspicion lurks that the span of the ultra-sensible difference is truncated to such an extent that it would no longer be a "silent difference" and that "'the Tacit,'" which the same text recalls with Granel, would once again be "forgotten."

Yet it is not only the silence and stillness, both of which can still accord with intentional comportments, but also the structural, thus non-intentional muteness which *Listening* considers, even if only at its margins: in a footnote and in a preamble with the title *"Interlude: Mute Music."* In this preamble one reads, without further commentary: "Muteness, *motus*, to become mute [*amuïr*], disappearance of a phoneme [*amuïssement*]: of the *t* at the end of the word *mot*."[46] This *t* at the end of the word *mot* does not resonate. It has no voice, does not sound, does not vibrate, remains without echo, even without the chance to be in unison with itself, even if it be a delayed one, or to ring out in harmony, even if that be one of no known convention. The *mutum t* may have a function within the body of the French language, namely what linguists call a *signe zéro*, yet it has this as a mark which functions as an infra- or ultra-sensible difference, not however as a sound, and does not even suggest a sound. The linguists' zero presents a negative mark, without which the linguistic occurrence cannot be formed into a functional system, but must, in order to do so—and these linguists do not specifically notice this—create from a functionally unoccupiable realm of the aphonic, in which there are no marks, no "signs," neither positions nor negations and no places in which they have a signifying or communicative effect. Without such aphonic differences, which, even this side of the linguistically graspable zeros, ground the entire linguistic field, there would be no articulated language, no music, no noises, not even a silence that could be intended or interpreted as intended with the resonances proper to it. Such muteness structures—without sensible, and before every intelligible, sense—all saying, but also all thinking, every attempt at a *philein*, *legein*, *homologein*, whether it be undertaken in the realm of Heraclitus's proto-ontology or that of the later *prima philosophia* and its *orexis*. Without that which does not let itself be heard, and which to this extent is not a being and does not have to be one, there would be nothing—and no Nothing—that could open up even the slightest possibility of apprehending and addressing beings, whether they be sensible or intelligible, possible or actual.

That mutenesses are constitutive and destitutive for language, history, and the world, for Being and for sense, cannot be denied by the fact that attention is turned away from them and toward the names for them, as occurs in a footnote of the same text. There one reads two questions which are as important as they are ambiguous: "And how can one not add that the word *mot* ('word') itself comes from *mutum*, which designates a sound deprived of sense, the *murmuring* emitted by repeating the syllable *mu*? . . . If the silent difference withdraws within music, doesn't sound deprived of sense withdraw into the heart (but not *from* the heart) of speech that is supposed to be meaningful?"⁴⁷ Even granting that these etymologies are correct, with their derivation of *mot* from *mutum* and *mu*, they thereby derive but one sound from another; they do not, however, derive it from the ana- and aphonemes of muteness and cannot justify speaking of a "sound deprived of sense," although the structural necessity of something non-sensuous and non-sense-laden prohibits speaking of "privation." The "silent difference" cannot be paralleled by a "sound deprived of sense," as Nancy suggests, because that "difference" must still precede every "sound," from which its "sense" could be taken; nor can it be integrated "into the heart" of a sense, whether it be one of sonority and its resonances, or one of significance and its reflections.

Yet the interrogative character of Nancy's questions about this sense and still more about the play between *sens, son, censée, au sein*, and *du sein* provides, especially through its connection with the "beyond" of the "beyond-sense or sense that goes beyond signification," an indication of what is "at stake" in *Listening*. This "beyond," namely, which in this text is used—and who knows whether consciously or unconsciously—with uncommon insistency and intensity, is a word that only acquires a sense *within* its and *through* its respective context, yet can also exceed this context and turn against it. "Beyond" can always also signify a "beyond" of the "beyond." Isolated from its immediate contexts, *outre* is the absolutely homophonous derivation of two, perhaps even four, Latin words, which, to all appearances, are hardly related—they are not "homologous" and not completely paronymous—the derivation, namely, of *ultra* and of *uter* (sack of goatskin), which for its part maintains the closest contact with *uterus*, with the Greek *gastēr*, the belly, especially with the *uterus maternus* (the womb) and, metonymically, with *sein*; moreover, *uter*, as in the sense of "one of two," converges with the *aut*—the *ou*—and the *alter*, the other. Without being able to pursue all the intricate contacts between the various connotations and resonances of these words in *À l'écoute* (*Listening*)—and without justifying why this title would perhaps have to be rewritten as *À l'écoutre*—it should nevertheless be emphasized that the "beyond-sense or sense that goes beyond [sense]," which demands a "beyond-phenomenological and beyond-philosophical ascent," leads in this text to the assumption of a "womb[*matrice*]-like constitution of resonance, and the resonant constitution of the womb,"⁴⁸ additionally to the auscultation of the "belly of a mother,"⁴⁹ and furthermore to that of a "belly that listens."⁵⁰ For, as Nancy reasons, "What is the belly of a pregnant woman, if not the space or the antrum where a new instrument comes to resound, a new *organon*. . . .

But, ... more womblike, it is always in the belly that we—man or woman—end up listening, or start listening."[51] And finally: "The ear opens onto the sonorous cave that we then become."[52] The ear opens and is an opening, an opening that, transitively, *outre-passant*, leads out into another opening, into a "belly" or "antrum" of another. Only as this opening is the ear in each case the possible beginning of a *nous* that, for its part, can in turn open up as an ear. One ear hears what is heard by the other ear. Yet, and this remains unsaid, hearing cannot hear *itself*; it is not the organ of an immediate self-affection, but, in all experienceable and thinkable relations, is always only the occurrence of a relation to another—and even to such another that for its part can sustain no relation to it.

The correspondence between ear and ear, the configuration of the ear *in* the ear and the ear *around* the ear, the ear *from* the ear and the ear *to* the ear, which is evoked in the scene cited above; also the correspondence between *oreille, ventre ou antre, outre, caverne,* and *sein* on the one side and the vibrating resonance of a timbre on the other; finally the phonetic correspondence between the *or* of *oreille, sonore,* and *alors* in the last of the cited sentences—*L'oreille ouvre sur la caverne sonore que nous devenons alors,* "The ear opens onto the sonorous cave that we then become"—prompts, as suggestive as it is, the conclusion that the ear, serialized, affected by itself, and mutated into the "antrum," impregnates and regenerates itself as a uterus in *generatio spontanea*; the conclusion, therefore, of a fundamental identifiability of self and other, of father, mother, and child in a familial fusion. This fusion in the "metaphysical circle" of a *eukyklos sphaira* does not know another that would not have always already been integrated into this circle; it knows no fourth and therefore no "beyond-sense" that would be irreducible to an intended silence or structurally mute. *Or* remains contained in an ear that is not an opening, without *dehors*; *outre* remains caught in an *uterus maternus*, a "womb[*matrice*]-like constitution of resonance" that permits no "beyond-philosophical ascent." *Outre* and *outre* have "forgotten" their difference and therefore themselves.

In order, however, for a "cave" to be able to become a "sonorous cave" and a "belly that listens," it must initially be *cave, creux,* hollow without sound; it must be empty and cannot be a matrix. That does not mean that this *cave* would have to be given already "of itself" *before* every sound or every *avec*, but rather that it must be given *with* this: with this Without-With. The *outre-sens* must still be *outre* of every *outre* of the uterus with which it is consonant and in homophony. The "*outre*-philosophical ascent" must therefore become an ascent that is *outre*-matrix, *outre*-resonant, and *outre-nous*. Since, however, *nous* means *être-avec*, the anagrammatic *cave* of the *avec*, together with its *être*, must be abandoned if one is to be able to think an *outre-être*, an *outre de l'être* even beyond the *être de l'outre*—and moreover to think it as an *outre sans génétif et sans génération*.

*Ou*t*rance*—and ou*trance*: nothing other is the movement of Being in *différance*, nothing other is the *mutum*—even if this be but the tiny *mutum* of the *t* at the end of the word *mot*, another word for *logos*.

N'outrance—or n'ous*trance*—so may, in the style of *Finnegans Wake*, the movement of Being-with and Being-we even beyond the With, the We, and Being be written: written apart and thus in such a way that even what is not written and not heard can be read, the intervals, the diacritical marks, the *muta*. For the French *nous* can also only be spoken with a silent *s*.

This *mutum* may, as one says, be "motivated," but it is "motivated" only by the language that names "itself" in it, yet one that must have *ex*posed "itself" in the named and already in the naming: exposed to something not merely provisionally unaddressed, but to something without resonance, something free of correspondence, something unaddressable. The mutisms of this—namely of every thinkable—language may accompany, scan, and cut across all apprehensible and even possible sounds, tones, resonances, and timbres, yet they themselves do not ring out, resound, and resonate *of* themselves or *with* themselves alone. For this reason, the *con*sonantics of the *muta* are of a different sort than that of "metonymic"—or *meter*nymic— "contiguity";[53] they are irreducibly infra-*con*tingent, as only what one calls death or the nothing could otherwise be. *Muta* do not belong to the order of the phenomenal, but rather—if this can still be called "belonging"—to the orderlessness of aphanisis,[54] aphonisis, asemeiosis, and asomiosis. They are, even when they do not remain it in every respect, *inouis*.[55]

The urgency to think an "outre-être" and "outre-être-avec," as sketched in *Listening*, but also in earlier and later works of Jean-Luc Nancy, results, succinctly, from the thought that Being-with is Being-with-others and can only be Being-with with such others as are incommensurable and therefore distinguished by the fact that they do not share with others the same With, the same understanding, or the same sense of the With. Being-with must, therefore, insofar as it is With-*another*-With, be structured in such a way that it always also remains With-another-*than*-With and thus—*a limine, ultra liminem*—With-without-With. But even the reduced formula "With-without-With" grants too much constitutive power to Being-with, insofar as it lets the "Without-With" appear to be but a negative modification of its coexistence. The Without must, namely, necessarily be understood in the sense that it not only marks the privation of a Being-with that is posited as primary, but is also, from the perspective of the unprogrammable otherness of the With-*another*-With, to be left open as a Without that is other than privative and other than assertive, as an *other*

Without, an other-*than*-Without and for this reason as something indeterminable: as a Without that does not function *as* a Without, that can be spoken of neither in the sense of an apophantic, nor in the sense of a hermeneutic *as*, least of all in the sense of an *as-if*, but rather can only be *un*spoken. From this *un*speaking of the Without, from this Without-without-Without, one may first experience what Being-with means: We are not *we*, but rather exposed to the Without-we in its Without-Being, delivered over to the Without-Being-with and therefore accomplices of an illimitable untogether and accomplices *from out of* it. It is not from out of the With that the Without-With is to be thought of as a troublesome, but transient privation, but rather vice versa: from out of the Without-With, every With, together with its ontological parameters, is and remains to be thought. *This* turn, which heads not for the Being of community, but rather for its nonappearance, is still, and has been for a long while, to come.

A few steps in this other direction can be recognized in early modernism, for example in Valéry's *Monsieur Teste*, where, shortly after there was talk of a "mystic without God," one reads: "They are scholars, lovers, old men, priests, and the disillusioned; all *dreamers* [absents], of every possible kind. They seem to be seeking their mutual distances. They must like to see but not to know one another, and their separate sorts of bitterness are accustomed to encountering each other."[56] And in Heidegger's *Being and Time*, where one could read in 1927: "As the *nonrelational* possibility, death individualizes, but only, as the *insuperable* possibility, in order to make Dasein as being-with understand the potentialities-of-being of others."[57] The extensive commentary that both of the cited passages require will here be replaced by a third, in which Georges Bataille, in a sketch for the afterword of a new edition of *L'expérience intérieur*, noted in 1953: "insist on the idea of negative community: the community of those who don't have community."[58] The three passages mark an irresolvable aporia. They speak of a With of the Without-With, of a Being-with of those who cannot claim for themselves such a Being-with, of "mutual distances" that are not deficits, but rather the inconceivable facts of all relations called "social" and "linguistic." The path—the pathless path—that they forge, their diaporia, does not lead in the same direction as that which philosophy has taken since Aristotle. This path can only be called a "path back" in the sense that it leads into that movement from which it can first of all become a path. Philosophy only becomes a "rewriting" of the ontological tradition where it proceeds as a writing-*back*, as an erasure of writing, as *un*writing or, to use a stark word of Nancy's, as *excriture*.

As soon as a word is spoken, it is exposed to its *un*speaking; as soon as it is thought, it is also *un*thought. But both movements do not necessarily advance in a complementary fashion. What can be conceived as a countermovement, inversion, or negation must not find its correlate in a previous movement or positing. The distance, nonrelationality, and negativity of which Valéry, Heidegger, and Bataille speak is not a secondary one and it is not negative, without however already being therefore positive. It could be characterized as ultra- or infra-negation, for it does not posit and it does not negate, but first of all opens the field in which positions and negations, attributions and denials, assumptions and rejections are possible. What, with the incommensurability of Being-with, enters into speaking, thinking, and even into the clarification of thinking also known as philosophy is not the formal negation of speaking, thinking, philosophizing, but rather an other that slips away from the genealogical, etiological, and in general categorial orderings. The "incommensurable 'with'"[59] of which *Being Singular Plural* speaks without completely satisfying its bizarre alogic would, as a mere negation of the commensurable, still be oriented to the latter, and would be in ward of a "we" that could secure only its selfsameness. The incommensurability of the "incommensurable 'with'" must, therefore, be thought without negation, its Not without Not, its Without as a Without without compare. Only thus is it the end of ontology, without ever having been its goal. Only thus is it also the end of the *anēr philosophos*, as Heidegger last presented him in harmonizing fashion. Only this *other* incommensurability is perhaps a further beginning for an *outre-philosophie* that does not speak a compact, univocal, self-enclosed language, but rather—as that of Joyce and already of Mallarmé—several languages which are not coordinated with one another, languages which hold themselves open to further languages—and to languages which are never given: to languages of the perhaps of the With-one-another of these languages and of the perhaps even of their correspondence with that which they indeed intend, but which they are not.

Of a sort of relation that transitions into a relation to irrelation and is the errancy of this transition; of a relation without relata, thus of a free—even free from itself—of an independent, un-conditioned relation; of such a transition—such a transcendence, yet trans-sans-trans and thus impassible for every transcendental, let alone transcendent refuge—of this do the sentences at the beginning of *Being Singular Plural* speak, sentences which deal with an "impossible thought, a thinking that does not hold itself back from the circulation that it thinks, a thinking of meaning right at [*à même*] meaning." There one reads in parentheses, surpassing even the thought of "meaning right at meaning": "(For instance, at the moment at which I am writing, a brown-and-white cat is crossing the garden, slipping mockingly away, taking my thoughts with it.)"[60] This parenthetical cat is not a cat that obeys the requirements of objectivity; it is a cat that carries away both the thinking that is directed to it and even what is thought in this thinking: *un des chats de tout un chacun*, which is their Being-noone and not-Being, *un chat-du-pas-d'être* and of its sense, *un chat-du-sanssens*, a cat of languages and of not-speaking. It does not hold and it does not hold *itself* in a relation, it slips. It marks, but *de*marks and mocks itself at the same time, always, "at the moment at which I am writing." "*Mund*," as one reads in another passage in several languages, "mouth—*mucken, mokken*, mockery, *moquer*."[61] It slips away from the circular motion of thinking and speaking, and carries away even the thought of the philosopher who attempts to think its slipping away, without success. It is not a philosophical cat, nor a cat of "art," of "literature," of technical figuration. It does not belong. It goes its ways, without needing the assurance that they are its own. The *t* of *chat* is also mute.

A poem by Paul Celan speaks about muteness within language and without, about the mere "perhaps of a language" and about still more besides. This poem was first published from his literary remains, since he did not himself send it out for publication. It bears the title "MUTA." It cannot be translated into French, because it is partly written in French. In contrast to the *Seul* that opens the poem, the second, with its mute final letter, is in the plural. Not only can it therefore not be translated; it cannot be completely spoken. That first *Seul* is, one reads, "spoken to three," thus it is not simply spoken *of* three, but addressed *to* three—here presumably a woman, her child, and the speaker himself, which together form a familial triad—although the bow which is then discussed—"held / taut toward the perhaps of a language"—is directed toward this "perhaps" as to that *one* language which, as a fourth instance, could for the first time help provide the aforementioned three, and thus also the speaker himself, with a "language": with a sort of language from which the "perhaps" has not vanished, the "perhaps" to which it could owe a multiplicity that lets the singular *Seul* mutate into a plural *Seuls*, together with its muteness.[62]

MUTA

Seul—: zu dreien gesprochen, stummes
Vibrato des Mitlauts.
Seuls.

. . . .

Ein Bogen, hinauf
ins Vielleicht einer Sprache gespannt,
aus der ich, souviens-

t'en,—aus der ich
zu kommen
glaubte. Und

une corde (eine Saite, eine
Fiber) qui
répondrait.

MUTA

Seul—: spoken to three, mute
vibrato of the consonant.
Seuls.

. . . .

A bow, held
taut toward the perhaps of a language,
from which I, souviens-
t'en,—from which I
believed
to come. And

une corde (a string, a
fiber) qui
répondrait.

—Translated by Ian Alexander Moore

Notes

1. "*philein*, lieben, bedeutet hier im Sinne Heraklits: *homologein*, so sprechen, wie der *Logos* spricht, d. h. dem *Logos* entsprechen. Dieses Entsprechen steht im Einklang mit dem *sophon*. Einklang ist *harmonia*. Dies, daß ein Wesen dem anderen wechselweise sich fügt, daß sich beide ursprünglich einander fügen, weil sie zueinander verfügt sind, diese *harmonia* ist das Auszeichnende des heraklitisch gedachten *philein*, des Liebens." Martin Heidegger, *Was ist das—die Philosophie?* (Pfullingen: Neske, 1956), 13 / *What Is That—Philosophy?*, trans. Eva T. H. Brann (Annapolis, MD: St. John's College, 1991), 15–16.

2. Heidegger, *What Is That—Philosophy?*, 16; translation modified.

3. Martin Heidegger, *Being and Time*, trans. John Stambaugh, revised and with a foreword by Dennis J. Schmidt (Albany: State University of New York Press, 2010), German p. 38.

4. Heidegger, *What Is That—Philosophy?*, 26.

5. Heidegger, *What Is That—Philosophy?*, 29–30; translation modified.

6. Cf. Heidegger, *What Is That—Philosophy?*, 22.

7. Jean-Luc Nancy, *Listening*, trans. Charlotte Mandell (New York: Fordham University Press, 2007), 77.

8. Jean-Luc Nancy, *Being Singular Plural*, trans. Robert D. Richardson and Anne E. O'Byrne (Stanford, CA: Stanford University Press, 2000), 204n81; cf. 194n1.

9. Georg Wilhelm Friedrich Hegel, *Phenomenology of Spirit*, trans. Terry Pinkard (Cambridge: Cambridge University Press, 2018), 108 (¶177).

10. Nancy, *Being Singular Plural*, 83.

11. Nancy, *Being Singular Plural*, 5.

12. Nancy, *Being Singular Plural*, 94.

13. Nancy, *Being Singular Plural*, 94–95.

14. Cf. one of Nancy's *co*-lists in *Being Singular Plural*, 75.

15. One of the interim results in the analyses of Being-with-one-another from *Being Singular Plural* will be cited here in order to make clear that the structure of Being-with itself, and not just an accidental deformation, effects the most complete expropriation—and de-authenticization—imaginable of this and thus every Being: "So it appears to us that what is proper to community is nothing more than the generalized impropriety of banality, of anonymity, of the lonely crowd and gregarious isolation. The simplest solidarities, the most elementary proximities seem to be dislocated. As such, then, 'communication' is only the laborious negotiation of a reasonable and disinterested image of community devoted to its own maintenance, which constantly reveals itself as nothing but the maintenance of the spectacular-market machine. / It must be said, however, that co-appearance might only be another name for capital." Nancy, *Being Singular Plural*, 63.

16. Nancy, *Being Singular Plural*, 3; translation modified.

17. Nancy, *Being Singular Plural*, 3; translation modified.

18. Jean-Luc Nancy, *The Creation of the World or Globalization*, trans. François Raffoul and David Pettigrew (Albany: State University of New York Press, 2007), 106.

19. Nancy, *Creation of the World*, 109.

20. Nancy, *Creation of the World*, 103.

21. Martin Heidegger, *Introduction to Metaphysics*, trans. Gregory Fried and Richard Polt, 2nd ed. (New Haven, CT: Yale University Press, 2014), German p. 122.

22. Heidegger, *Introduction to Metaphysics*, German p. 124.

23. Nancy, *Creation of the World*, 102; translation modified.

24. Nancy, *Creation of the World*, 103.

25. Nancy, *Being Singular Plural*, 50.

26. Nancy, *Being Singular Plural*, 57–58.

27. Nancy, *Being Singular Plural*, 58–59.

28. Nancy, *Creation of the World*, 53.

29. In his 1953 Rome discourse ("The Function and Field of Speech and Language in Psychoanalysis"), in which he draws closely on analyses of Roman Jakobson and Claude Lévi-Strauss, and not without some connection to Heidegger, Lacan, from whom Nancy distances himself in the cited passage,

made the attempt to do justice to this structure of "coexistence" by characterizing it through the non-usage of the "symbolic object." Even sea swallows form a group by not eating the fish that they pass from beak to beak while in flight. In the domain of humanization this non-usage is, according to Lacan's presentation, radicalized by the fact that language is in each case language of and toward what is absent and that linguistically constituted social structures bear the latter as a "trace of a nothingness," as he writes. What he calls the "symbolic order" is accordingly an order not of symbolic complementarity, but rather of the structural impossibility—and of the psychic incapacity resulting from it—of perfectly joining together the parts of a symbol. If there is something like a "trace of a nothingness," then human languages and societies are characterized by a With-the-impossibility-of-a-With. In Lacan's usage—or nonusage—of the term, a symbol is an antonym. The imaginary, thus the entire realm of figuration, serves to suppress, deny, and reject the impossibility of a Being-with that would be consistent with itself. See Jacques Lacan, *Écrits: The First Complete Edition in English*, trans. Bruce Fink in collaboration with Héloïse Fink and Russell Grigg (New York: Norton, 2006), 225, 229, 231.

30. Martin Heidegger, *Off the Beaten Track*, ed. and trans. Julian Young and Kenneth Haynes (Cambridge: Cambridge University Press, 2002), 30.

31. Thus in Thomas Aquinas: *De ente et essentia*, I, 30–34. After Thomas has ascertained there that *nomen essentiae a philosophis in nomen quiditatis mutatur*—thus that the name of essence has been changed by the philosopher into the name of whatness—he continues: *et hoc est etiam quod Philosophus frequenter nominat quod quid erat esse, id est hoc per quod aliquid habet esse quid*—according to the translation of Armand Maurer, "The Philosopher frequently calls this 'what something was to be'; that is to say, that which makes a thing to be what it is." Thomas Aquinas, *On Being and Essence*, 2nd rev. ed. (Toronto: Pontifical Institute of Mediaeval Studies, 1991), 31.

32. In the passage from the first of the books on substance in the *Metaphysics* (Z) discussed here, there is hardly a single sentence on whose interpretation commentators agree. The concept of *to ti ēn einai*, which stands at the center, is taken by some to be "the most obscure, not to say the most grotesque, expression in Aristotle's conceptual language" (Hermann Schmitz, *Aristoteles: Kommentar zum 7. Buch der Metaphysik* [Bonn: Bouvier, 1985], 13). Aside from the explanations offered by the contributions in *Metaphysik: Die Substanzbücher*, ed. Christof Rapp (Berlin: Akademie, 1996), cf. in particular the astute study by Friedrich Bassenge, "Das to heni einai [. . .] und das to ti ēn einai bei Aristoteles," *Philologus* 104 (1960): 14–47, 201–22, as well as the article by Jean-François Courtine and Albert Rijksbaron, "TO TI ÊN EINAI," in *Dictionary of Untranslatables: A Philosophical Lexicon*, ed. Barbara Cassin, trans. Steven Rendall et al., translation edited by Emily Apter, Jacques Lezra, and Michael Wood (Princeton, NJ: Princeton University Press, 2014), 1133–37.

33. Cf. the commentary by Horst Seidl in *Aristoteles' Metaphysik*, vol. 1 (Hamburg: Meiner, 1989), 387.

34. Nancy, *Being Singular Plural*, 88; translation modified.
35. Nancy, *Being Singular Plural*, 88.
36. Walter Benjamin, "The Metaphysics of Youth," in *Early Writings 1910–1917*, trans. Howard Eiland and Others (Cambridge, MA: The Belknap Press of Harvard University Press, 2011), 145.
37. Martin Heidegger, *Contributions to Philosophy (of the Event)*, trans. Richard Rojcewicz and Daniela Vallega-Neu (Bloomington: Indiana University Press, 2012), 63.
38. Nancy, *Listening*, 19.
39. Nancy, *Listening*, 20.
40. Nancy, *Listening*, 30.
41. Nancy, *Listening*, 31.
42. Nancy, *Listening*, 31.
43. Nancy, *Listening*, 29–30, 77n7.
44. Nancy, *Listening*, 32.
45. Nancy, *Listening*, 34–35.
46. Nancy, *Listening*, 23.
47. Nancy, *Listening*, 75n41.
48. Nancy, *Listening*, 37.
49. Nancy, *Listening*, 41.
50. Nancy, *Listening*, 43.
51. Nancy, *Listening*, 37.
52. Nancy, *Listening*, 37.
53. Nancy, *Listening*, 42.
54. The concept "aphanisis" was introduced by Ernest Jones to clarify Freud's concept of castration and was later taken up by Lacan.
55. This *inouï*, the *inauditus*, the unheard, never-heard, unfamiliar, *hors du commun*, plays a peculiar double role in Nancy's *Inoperative Community*. On the one hand, it characterizes the "exigency of community," of which it is said that it "is still unheard and remains to be discovered and thought," indeed, that all communitarian promises already "missed the unheard 'meaning' of 'community,'" that accordingly "Nothing has yet been said" and "we must expose ourselves to what has gone unheard in community." On the other hand, this *inouï* characterizes the fundamental structure of every society, namely its linguisticality and thus sociality itself according to a model that does not silence its provenance in Hegel's thoughts of immediate externalization. For every discourse, so runs the argument, "exposes" (obviously in the sense of externalization) the "inner" to an "outer," without which it would not be the "inner." Language is thus not a *means* (Mittel) of communication (*Mitteilung*), but rather this communication and, with it, community itself. According to this argument, community can never be missing, it cannot be an empty promise, since it always already takes place as "exposition" (in the sense of externalization)—"including silence." Indeed, as a parenthetical remark specifies: "(similar to the way the Inuit Eskimos sing by making their own cries

resonate in the open mouth of a partner)." Jean-Luc Nancy, *The Inoperative Community*, ed. Peter Connor, trans. Peter Connor et al. (Minneapolis: University of Minnesota Press, 1991), 23, 26, 30–31. *Inoui* or *Inuits*, that is not the question here, for they are supposed to be the same and yet incapable of being made one. The tension between Hegelian and Heideggerian arguments pervades almost the entire corpus of Nancy's works.

56. Paul Valéry, *Monsieur Teste*, trans. Jackson Mathews (Princeton, NJ: Princeton University Press, 1973), 31, 33; translation modified.

57. Heidegger, *Being and Time*, German p. 264; emphasis added.

58. Georges Bataille, *Oeuvres complètes* V (*La Somme Athéologique*) (Paris: Gallimard, 1973), 483.

59. Nancy, *Being Singular Plural*, 83.

60. Nancy, *Being Singular Plural*, 4.

61. Nancy, *Listening*, 24.

62. Celan's poem is published in Paul Celan, *Die Gedichte aus dem Nachlass*, ed. Bertrand Badiou, Jean-Claude Rambach, and Barbara Wiedemann (Frankfurt am Main: Suhrkamp, 1997), 63 (translated here by I. A. Moore).

On this see Werner Hamacher, "HÄM: Ein Gedicht Celans mit Motiven Benjamins," in *Jüdisches Denken in einer Welt ohne Gott: Festschrift für Stéphane Mosès*, ed. Jens Mattern, Gabriel Motzkin, and Shimon Sandbank (Berlin: Vorwerk 8, 2000), 177–78; on the problem of *mutating*—in every, and no, sense of the word—see "HÄM," passim.

I also take the liberty here of referring to the motif of a relation without relata in Werner Hamacher, *Entferntes Verstehen: Studien zu Philosophie und Literatur von Kant bis Celan* (Frankfurt am Main: Suhrkamp, 1998), e.g., 10, 24, etc. Translated into English by Peter Fenves as *Premises: Essays on Philosophy and Literature from Kant to Celan* (Cambridge, MA: Harvard University Press, 1997).

On the complex of the With-without-With, which I have already investigated elsewhere, especially and in great detail in Werner Hamacher, "What Remains to Be Said: On Twelve and More Ways of Looking at Philology," trans. Kristina Mendicino, in *Give the Word: Responses to Werner Hamacher's 95 Theses on Philology*, ed. Gerhard Richter and Ann Smock (Lincoln: University of Nebraska Press, 2020), I should point out the fine and important remarks by Marcia Sá Cavalcante Schuback in her edited volume *Being With the Without* (Stockholm: Axl Books, 2013). Irving Goh kindly drew my attention to this volume while I was writing this text.

Infinitely Passing (or, Pascal Passes)

JEAN-LUC NANCY

1.

> *What a chimera man is, therefore! How novel, how monstrous, how chaotic, how contradictory, how prodigious! Judge of all things, imbecilic earthworm, repository of truth, cesspool of doubt and error, glory and refuse of the universe!*
> *Who will unravel this entanglement?*
> *This is certainly beyond dogmatism and scepticism, beyond all human philosophy. Man transcends [passe] man.*[1]

To pass: to go beyond, to exceed, to surpass, to bypass, and first of all, very simply, to traverse. To not stop. Man does not stop at being man. He moves incessantly. Indefinition defines him.

This passage exceeds human philosophy. But is there any other? This is not certain and yet this could well be the question. Human philosophy is so circumscribed by categorical affirmation and integral doubt. To move past human philosophy would be to undertake a philosophy that neither affirms nor suspends.

> *Let us then concede to the sceptics what they have so often proclaimed: that the truth is neither within our reach nor our game* [gibier], *that it does not dwell on earth but is at home in heaven, lodged in the bosom of God, to be known only in so far as it pleases him to reveal it. Let us learn our true nature from the uncreated and incarnate truth.*[2]

205

All-encompassing doubt [*doute integral*] wins out despite everything: one must concede to it the sending back [*renvoi*] of truth to a revelation that does not depend on us. What is named "revelation" is exactly what we cannot acquire but only receive—and receiving on a whim that alone decides what and in which manner to reveal.

The source of such a revelation is uncreated and incarnate truth, which is to say, the word made flesh. Jesus is not the messenger of the revelation; he is the revelation itself. In other words, it is necessary to receive him as uncreated and incarnate truth in order to receive the revelation. It is up to God to reveal himself so that we receive his truth. However, incarnation is not a manifestation: it is the pure and simple fact of the word made flesh. And this "fact" of "being made" is only a fact insofar as it is the fact of revelation.

2.

Now the same fact—the word made flesh or the uncreated incarnate—is the fact of a disproportion, an incommensurability between word and flesh. Each of these terms signifies nothing other than the exclusion of the other. In the incarnate truth, the uncreated truth passes outside of itself precisely by remaining itself. And the flesh corresponds [*s'égale*] to that which surpasses it.

Such is revelation: it is neither the manifestation nor the unveiling of anything; it is its own prior passage outside of itself as it makes itself received as such like the flesh that, by itself, is incapable of recognizing it. Revelation reveals me to myself as I surpass myself.

There were two ways: that of Immortals and that of Mortals. There is only one now, which is that of the passage between word to flesh and vice versa. This is to say—and to say it in a word—what I sense makes sense. Or, more precisely: in me, a human, the fact of sensing makes sense. But this "making sense" does not arise from any given measure, and that in itself designates the human.

This revelation is a humiliation: not because it submits me to some higher power but because it raises me above myself, hence outside myself too. But it does not subsume [*emporte*] me in this outside, for then it would no longer be revelation but metamorphosis, transfiguration. It places me in the condition of passage or passing. It makes me pass myself infinitely.

> *Know then, proud man, what a paradox you are to yourself! Be humble, impotent reason! Be silent, foolish nature! Learn that man in-*

finitely transcends [passe] *man, and hear from your Master your true condition, which is unknown to you.*

Listen to God.[3]

This passage is registered in me [*se signale en moi*]. If revelation is a fact without proof, it touches nonetheless upon a wellspring in us. We cannot not think ourselves imperfect since we can think perfection at least as that which we lack.

> *[. . .] if man had never been corrupted, he would, in his innocence, confidently enjoy both truth and felicity. And if man had never been anything but corrupt, he would have no idea neither of truth nor beatitude. But, unhappy as we are (and we should be less so if there were no element of greatness in our condition), we have an idea of happiness but cannot attain it. We sense* [sentons] *an image of truth and possess nothing but falsehood, being equally incapable of absolute ignorance and certain knowledge; so obvious is it that we once enjoyed a degree of perfection from which we have unhappily fallen.*[4]

What we lack is present to us in the mode of thought or language, which is to say, according to the mode whereby it is possible to recognize that we can neither know nor attain. If we did not have this capacity, we would simply have neither thought nor language. The word that was in question is not language: it is the animating or creative breath that traverses language. The latter in effect neither animates nor creates things, but it names them and hence designates exactly its distance from things. Language—as speech and as thought—constitutes the gap [*écart*] without which there would be neither "idea," nor "truth," nor "knowledge"—nor even their opposites (facts, lies, ignorance).

3.

The above is interpreted as a fall from grace [*déchéance*]. However, without the latter there would not be "passage" either. In fact, the passage of falling from grace and that of salvation [*salut*] are one and the same thing: the revelation of that to which man himself is a stranger. All of Western antiquity and Christianity can be summed up by this. Man no longer has his place and measure. He passes and passes himself.

> *It is, however, an astounding thing that the mystery furthest from our knowledge, that of the passing on* [transmission] *of sin, should be something without which we can have no knowledge of ourselves.*[5]

Here, Pascal introduces a "mystery" that is not part of the canonical great mysteries—those concerning God himself—but refers to an old difficulty debated at length since Augustine. The passing on [*transmission*] of Adam's sin to his descendants would imply an injustice toward the latter. It is thus necessary to think of Adam as the bearer of a reality or of a human nature affected by his fault. This is not more illuminating, since it involves the creator of this double nature.

In effect, it is necessary to understand that corruption is necessary for redemption, which is to say, it is necessary for revelation.

> *Without doubt nothing is more shocking to our reason than to say that the sin of the first man has implicated in its guilt men so far from the original sin that they seem incapable of sharing it. This flow of guilt does not seem merely impossible to us, but indeed most unjust. What could be more contrary to the rules of our miserable justice than the eternal damnation of a child, incapable of will, for an act in which he seems to have so little part that it was actually committed 6,000 years before he existed? Certainly nothing jolts us more rudely than this doctrine, and yet, but for this mystery, the most incomprehensible of all, we remain incomprehensible to ourselves. The knot of our condition was twisted and turned in that abyss, so that it is harder to conceive of man without this mystery than for man to conceive of it himself.*[6]

There is something inconceivable that is necessary just to conceive that man is inconceivable to himself. This is precisely the opposite or the negative of revelation: the latter precedes itself as incarnation and sin precedes itself as division. Division had to precede incarnation, which suppresses it, but incarnation by right had to precede division, which it must suppress. Without this double logic, there would be no human "paradox" or "passage."

The underlying principle here is an incommensurability of man to himself. And this incommensurability is resolved in itself: in the incommensurability of the word and the flesh, which is also the incommensurability of life and death, which gives rise to the "resurrection," which is to say, the mysterious consequence of the original mystery [*mystère initial*].[7]

4.

> *It appears thence that God, in his desire to make the difficulties of our existence unintelligible to us, hid the knot so high, or more precisely, so low, that we were quite unable to reach it. Consequently, it is not through the proud activity of our reason but through its simple submission that we can really know ourselves.*

> *These fundamental facts, solidly established on the inviolable authority of religion, teach us that there are in faith two equally constant truths. One is that man in the state of his creation, or in the state of grace, is exalted above the whole of nature, made like unto God and sharing in his divinity. The other is that in the state of corruption and sin he has fallen from that first state and has become like beasts. These two propositions are equally firm and certain.*[8]

It appears thence that Christianity was the product of a profound transformation, through which the dimension of Mediterranean man changed. Previously he had been mortal and incommensurable to the Immortals, with whom he nevertheless entertained relations oscillating between piety, for which he was rewarded, and presumptuousness, for which he was severely chastised. But he became incommensurable to himself, entering into correspondences in various ways with a divinity that itself underwent metamorphosis. The very complex theological development of Christianity was the phantasmatic and simultanesouly ultra-logical translation of this mutation.[9]

After sixteen centuries of incubation and development, this metamorphosis attained a new level: it is rendered henceforth explicit in a duality henceforth clearly divided, conflictual or divergent even. Of this critical stage, which inaugurates the modern age, Pascal is its most sensitive witness.

February 2020
—Translated by Irving Goh

Notes

1. Translator's note (hereafter abbreviated TN): "Pascal Passes" was Nancy's original title for the piece, but we went with "Infinitely Passing" in the end. I am including the original title in parentheses here to signal to Nancy's focus on Pascal in this piece, based on §434 of Pascal's *Pensées*. Nancy uses the Brunschvicg edition. Pascal's text is in italics here, and the translations, slightly modified in places, are based on A. J. Krailsheimer's. The section §434 can be found on pp. 33–36 of the translation (in Pascal, *Pensées* [London: Penguin, 1995]), and the passage cited here is on p. 34.

On another note, Pascal's phrase of "*l'homme passe l'homme*" (or "*l'homme passe infiniment l'homme*" in a later iteration), translated by Krailsheimer as "man transcends man," is what has always fascinated Nancy. I have kept to Krailsheimer's translation here, but it might be evident from this piece (and elsewhere) that Nancy would have preferred the translation of "to pass" for the French "passer" rather than "to transcend," for which the French has "transcender." The notion of transcendence is too much associated with the sacred. And as

I have noted in my introduction to this volume, if Nancy has to use the term *transcendence*, for example in relation to community, he disavows that sacred dimension, which we in fact see here too. This is also in "Shattered Love," where he brings transcendence to the level of love between mortals, if not to that of a human lover: "Love is the act of a transcendence. . . . But this transcendence is not the one that passes into—and through—an exteriority or an alterity in order to reflect itself in it and to reconstitute in it the interior and the identical (God, the certainty of the *cogito*, the evidence of a property). It does not pass through the outside, because it comes from it" (*The Inoperative Community*, ed. Peter Connor, trans. Peter Connor, Lisa Garbus, Michael Holland, and Simona Sawhney [Minneapolis: University of Minnesota Press, 1991], 97).

I am grateful to both Georges Van Den Abbeele and Philip Armstrong for all their help in translating this text.—Trans.

2. Pascal, *Pensées*, 34, translation modified.

3. Pascal, *Pensées*, 35, translation modified.

4. Pascal, *Pensées*, 35, translation modified. TN: Krailsheimer translates "*sentons*" as "perceive," for which the French actually has "*percevoir*" or "*apercevoir*." I choose to translate it as "sense" to keep with Nancy's preference for this term, which, in Nancy's understanding, pertains to sense in all its senses (and not just visual perception).

5. Pascal, *Pensées*, 35, translation modified. TN: While Krailsheimer chooses the literal translation of "transmission" for the French "transmission," I have chosen to translate it as "passing on" to build on Nancy's interest in the semantic valences of "passing."

6. Pascal, *Pensées*, 36.

7. TN: I have translated *mystère initial* as "original mystery" only in keeping in mind the context of original sin in this section. I am aware that Nancy, like Derrida, is suspicious of anything that claims to be original, or to be the point of origin, or an original source.

8. Pascal, *Pensées*, 36, translation modified.

9. TN: On the changing dimensions and contours of divinity, see of course Nancy's first volume, titled *Dis-enclosure,* of *The Deconstruction of Christianity*, trans. Bettina Bergo, Gabriel Malenfant, and Michael B. Smith (New York: Fordham University Press, 2009).

Contributors

Georges Van Den Abbeele is Professor of French, English, and Comparative Literature at the University of California at Irvine. His publications include *Travel as Metaphor, Community at Loose Ends, A World of Fables, French Civilization and Its Discontents,* and numerous articles on travel narrative, critical theory, and early modern French literature, as well as translations into English of Jean-François Lyotard. His latest book, *Sense and Singularity: Jean-Luc Nancy and the Interruption of Philosophy,* is due out from Fordham University Press in Spring 2023.

Emily Apter is Julius Silver Professor of French Literature, Thought and Culture and Comparative Literature, and Chair of French Literature, Thought, and Culture at New York University. Her books include *Unexceptional Politics: On Obstruction, Impasse, and the Impolitic* (Verso, 2018); *Against World Literature: On the Politics of Untranslatability* (2013); *Dictionary of Untranslatables: A Philosophical Lexicon* (coedited with Barbara Cassin, Jacques Lezra, and Michael Wood) (2014); and *The Translation Zone: A New Comparative Literature* (2006). Her current project, *What Is Just Translation?* takes up questions of translation and justice across media. Her essays have appeared in *Public Culture, diacritics, October, PMLA, Comparative Literature, Art Journal, Third Text, Paragraph, boundary 2, Artforum,* and *Critical Inquiry*. In 2019 she was the Daimler Fellow at the American Academy in Berlin. In 2017–18 she served as President of the American Comparative Literature Association. In fall 2014 she was a

Humanities Council Fellow at Princeton University, and in 2003–4 she was a Guggenheim Fellowship recipient. She edits the Translation/Transnation book series at Princeton University Press.

Rodolphe Gasché is SUNY Distinguished Professor & Eugenio Donato Professor of Comparative Literature at the State University of New York at Buffalo. His interests concern the history of aesthetics, German Idealism and Romanticism, phenomenological and post-phenomenological thought, hermeneutics, and critical theory. His most recent books include *Europe, or The Infinite Task: A Study of a Philosophical Concept* (Stanford University Press, 2009); *Un Arte Muy Fragile: Sobre la Retorica de Aristoteles*, trans. Rogenio Gonzalez (Santiago, Chile: Ediciones Metales Pesados, 2010); *The Stelliferous Fold: Toward a Virtual Law of Literature's Self-Formation* (Fordham University Press, 2011); *Georges Bataille: Phenomenology and Phantasmatology* (Stanford University Press, 2012); *Geophilosophy: On Gilles Deleuze and Félix Guattari's "What Is Philosophy?"* (Northwestern University Press, 2014); *Deconstruction, Its Force Its Violence* (SUNY Press, 2016); *Persuasion, Reflection, Judgment: Ancillae Vitae* (Indiana University Press, 2017); *Storytelling: The Destruction of the Inalienable in the Age of the Holocaust* (SUNY Press, 2018); *De l'Éclat du Monde: La "valeur" chez Marx et Nancy* (Editions Hermann, 2019); *Locating Europe: A Figure, A Concept, An Idea?* (Indiana University Press, 2020). His latest book-length study, *Plato's Stranger,* will be forthcoming from SUNY Press in 2022.

Werner Hamacher (1948–2017) was Professor for General and Comparative Literature at the Goethe University in Frankfurt and Global Distinguished Professor of German at New York University. Among his pathbreaking works of philosophy and literary criticism available in English are *Pleroma: Reading in Hegel*; *Premises: Essays on Philosophy from Kant to Celan*; and *Minima Philologica*.

Irving Goh is Associate Professor of Literature at the National University of Singapore. He is the author of *The Reject: Community, Politics, and Religion after the Subject* (Fordham University Press, 2014), which won the MLA Aldo and Jeanne Scaglione Prize for Best Book in French and Francophone Studies. His second monograph, *L'existence prépositionnelle*, was published by Galilée in 2019. With Jean-Luc Nancy, he published *The Deconstruction of Sex* (Duke University Press, 2021). He is also editor of *French Thought and Literary Theory in the UK* (Routledge, 2019), coeditor with Verena Andermatt Conley of *Nancy Now* (Polity, 2014), and coeditor with Timothy Murray of the *diacritics* special issue on "The Prepositional Senses of Jean-Luc Nancy" (2 volumes, 2014–15).

Eleanor Kaufman is Professor of Comparative Literature and English at the University of California, Los Angeles. She is the author of *The Delirium of Praise: Bataille, Blanchot, Deleuze, Foucault, Klossowski* (Johns Hopkins University Press, 2001), *Deleuze, the Dark Precursor: Dialectic, Structure, Being* (Johns Hopkins University Press, 2012), and *At Odds with Badiou: Politics, Dialectics, and Religion from Sartre and Deleuze to Lacan and Agamben* (forthcoming, Columbia University Press).

Ian Alexander Moore is Assistant Professor of Philosophy at Loyola Marymount University and a faculty member at St. John's College. He is the author of *Dialogue on the Threshold: Heidegger and Trakl* (SUNY Press, 2022) and *Eckhart, Heidegger, and the Imperative of Releasement* (SUNY Press, 2019/2020); editor of Reiner Schürmann's *Neo-Aristotelianism and the Medieval Renaissance* (Diaphanes, 2020); coeditor of Jean Wahl's *Transcendence and the Concrete* (Fordham University Press, 2017); and translator of texts by Heidegger, Gadamer, Levinas, Nancy, and Hamacher, among others.

Marie-Eve Morin is Professor and Chair of Philosophy at the University of Alberta in Canada. She is the author of many articles on Derrida, Nancy, Merleau-Ponty, Heidegger, Sartre, Latour, and Sloterdijk. She is also the author of *Merleau-Ponty and Nancy on Sense and Being: At the Limits of Phenomenology* (Edinburgh University Press, 2022) and *Jean-Luc Nancy* (Polity, 2012); editor of *Continental Realism and Its Discontents* (Edinburgh University Press, 2017); as well as the coeditor, with Peter Gratton, of *The Nancy Dictionary* (Edinburgh University Press, 2015) and of *Jean-Luc Nancy and Plural Thinking: Expositions of World, Politics, Art, and Sense* (SUNY Press, 2012). She has also translated some of Nancy's works into English, including *Ego Sum* (Fordham University Press, 2016).

Timothy Murray is Director of the Cornell Council for the Arts, Professor of Comparative Literature and Literatures in English, and Curator of the Cornell Biennial and the Rose Goldsen Archive of New Media Art. Publications include *Technics Improvised: Activating Touch in Global Media Art* (University of Minnesota Press, 2022); *Medium Philosophicum: Para un pensamiento tecnológico del arte* (Universidad de Murcia, 2021); coeditor with Shin-Yi Yang, *Xu Bing's Background Stories* (Mandarin) (Beijing: Life Bookstore, 2016); coeditor with Irving Goh, "The Prepositional Senses of Jean-Luc Nancy," 2 vols., *diacritics* (2014–15); *Digital Baroque: New*

Media Art and Cinematic Folds (University of Minnesota Press, 2008); *Zonas de Contacto: El arte en CD-Rom* (Centro de la Imagen, 1999); *Drama Trauma: Specters of Race and Sexuality in Performance, Video, and Art* (Routledge, 1997); and *Like a Film: Ideological Fantasy on Screen, Camera, and Canvas* (Routledge, 1993).

Jean-Luc Nancy (1940–2021) was a French philosopher and Emeritus Professor of Philosophy at the University of Strasbourg. He is especially known for works such as *The Inoperative Community*, *The Experience of Freedom*, *Being Singular Plural*, *The Sense of the World*, and *The Creation of the World or Globalization*. Translations of his later important works such as the two volumes of *The Deconstruction of Christianity*, *The Disavowed Community*, and *Sexistence* have been published by Fordham University Press.

John H. Smith is a Professor of German at the University of California, Irvine. He has published monographs on Hegel and philosophies of the will. He has essays on a range of literary and philosophical topics, most recently on Goethe and Idealism, on Nietzsche and the decadent will, and on *Ereignis* in Heidegger and the *Novelle*. His latest book is *Dialogues between Faith and Reason: The Death and Return of God in Modern German Thought*. He is currently working on a project entitled "How Infinity Came to Be at Home in the World," which explores the place of the infinitesimal calculus and the mathematical infinite in the German philosophical tradition. And he is coeditor of the *Goethe-Lexicon of Philosophical Concepts*.

Index

actuality, 34, 36, 47n8, 68, 112, 188
Adami, Valerio, 150
After Finitude (Meillassoux), 53
Agamben, Giorgio, 20n32, 92, 189–90
"Age of the World Picture, The" (Heidegger), 100, 152–53
Alquié, Ferdinand, 47n6
Analyst, The (Berkeley), 52
Anthropology of Ancient Greece, The (Gernet), 86
areality, 26–29, 40, 42, 45–46, 48n12, 51n28
Arendt, Hannah, 98–99
Aristotle, 92, 169, 181, 186–90, 202n32
art, 3, 8, 12–13, 15, 17, 20n24, 73n26, 113, 149–63, 165n47
Augustine, 208

Badiou, Alain, 9–10, 52–53, 60, 65–66, 70, 71n5, 72n14, 73n17, 139
Banality of Heidegger, The (Nancy), 10, 91, 101–2
Bataille, Georges, 38, 44, 61, 89n17, 163n17, 174, 181–82, 197–98
becoming, 38, 55–61, 66, 69–70, 190
being, 14, 19n14, 23, 56–70, 84, 89n14, 92–94, 103, 113–20, 139–42, 168–71, 173, 177–78, 180, 183, 185–88, 196
Being and Event (Badiou), 9, 71n5, 72n14
Being and Time (Heidegger), 83, 92, 94, 97, 107n21, 168, 197
being-essentially-with, 35
being-in-common, 10, 17, 35, 75, 84
being-in-the-world, 113
being-other, 177
being-other-in-itself, 189

being-perceived, 132n33
being-seen, 119
Being Singular Plural (Nancy), 3, 18n1, 31, 35, 83, 94, 170, 173–81, 183–85, 189, 198, 201n15
being-so, 14, 180, 184, 186–91
being-to, 121–22
being-toward, 121–22, 132n35
being-we, 172, 196
being-with, 14, 82–83, 87, 94, 99, 107n8, 172–78, 180–86, 189, 196–98
being-with-another, 14
being-with-one another, 35, 172
being-with-oneself-as-another, 14
being-with-others, 85
Benjamin, Walter, 186, 190
Benveniste, Émile, 33–34
Bergson, Henri, 82
Berkeley, George, 52, 57
Birth to Presence, The (Nancy), 31, 94, 96
Black Notebooks (Heidegger), 91, 101–2, 106n2
Blunden, Andy, 72n13
Boileau, 149, 154
Book of Questions, The: El, or the Last Book (Jabès), 91
Borges, Jorge Luis, 156
Boyarin, Daniel, 104
Broch, Hermann, 89n12
Buci-Glucksmann, Christine, 150
Buren, Daniel, 150
Burke, Edmund, 158

Cage, John, 160
calculus, 53–54, 58–61, 73n19

215

Calvez, Jean-Yves, 83
Canguilhem, Georges, 112
Cantor, Georg, 53
capitalism, 26, 76, 80–83, 155, 159
Categorical Imperative, The (Nancy), 3
Celan, Paul, 142, 199, 204n62
chaos, 26–27, 31–32, 36–38, 73n21
Christianity, 98, 102–3, 105, 176–77, 208–9. *See also* God
Christology, 64
Cicero, 188
Conley, Verena Andermatt, 47n8
Coming Community, The (Agamben), 189
consciousness, 31, 48n13, 53, 62, 67–68, 115–16, 119–20, 171–72, 191
contraception, 140–42
Contributions to Philosophy (of the Event) (Heidegger), 190
Copjec, Joan, 136, 141, 147nn13,15
Corpus (Nancy), 18n1
COVID-19 pandemic, 16
Creation of the World or Globalization, The (Nancy), 76, 82
Critique of Dialectical Reason, The (Sartre), 93
"Critique of the Gotha Programme" (Marx), 84

Dasein, 23, 32, 39, 56–58, 66, 72n14, 82–83, 94, 107n21, 113, 137, 143, 173, 178, 183, 185, 197
Deconstruction of Sex, The (Nancy and Goh), 146nn3,12
Deleuze, Gilles, 52, 113, 149–50
Derrida, Jacques, 18n1, 22, 48n12, 51n26, 62–63, 106n5, 112–14, 120, 129nn4,13, 130nn16,20, 141, 149, 169, 192
Descartes, René, 2–3, 21–24, 35–37, 44–45, 48n13, 49n17
désoeuvrement, 18n9
Deutscher, Isaac, 104–5
différance, 113, 120–22, 125, 130, 133n43, 169, 196
differend, 12, 158, 160–62
Discourse on Method (Descartes), 33, 36, 49n15
dualism, 38–40, 42, 109n37

Eco, Umberto, 48n13
Ego Sum (Nancy), 3, 21–46, 51n26
Esposito, Roberto, 98–99
Être et chair (Saint Aubert), 128
existence, 5–6, 19n14, 35, 57–58. *See also* being
experience, 27, 40, 67. *See also* sense
Experience of Freedom, The (Nancy), 3, 18n4, 31
Exploit, The (Thacker and Galloway), 159
"Eye and Mind" (Merleau-Ponty), 113, 115

Faith and Knowledge (Hegel), 65, 72n12
feminism, 12, 16, 135–36
Fiedler, Leslie, 98
"Finite History" (Nancy), 75–76
Finite Thinking, A (Nancy), 45, 94
flesh, 118–20, 125

Fold, The (Deleuze), 52
"Forgetting of Philosophy, The" (Nancy), 151, 157, 164n34
Fortenbaugh, William, 139
Foucault, Michel, 20n32, 51n26
freedom, 4–5, 15–16, 18nn4,7, 31, 45, 51n33, 78–79, 84–85, 89n8, 101
Freud, Sigmund, 104–5, 112, 115, 144, 182, 203n54
Fundamental Concepts of Metaphysics, The: World, Finitude, Solitude (Heidegger), 92–95

Gainsbourg, Serge, 142
Galloway, Alexander, 159–60
Gassendi, Pierre, 51n29
Gaston, Sean, 106n2
German Ideology, The (Nancy), 81
German Philosophy: A Dialogue (Badiou and Nancy), 52
Gernet, Louis, 86–87
globalization, 1, 13, 76, 78, 88n6, 161–62
Gnosticism, 109n37
God, 30–31, 70, 78, 88n7, 91–92, 96–97, 100, 106n3, 127, 170, 177, 197, 207–8. *See also* Christianity
Goh, Irving, 47n8, 48n9, 146nn3,12
Gorgias (Plato), 139
Goux, Jean-Joseph, 55, 61–62
Granel, Gérard, 191
Gravity and Grace (Weil), 97, 99–100
Ground of the Image, The (Nancy), 155

habit, 131n25
Hegel, Georg, 2–3, 16, 22, 53–70, 71n8, 72nn12, 15–16, 73n18, 88n4, 124, 167, 171–72, 174, 177, 181, 192, 203n55
Hegel: The Restlessness of the Negative (Nancy), 3, 67
Heidegger, Martin, 2, 16, 22–23, 49n16, 70, 82–83, 89nn14,17, 91–103, 105, 106nn2,3, 107n21, 109nn35,37, 129n10, 152–53, 167–69, 173, 177, 179, 182–83, 186, 190, 197–98, 201n29
Heraclitus, 167
history, 75–76, 78–79, 88n7, 89n14
Hobbes, Thomas, 181
humanism, 78–79, 81–82, 89n14, 130n20
Husserl, Edmund, 112, 130n16, 134n53, 191

Infinite Thought (Badiou), 53
infinity, 52, 206–7; existence and, 57–58; Hegel and, 53–55, 58–59, 64–67, 71n8, 72nn12,14; mathematical, 52–53, 58–61, 73n18,19; negation and, 57; spirit and, 66; thought and, 69; writing and, 63–64
Inhuman, The (Lyotard), 156–57, 160, 165n47
Inoperative Community, The (Nancy), 3, 25–26, 31, 38, 203n55
Irigaray, Luce, 142–43

Jabès, Edmond, 91
Jakobson, Roman, 201n29
James, Ian, 129n13
Johnston, Adrian, 145
jouissance, 66, 127, 138, 140–41, 147n13
Judaism, 91–92, 95–97, 99–105, 106n2, 109n33

Kacem, Mehdi Belhaj, 137
Kant, Immanuel, 3, 22, 55–56, 66, 73n19, 82
Kellner, Douglas, 147n21
Kierkegaard, Soren, 177

Lacan, Jacques, 137–39, 141, 143–44, 201n29
Lacoue-Labarthe, Philippe, 18n1, 63–64
language, 10, 14, 28, 42, 66–67, 83, 89n17, 138, 141–42, 145, 158, 166–68, 189–93, 198–99, 203n55
Lee, Kyoo, 48n13
Leibniz, Gottfried, 52, 59
Levinas, Emmanuel, 172–73, 178
Lévi-Strauss, Claude, 201n29
Listening (Nancy), 170, 191, 193–94, 196
Literary Absolute, The (Lacoue-Labarthe), 63
Longinus, 149
Love, Heather, 144
Lyotard, Jean-François, 150, 154–62, 165n47

Madison, Gary, 130n20
Maimon, Salamon, 52
Malabou, Catherine, 73n26
Mandell, Charlotte, 138
Marcuse, Herbert, 144, 147n21
Marin, Louis, 150
Marion, Jean-Luc, 141, 143, 146n5
Marx, Karl, 2, 16, 75–84, 86–87, 88nn4,7, 89nn14,17, 100, 105
materialism, 19n20, 100, 135, 141, 143, 157
Meditations on First Philosophy (Descartes), 22–24. *See also* Descartes, René
Meillassoux, Quentin, 9, 53
Menard, Pierre, 170
Mendieta, Eduardo, 110n45
Merleau-Ponty, Maurice, 2, 11–12, 15–16, 111–28, 129nn10,13, 130nn16,20, 131nn25,26, 132n33, 133nn45,52, 134n53
"Metaphysical Anti-Semitism and Worldlessness" (Mendieta), 110n45
Metaphysics (Aristotle), 202n32
"Metaphysics of Youth, The" (Benjamin), 190
MeToo, 16
Monsieur Teste (Valéry), 197
Muses, The (Nancy), 18n1, 150
MUTA (Celan), 199–200
mutuality, 190

narcissism, 120, 122–24, 133n43
Nazis, 100, 109n35
Need for Roots, The (Weil), 109n35
Negri, Antonio, 165nn47,54

Nicholas of Cusa, 73n19
Nietzsche, Friedrich, 23, 174, 177, 180
"Non-Jewish Jew, The" (Deutscher), 104
Novalis. *See* von Hardenberg, Friedrich

One-Dimensional Man (Marcuse), 144, 147n21
On the Way to Language (Heidegger), 190
On Touching (Derrida), 114
Origin of German Tragic Drama, The (Benjamin), 186
Origin of the Political, The: Hannah Arendt of Simone Weil? (Esposito), 98–99

"Painting as Libidinal Apparatus" (Lyotard), 160
pandemic, 16
Parmenides, 167
passing, 3, 5–8, 10, 12, 15–16, 19n14, 33, 205–9
passivity, 114–16
pathos, 139, 141
Paul, Apostle, 95–96, 102–4, 139
Pensée de Karl Marx, La (Calvez), 83
perception, 28, 43, 71n4, 95, 116–18. *See also* sense
Phénoménologie de la perception (Merleau-Ponty), 112, 116–18
Phenomenology of Internal Time Consciousness (Husserl), 191
Phenomenology of Religion (Heidegger), 104
Phenomenology of Religious Life, The (Heidegger), 95–96
Phenomenology of Spirit (Hegel), 65, 67, 167, 171
Phenomenology or Deconstruction? (Watkin), 128
"Philosopher and His Shadow, The" (Merleau-Ponty), 134n53
Pinkard, Terry, 60, 72n15
Plaisir au dessin, Le (Nancy), 113
Plato, 139, 166–67, 169, 179
Pleasure in Drawing, The (Nancy), 151
Postmodern Condition, The (Lyotard), 155–56

"Question concerning Technology, The" (Heidegger), 152

Radical Jew, A: Paul and the Politics of Identity (Boyarin), 104
Reinhard, Kenneth, 139
Reject, The (Goh), 48n9
representation, 150–51
Republic (Plato), 166–67
Reynolds, Jack, 130n20
Ricoeur, Paul, 129nn4,13
Robinson, Abraham, 53, 73n17

Saint Aubert, Emmanuel, 127–28, 129n10
Sartre, Jean-Paul, 44, 93, 112
Schelling, Friedrich Wilhelm Joseph von, 192
Schlegel, August Wilhelm, 63
Schlegel, Friedrich, 63–64
Schleiermacher, Friedrich, 63

Scholem, Gersholm, 104, 109n42
Science of Logic (Hegel), 54–56, 58, 61
self-consciousness, 172
selfhood, 120–22, 132n38
self-identification, 121
sense, 5, 28, 43–44, 94, 116–18, 121, 125–26, 194
Sense of the World, The (Nancy), 3, 18n1, 53, 94
sexistence, 135–39, 143, 145
"Sexistence" (Nancy), 146nn4,17
Sexistence (Nancy), 3
sexual difference, 145
Shakespeare, William, 142
Simmel, Georg, 89n13
Situationism, 184
Sontag, Susan, 98
Speculative Remark, The (Nancy), 3, 52, 54, 62–63, 66–67
Spinoza, Baruch, 88n4, 105
Stiegler, Bernard, 149
"Strange Foreign Bodies" (Nancy), 114
Structure du comportement, La (Merleau-Ponty), 112
subject, 23–27, 30–33, 35, 42–44, 68
sublimity, 151–56

Taubes, Jacob, 104–5
technology, 89n14, 100, 149, 151–63
Thacker, Eugene, 159–60

thought, 4, 24–25, 43–45, 64, 69
"Time in Nancy" (Conley and Goh), 47n8
touch, 19n10, 73n26, 108n21, 113–14, 118–20, 122–27, 130n16, 134n53
Treatise on the World (Descartes), 36
Truth of Democracy, The (Nancy), 31

Valéry, Paul, 197–98
value, 78–83, 86–87
Virilio, Paul, 150
Visible and the Invisible, The (Merleau-Ponty), 117, 122–23, 126, 133n52
vision, 119–20, 127
von Hardenberg, Friedrich, 63

Wagner, Adolph, 80
Waiting for God (Weil), 98
"War, Law, Sovereignty—*Techné*" (Nancy), 161
Watkin, Christopher, 128, 129n13
Weierstrass, Karl, 61, 101–2
Weil, Simone, 2, 16, 91–92, 96–100, 103, 105, 109n35
"What Is That—Philosophy?" (Heidegger), 167
Wittgenstein, Ludwig, 82
worldliness, 80, 90n30, 162

Žižek, Slavoj, 136
Zupančič, Alenka, 136, 138

Perspectives in Continental Philosophy
John D. Caputo, series editor

Recent titles:

Irving Goh, ed., *Jean-Luc Nancy among the Philosophers*.
Neal DeRoo, *The Political Logic of Experience: Expression in Phenomenology*.
Marika Rose, *A Theology of Failure: Žižek against Christian Innocence*.
Emmanuel Falque, *The Guide to Gethsemane: Anxiety, Suffering, and Death*. Translated by George Hughes.
Emmanuel Alloa, *Resistance of the Sensible World: An Introduction to Merleau-Ponty*. Translated by Jane Marie Todd. Foreword by Renaud Barbaras.
Françoise Dastur, *Questions of Phenomenology: Language, Alterity, Temporality, Finitude*. Translated by Robert Vallier.
Jean-Luc Marion, *Believing in Order to See: On the Rationality of Revelation and the Irrationality of Some Believers*. Translated by Christina M. Gschwandtner.
Adam Y. Wells, ed., *Phenomenologies of Scripture*.
An Yountae, *The Decolonial Abyss: Mysticism and Cosmopolitics from the Ruins*.
Jean Wahl, *Transcendence and the Concrete: Selected Writings*. Edited and with an Introduction by Alan D. Schrift and Ian Alexander Moore.
Colby Dickinson, *Words Fail: Theology, Poetry, and the Challenge of Representation*.
Emmanuel Falque, *The Wedding Feast of the Lamb: Eros, the Body, and the Eucharist*. Translated by George Hughes.
Emmanuel Falque, *Crossing the Rubicon: The Borderlands of Philosophy and Theology*. Translated by Reuben Shank. Introduction by Matthew Farley.
Colby Dickinson and Stéphane Symons (eds.), *Walter Benjamin and Theology*.

Don Ihde, *Husserl's Missing Technologies.*
William S. Allen, *Aesthetics of Negativity: Blanchot, Adorno, and Autonomy.*
Jeremy Biles and Kent L. Brintnall, eds., *Georges Bataille and the Study of Religion.*
Tarek R. Dika and W. Chris Hackett, *Quiet Powers of the Possible: Interviews in Contemporary French Phenomenology.* Foreword by Richard Kearney.
Richard Kearney and Brian Treanor, eds., *Carnal Hermeneutics.*

A complete list of titles is available at www.fordhampress.com.

www.ingramcontent.com/pod-product-compliance
Lightning Source LLC
Chambersburg PA
CBHW020407080526
44584CB00014B/1207